No one is more qualified to write about today's
toughest competition, spo̶r̶t̶...
No other book .... than

THE .... ME

On Brent ...., outrageous
things beca......................stem that created him
also grants ....total immunity."

On Howard Cosell: "Howard was at the depths of
impossibility in 1980. . . . . no one dared cross
him . . . . Howard the High Priest defiled *Monday Night*'s sacred prime-time altar for 14 years."

On John Madden: "Underneath the teddy bear TV
personality, the Oakland Raider still clenched a
dagger in his teeth."

On Roone Arledge: "Like Napoleon and Alexander
the Great, Arledge was bent on conquering the
world—annexing territor[ies]. . . . These became
a confederation called *Wide World of Sports,* one of
the longest-running shows in television history."

Read the raves behind this page!

GAME

Behind

GAME

HIGH STAKES, HIGH PRESSURE
IN TELEVISION SPORTS

TERRY O'NEIL

SMP

ST. MARTIN'S PAPERBACKS

The lines from "Night Moves," written by Bob Seger, which appear on page 183, copyright © 1976 by Gear Publishing Co.

The lines from "For Everyman," words and music by Jackson Browne, which appear on page 336, copyright © 1973 by Swallow Turn Music. All rights reserved; used by permission.

Published by arrangement with HarperCollins

THE GAME BEHIND THE GAME

Copyright © 1989 by Terry O'Neil.

Library of Congress Catalog Card Number: 88-45545

ISBN: 0-312-92423-2

Printed in the United States of America

Harper & Row hardcover edition published 1989
St. Martin's Paperbacks edition/January 1991

10 9 8 7 6 5 4 3 2 1

In memory of the great Louise O'Neil

Contents

Acknowledgments

WRITING FOR PUBLICATION is far more a team game than one might suspect. This project was represented in skillful and professional manner by Arthur Kaminsky and his colleague at Athletes & Artists, Janet Pawson. Perhaps the most important of their many contributions was an immediate instinct to phone Ed Burlingame at Harper & Row.

Ed easily persuaded me that writing about oneself induces blurred perspective. Fortunately, he was willing to serve as the corrective lens. Without him and his assistants, Kathy Banks and Scott Prentzas, this would be an altogether different book.

Elsewhere on his team, an author needs unofficial editors—the truest of friends—to read early drafts and be encouraging. Patrick and Isabella Mulligan somehow did this with straight faces. Bill Sawch surrendered lunch hours and late nights to the task. His criticisms, delivered with the subtlety of a Princeton diplomat and the precision of a Georgetown lawyer, helped shape the final manuscript.

Likewise, my sister, Kathy, and brother-in-law, Steve Hilgartner, made deft suggestions. As important, they conducted a Berlitz course for me in word processing and computers.

The author's team should also include supporters who cannot yet read. For roster depth, it is preferable that they come in a matched set, such as Arabella and Geneviève von Walstrom. Together with big sister Cristobel, these are the precious godchildren who took me on a ski holiday when I most needed it. Only occasionally did they ask, "Teely, when are you going to be done with that silly book?"

Rod Crowley and Roger Knight brooded over the title. Bob DeFruscio and Fred Torrez also deserve thanks, and they know why. These are the good guys who make Greenwich so special, such home.

In acknowledging editorial sources, let's begin in the National Football League: Ken Valdiserri of the Bears, John Konoza of the Redskins, Greg Aiello of the Cowboys, Pete Donovan of the Rams, Gary Heise of the Chiefs, Dave Houghton of the Raiders, Scott van Hoover of the Bills, Jerry Walker, Rodney Knox, Dave Rahn, and Bill Walsh of the 49ers.

Also John Kosner of the NBA, Jim Marchiony of the NCAA, Jo Laverde of A. C. Nielsen, Leslie Slocum of the Television Information Bureau, Peter Lambert of *Broadcasting,* George Maksian of the New York *Daily News,* Marvin Bader, Kent Gordis and Al Michaels of ABC Sports, Beano Cook, Donn Bernstein, Chuck Howard, Jeff Fahrer, Kay Wight, John Tesh, Ed Joyce, Mike Trager, Pete Dey, Brenda O'Connor, Eddie Hart, Rey Robinson, James L. Brooks and his assistant, Patty MacDonald, plus two of my assistants at CBS, Lori Diver-Ehret and Ashley O'Neil (no kin). Special thanks to the Greenwich Library information desk, which never flinched, even at the oddest questions.

Terry O'Neil
July 1988

Prologue

AMBIENCE at the San Francisco 49ers' training complex in Redwood City, California, was normally optimistic, sometimes even bubbly. The offensive players, especially, felt challenged and proud to execute the most creative schemes in pro football. But on this weekend, their mood was off the scopes.

"We got some different stuff for this one," Keith Fahnhorst, the right tackle, told us. "Weird stuff. Yeah. *Weird.*"

I mentioned Fahnhorst's comment to Freddie Solomon, the wide receiver. Always a sunny personality, Freddie glowed brighter than I had ever seen him.

"Some shit be goin' down tomorrow," he giggled.

Adding to the mystery, San Francisco's public relations director had told Pat Summerall, John Madden, director Sandy Grossman, and me that practice would be closed. We were invited to wait in the team's offices. But for the first time in a friendly, four-year association with Coach Bill Walsh, we would not be invited to his Saturday practice.

Taking Madden aside, I said, "John, we've got to find out what's going on. Walsh'll leave us naked tomorrow."

"I know," he replied.

After practice, Russ Francis, the tight end, stopped by our waiting room—actually the office of owner Ed De

Bartolo, Jr. When we nudged him for information, Francis could only shake his head about Walsh's compulsiveness:

"Can you believe he tried to put in another dozen pass plays this morning? Jesus Christ, we already have 114 for this game. He says, 'Men, I got a few ideas last night.'

"The players said, 'No, Bill. You can't! Not the day before the game!' "

A few minutes later, our scheduled meeting with Walsh came and went without further enlightenment. This was a complete reversal of the candor we'd come to expect from him. Dressed in tennis warm-ups and wearing a look of total preoccupation, he jumped out of his chair after our second question and announced, "I should let you fellows go."

He left us in open-mouthed disarray, but Madden reassured me, "Don't worry. We'll get it from Montana."

Joe Montana, the All-Pro quarterback, was an open book. On prior occasions, he'd given us audibles, pass patterns, attack points against the opposing defense, anything we asked. Together with Chicago's Jim McMahon and Gary Fencik, he was among our top sources in the league. But on this day, Montana was glassy-eyed, mumbling generalities and fidgeting with the cuff of his sweatpants.

Madden and I grew panicky, every bit as uptight as the 49ers themselves. There was only one hope. Dick Vermeil, our CBS Sports colleague and former coach of the Philadelphia Eagles, was on site for the pregame show. Vermeil had been a junior quarterback at San Jose State when Walsh was a graduate assistant. Later, they were assistants together at Stanford. The two had remained close friends, frequently each other's house guest.

Whatever secrets lurked in the San Francisco game plan, they were too bizarre for the players to reveal. Leaving Pat, John, and Sandy for a moment, I found Vermeil in the locker room and asked him to approach Walsh directly. He agreed to give it a try.

Returning to our meeting room, I asked, "Who're we waiting for?"

"Bubba Paris," said Grossman.

William "Bubba" Paris was a 6-foot 6-inch, 299-pound tackle. He'd been a top draft choice from Michigan, but, in two seasons, the NFL's jungle-cat pass rushers had made him look slow and awkward.

Bubba was now within 24 hours of the toughest test of his athletic life, lining up against Richard Dent of the Chicago Bears. Dent was fierce and super-quick, the league leader that season with 17½ quarterback sacks. San Francisco fans shuddered at the match-up: On Joe Montana's backside, his blind side, Dent would be undressing poor Bubba.

Poor Montana.

I'd spotted the rounded, soft-looking lineman that morning in a hallway. Introducing myself, I mentioned that our group looked forward to speaking to him after practice. Then, as he stepped away, I called after him thoughtlessly, "Bubba, you've got the isolate tomorrow. All day long."

A couple of veterans, Ronnie Lott and Carlton Williamson, overheard me and leaped on their favorite target:

"Ooooh, Bubba. The isolate, man. You and Dent. All day long."

Paris kept ambling toward the locker room without rejoinder.

Suddenly, my memory of this scene was broken by the behemoth himself. Charging through our doorway, he pointed a finger into Madden's face.

"Look!" he demanded. "If Dent kicks my ass, you can say anything you want. But if I kick *his* ass, I want the credit!"

Bubba was a changed man. We calmed him down long enough to hear the technique that line coach Bobb McKittrick had taught him. McKittrick told him to imagine a line extending from Dent's lower abdomen to Montana's lower abdomen, an axis that would be ever changing as both men moved during the play. As long as Bubba kept himself on that axis or plane, bisecting it, he'd be okay.

Our expressions must have indicated we weren't getting it.

"Look," he said, grabbing his crotch, "as long as I keep my balls between Dent's balls and Montana's balls, I'll be all right."

This was a principal story line for us. Could Bubba neutralize Dent? Could the 49ers handle Chicago's vicious, varied blitzes, the most potent defensive weapon in the NFL that year? All the tricks in Walsh's bag were useless if Montana was going to spend the afternoon on his back.

It was time to leave. Grossman and I were scheduled to meet with our cameramen and videotape operators at Candlestick Park. Stepping outside, we found Vermeil wearing a smile of wonderment on his handsome face. He'd gotten the goods from Walsh.

Vermeil's news was so stunning, I asked him to repeat it, slowly. Then Grossman and I raced up the freeway to meet our technicians in a stadium restaurant.

There were 30 of them, casually seated on folding chairs and luncheon tables. They were already studying typewritten copies of the coverage pattern that Grossman and I had devised for this game. It detailed an assignment for each cameraman and videotape operator on every play. At the front of the room, a portable chalkboard awaited me.

I diagrammed several formations for both teams, highlighting potential confusion for us. Then, reminding the group of its obligation to secrecy, as I did almost weekly, I dropped Walsh's double-headed bombshell. It sent the room into an uproar.

"Terry, let's go over this again," asked one cameraman. "Are you saying that, right before the snap, Montana and Solomon are going to trade positions? . . . Montana's gonna go out to wide receiver? . . . and Solomon's gonna become the quarterback? . . . Then he's gonna take the ball and run the option play, like in a college game? Is that right?"

"Hell, that's the easy one," I said. "You guys'll get that. What I want to see is how you react when he sends a guard into the backfield to block on short yardage and goalline."

"It'll never happen," said one videotape editor. "This time, they're pullin' your leg."

"Hey, guys," I said. "Remember, it's Walsh."

"Ten seconds to air . . . Nine . . . Eight . . ."

Only the voice of associate director Joan Vitrano was heard. Twenty other people sat tense and silent in a 40-foot CBS mobile unit, alternately watching their monitors and the ticking clock. They were like tourists on an ocean liner helplessly watching an oncoming tidal wave.

Vitrano was standing directly behind me. Sandy Grossman sat at my side. Reaching across our common console, I squeezed his forearm.

"Have a good one," he acknowledged.

Depressing two small levers at my fingertips, I spoke to Summerall and Madden in the commentary booth:

"Hit 'em hard, you two."

Summerall was blank of expression, lost in thought. Madden mugged for the camera, knowing his "game face" wasn't going any farther than our truck at this point.

". . . Seven . . . Six . . . Five . . ."

"Roll 'A'!" Grossman commanded. "Put 'A' on the line. And track it."

". . . Three . . . Two . . . One . . . We're on!"

Film coverage of a 1963 football game filled our monitors and, simultaneously, appeared in 26.4 million homes across the country. Summerall's voice was heard:

"How tough was Mike Ditka as a player? Well, you might ask the Pittsburgh Steelers of twenty-one years

5

ago. Five of them fell off Ditka, like leaves falling from a tree, on this memorable play. They called him 'Iron Mike,' the son of a steelworker from Aliquippa, Pennsylvania. And he played like it. . . ."

This videotaped "tease," prepackaged with narration and graphics an hour earlier, was 75 seconds in length. It offered one last chance to gather my thoughts before producing three-and-a-half hours of live television.

The date was Sunday, January 6, 1985, a typically cool, overcast afternoon in San Francisco. The 49ers were about to play the Bears for the National Football Conference Championship and a berth in Super Bowl XIX.

". . . How brilliant is San Francisco Coach Bill Walsh? How sophisticated his offense? Well, you might ask his players. Some weeks, their game plan will include more than a hundred pass plays. Most of them come with exotic names like '325 hitch and lateral,' the first play in last week's victory over the Giants. Other plays, like 'slow draw right,' display a subtlety and artistry that are uniquely Bill Walsh. . . ."

These final few seconds during the tease were often dominated by irrational fear: "My God, it's here. Have we forgotten anything?"

Only after kickoff could I savor this delicious process—the surety of being so focused, so fully prepared, that nothing could surprise us. On the best of days, I actually *welcomed* the unexpected as verification of our team's single-minded dedication.

"In the zone" is the athlete's common expression for this feeling. Before practice the previous day, Freddie Solomon and I had fallen into a discussion of the "zone." We marveled at the parallels between our jobs, finishing each other's sentences with a kind of shared spiritualism.

Freddie, an amateur vocalist, had titled his first song "All Alone in the Zone." Football fans assumed he meant zone pass coverage. But on the day before our respective moments at Candlestick Park, we traded knowing glances about a truer location of the "zone."

Our expressions for this topic were not smiles, but they weren't grimaces, either. The "zone" was strange. It made you powerful, capable of great feats. But it was also lonely. You had to go in there by yourself. Four days before producing my first Super Bowl telecast, I told Solomon, I was so deeply isolated in the "zone" that I phoned my girlfriend and broke into tears. He nodded.

". . . And so, from one perspective, today's game is Walsh // versus Ditka. // It's finesse // versus force. // The Pacific Coast // versus the Midwest. It's San Francisco versus Chicago—coming up."

In the first quarter, San Francisco looked ready to run Chicago out of the stadium. Leading 3–0, the 49ers had first-and-goal at the Bears' 2 yardline. But Montana's pass to Solomon was intercepted by Gary Fencik in the corner of the endzone.

Instantly, I ordered into my headset: "Cue it 'B,' cue it 'X,' cue it 'H,' cue it 'F'!" These were four of our eleven videotape machines.

"Ready 8, take 8!" cried Grossman, calling a shot of the Chicago sideline.

Summerall followed: "Mike Ditka lets you know he approves."

"What 'ya got?" Grossman asked me.

To both him and the commentators, I replied, "Isolate of Solomon. Then reactions—Walsh, Ditka, and Montana."

Madden: "You know Freddie Solomon was wide open early on that play and Montana thought it was a 'gimme.' And he threw it like a 'gimme.' But Fencik didn't 'gimme.'"

Meanwhile, I was giving Grossman the sequence of replays: "Sanford, it's 'B,' 'X,' 'H,' 'F.'"

"Stand by 'B,' " he barked. "Fly 'B,' and roll it."

We wedged four replays into 25 seconds, including the three explosive reactions: Walsh mouthing "Oh, shit," on his sideline, Ditka pumping his right arm like a human piston, Montana hanging his head and clapping hands in frustration.

The score was still 3–0 with 13 minutes remaining in the second period when San Francisco began moving from its 30 yardline. The seventh play of the drive was one of Walsh's special creations, and our technicians pounced.

Just before the snap, Montana shifted from under center to the left flank. Our reverse-angle cameraman panned with him, then whipped to Solomon, suddenly playing quarterback for the first time since his days at the University of Tampa.

The knowledgeable Candlestick crowd yelped as Solomon ran a true split-T, down-the-line option. The play might have gone for a touchdown, but Keith Fahnhorst, who'd called it "weird" the previous day, missed his block at right tackle. Solomon's pitch man, Roger Craig, was stopped for no gain.

Four plays later, with the ball on Chicago's 4 yardline, Walsh came with the second of his specials. Guard Guy McIntyre lined up in the backfield and blocked for fullback Craig. I ordered another Chalkboard replay, and Madden was more than ready:

"What would you think if you're the safety," he wondered, "and you look up and see a guy comin' at you, and he's a 260-pound guard? Watch McIntyre come, and Fencik says, 'Well, they told me I was supposed to take on a running back out here. Where'd that guard come from?!' "

Still, Chicago held. The 49ers' 14-play drive yielded only a field goal, and they settled for a halftime lead of 6–0.

Midway through the third quarter, however, San Francisco had goal-to-go again. This time, there was no stopping Walsh's offense, nor his new running back.

On a simple off-tackle play from the Bears' 9 yardline, McIntyre's assignment was to block middle linebacker Mike Singletary. Instead, he caved in the entire left side of Chicago's defense, springing halfback Wendell Tyler for the game's decisive touchdown.

From that point, the 49ers were in total command. Richard Dent never laid a hand on Montana. Our "Dent isolate" became a "Bubba Paris isolate," and we replayed a bunch of them. Madden lavished the big tackle with praise, though his explanation of technique was not quite so vivid as Paris's had been.

As San Francisco's 23–0 victory was winding down, I played a hunch. Walsh had a habit of giving his innovations distinctive names, the better to aid his players' memories through these massive game plans. In the final few minutes, I told my stage manager to dispatch his assistant to the San Francisco coaches' booth. I wanted the name of McIntyre's formation.

The answer came back: "It's called 'Angus,' Terry. Walsh named it for a local Black Angus restaurant. The coaches say McIntyre is known to inhale an occasional sirloin there."

When I passed the information to Madden, he exulted on the air: "It's a bull backfield! Bull! Angus! Big guy! Collapsing piles! Knocking guys down! Little backs running through! Touchdowns! Angus formation!"

1

Munich

IN THE TELEVISION business, there was never anything quite so good as working for ABC Sports in its dominant era, the 1960s and 1970s. You joined Roone Arledge's army and traveled the globe. One week, you were in Kitzbühel, Austria, the next week Tokyo, the following week Madison Square Garden.

Like Napoleon and Alexander the Great, Arledge was bent on conquering his world—annexing territory. He started by invading the little duchies that his competition dismissed as insignificant—skiing, figure skating, gymnastics. These became a confederation called *Wide World of Sports*, now, in its twenty-eighth year, one of the longest-running programs in television history. Next, he raided college football from NBC; track and field, swimming, the Preakness Stakes, and even the Kentucky Derby from CBS.

When his rivals sought refuge in long-standing relationships with major sports, Arledge attacked from nowhere to full parity in one negotiation (for example, major league baseball). Ignoring two decades of entrenchment by the others in pro football, he divided their kingdom into thirds and immediately elevated his share to a higher level (see *Monday Night Football*).

When they dared try his tactics, as CBS did with its NBA basketball takeaway of 1973, Arledge simply created hits out of thin air. *The Superstars* and *The American Sportsman*, his double-bladed counterthrust, did twice the ratings of CBS's basketball and left NBA owners feeling they'd defected to the wrong side in this war.

It wasn't just the *best* place to work back then; it was the *only* place. What arrogance it bred. At luncheons or banquets where professionals normally socialize, ABC Sports people sat among themselves, discussing their upcoming shows. They never knew, or cared to meet, their counterparts from NBC or CBS. What was the point? Unlike the news and entertainment divisions, there was no free exchange of personnel in sports. Roone never hired someone else's damaged goods. He simply recruited the brightest, most willing, most creative minds, right out of college, and trained an exclusive, superior work force.

The chosen few had typically endured a year or so shoveling elephant manure in ABC Sports' traveling circus—doing gofer work at $50 a day, *no expenses*, sleeping eight to a room—all for the honor of being one candidate in 30 to interview for a production assistant's job. This was the entry-level staff position, paying a princely $130 per week in the early '70s.

One could reject this process as extreme—the freakish, bastard child of fraternity rush and corporate business—but it was almost the only way to crack ABC's door. The one exception occurred every fourth year when Arledge sent telegrams to 50 colleges and universities, asking nominees for his Olympic researcher position.

Ah, the Olympics. This was ABC Sports' quadrennial opportunity to strut and preen and remind the world—as if every weekend wasn't often enough—that no other network was even close. CBS's 1960 broadcasts from Rome and Squaw Valley were so bad that it wouldn't try again until 1992. NBC's 1964 Tokyo and 1972 Sapporo Games were nearly as poor.

No, even the competition was now reluctantly agreed—the Olympics were best left to Arledge. After all, he had that *Wide World* team in place. They covered these sports every week.

And look at Roone's thoroughness: He hired a relentless specialist every four years to do nothing but scour the world for Olympic hopefuls, then assemble his research in huge volumes for ABC's commentators and production personnel.

In March 1971, Roone's telegram reached the desk of Roger Valdiserri, the best-known publicist in college sports and my mentor at Notre Dame. Roger must have suspected that the long Indiana winter had frozen my brain.

"Thanks for thinking of me," I told him, "but I really want to take the master's program at Columbia."

"Terry," he protested, "I don't know for sure, but I think Columbia will still be there in a year or two. This ABC opportunity is once in a career."

I was hoping to become a political reporter, maybe cover Capitol Hill or the White House for a major metropolitan newspaper some day. But there didn't seem any harm in flying to New York for the ABC interview. Or in submitting some articles from the student publications. Or in returning for the second interview.

As the process evolved, graduate school began losing its appeal. Returning from that second visit to ABC, I finally had to admit it: These people were special. I was dying to work for them.

Such sudden vulnerability. I'd felt so secure throughout senior year, flaunting my early acceptance to Columbia. Now I was like most of my classmates—hanging by my fingertips on the edge of an emotional cliff.

Two days after graduation, I went to work as a housepainter in my hometown, Natrona Heights, Pennsylvania, 30 miles up the Allegheny River from Pittsburgh. I told the foreman to expect either three days' or three months' work from me, depending on ABC's decision.

Arriving home that first evening, I was covered in satin

latex. Paint had actually soaked through the coveralls into my underpants. I crawled into the shower, wondering if I could survive three months of this. An hour later, Chuck Howard, Roone's vice president of production, phoned to ask how soon I could start at ABC.

Next thing I knew, I was in Paris and Rome, Australia and New Zealand. The Games of the XX Olympiad became a looming, singular goal. The network gave me almost total freedom to make my own schedule. There was only one deadline: On August 26, 1972, some 7,830 athletes from 121 nations would march in the opening ceremonies. I was to ensure that Roone Arledge, Jim McKay, Howard Cosell, Chris Schenkel, Frank Gifford, Keith Jackson, and all the others knew who was who.

They paid me $150 a week, virtually poverty level in New York City, but a pair of ABC Sports producers, Geoff Mason and Fred Hutchison, took me into their East Side penthouse like a vagrant off the streets. I made a bedroom of their dining room, even parked my motorcycle there.

But most often, I was on the road. I wanted to collect my research "up close and personal," as we came to say at ABC, not out of magazines and press guides. For reasons deeper than I immediately understood, Arledge agreed. He assured me that ABC's credit card was good at airline ticket counters on all six continents.

Without exaggeration, this was the most unusual job in sports television—free of weekend-to-weekend obligations and as close to the athletes as one can be. I squinted at the New Zealand rowing eight, training in virtual darkness at 5 A.M. so they could be at work by 8:30 . . . drank beer and sake with the hell-raising Japanese gymnastics team . . . watched Valery Borzov's Ukrainian blue eyes scan for Soviet officials as he broke regulations and spoke to me in English . . . heard Ugandan John Akii-Bua tell me he was one of 43 children born to his father's eight wives . . . learned that Jean-Louis Ravelomanantsoa's French

East Indian name translated to "man of good health" . . . and confirmed that sprinter Motsapi Moorosi would constitute the entire team from the tiny African nation of Lesotho.

With great relief, I thumbed 1,300 pages of this trivia, three thick books, on my Lufthansa flight to the Games. The rest of the job would be easy—updating a few bios, distributing start lists and official results, sitting just off-camera next to Schenkel, the overall host and studio anchor, making sure he had correct information. This would be the fun part.

The morning after arrival in Munich, I hustled through the ABC Broadcast Center, past the brightly lit studio and darkened control room, past Roone's comfortable suite, to find my cramped office. It was a windowless 20-foot square, packed with desks and chairs; AP, UPI, and Reuters tickers; Siemens computer terminals; and three dozen cartons I'd shipped from New York. Four research assistants, multilingual college students, awaited me.

I had barely shaken their hands when Peter Jennings appeared in the doorway. Jennings was then Middle East correspondent for ABC News, based in Beirut, Lebanon, and assigned to the Games in case of political developments. Unfamiliar with sports, he asked if I'd walk him through the Olympic Village and major venues. I almost begged off, wanting to get unpacked and keep myself available to the whole staff as instructed. But Jennings was persistent and, hell, the Games were still ten days away.

Our tour of the Village brought us to Buildings 12 and 14 Nadistrasse, home of the American team, where a dozen reporters were gathered. One of them was Sam Skinner, a black man of 270 pounds—an immense mound of high-caliber humanity and radio personality in the San Francisco Bay Area. I'd come to know him along the track circuit.

Something about seeing each other in a foreign country —it felt right to have Sam wrap me in a bear hug. We did our series of ritual handshakes, enjoying reunion so thoroughly that Jennings looked surprised.

Then, shifting to a dramatic whisper, Skinner astonished us with big news: Blacks on the U.S. track and field team were suddenly thinking of joining the threatened African boycott of Rhodesia.

In 1968, Rhodesia and South Africa had been barred from the Olympic movement for their apartheid racial discrimination. South Africa was still out, but Rhodesia had been reinstated in 1971 according to an International Olympic Committee compromise: The former British colony would compete under the Union Jack, with "God Save the Queen" as its anthem, rather than under the independent colors it declared in 1965. Black African nations had endorsed the compromise, never figuring that Rhodesia would accept these conditions. But Prime Minister Ian Smith stunned them and said okay, see you in Munich.

Now as the Games drew closer, Kenya and Ethiopia, particularly, searched for a technicality. Citing the Olympic charter, they said these Rhodesian athletes must have more than British uniforms—they must have British passports. This, of course, was impossible; they weren't British subjects. All right, said the black Africans, either they go or we go—all 34 nations.

This threat was menacing enough, encompassing the potential loss of Uganda's Akii-Bua (favorite in the 400-meter intermediate hurdles), Kenya's Kip Keino and Ben Jipcho (favorites in the 1,500 meters and 3,000-meter steeplechase), plus a host of top distance runners. But the Africans wanted added strength—black American support. The problem was that most U.S. athletes weren't yet in the Village. They were still being outfitted and processed for departure back in the States—all except the men's track and field team.

What a stroke of luck for the Africans. Early arrivals in Munich after a month-long training tour of Europe, the black American trackmen were the very stars of these Games, figures commanding enough to have their threat taken seriously.

There were two generations in this group. Lee Evans, 25, and Willie Davenport, 29, were the unquestioned leaders—thoughtful, experienced men. These were true international sports celebrities, both gold medalists in 1968 at Mexico City. There, both had seen Tommie Smith and John Carlos raise gloved fists in a "Black Power" protest during the playing of the American anthem. They also saw those teammates expelled from the Village next day, out of the Olympic movement for life.

John Smith and Wayne Collett were just out of high school then, watching Smith and Carlos on television. Now it was their turn, making this Munich team as 22-year-old recent graduates of UCLA. They were '60s children, familiar with Vietnam and civil rights disobedience. When their African brothers asked united opposition to apartheid, the issues were not lost on them, either.

Jennings knew the political angle of this story, but now Skinner and I explained the athletic consequences of black American pressure: Evans, Smith, Collett, and Vince Matthews in the 400, Davenport, Rod Milburn, and Tom Hill in the high hurdles, Arnie Robinson and Randy Williams in the long jump, et cetera.

Conjecturing on a possible boycott, *The New York Times* wrote that week: "A wholesale walkout by black athletes, Africans and Americans, would wipe out any meaningful competition in the glamour sport of the Games, men's track and field."

Sports fans everywhere would feel cheated, angry. And what about television? What about ABC and its $13.5 million investment? The world might finally understand and confront these racist governments, the Africans believed.

Skinner said U.S. athletes realized they had to make a quick decision in order to have any effect. The International Olympic Committee was still mulling Africa's threat, promising a decision in five days. If the Americans were aligning, they'd have to announce by the next afternoon, so aftershocks could reverberate into the IOC meeting room.

When Skinner suggested that we bring a camera crew the next day, Jennings and I nodded to each other. Sam, clearly, was more confidant than radio interviewer to these athletes, twice as close emotionally as any coach, black or white. At the Olympic Trials, victorious runners embraced him before seeking out their families, teammates, girlfriends—before anybody. Watching him amble back toward the door of Building 14, I predicted to Jennings that he'd have major influence in this decision.

Next afternoon, Peter and I waited with the world press, perhaps 80 journalists altogether. Just nine days to the Games, most reporters already in Munich, one story suddenly had become the only story.

Remember, this was before the boycotts of Montreal, Moscow, and Los Angeles. Granted, a similar African threat had been made in Mexico City, just before the last-minute expulsion of Rhodesia and South Africa. But that action didn't nearly involve a nation so high-profile as the United States. No Olympic Games had ever known such potential disaster as this.

Jennings and I stood side by side with his crew. They were planning to feed a lead item for that day's *ABC Evening News*. We waited, shifting and fidgeting anxiously, facing a ten-story dormitory building of gray concrete. The athletes were in there. We'd seen them return from workout. But for two hours, nobody emerged. Jennings looked at his watch.

Then Lee Evans, the 400-meter world record holder, appeared. His big jaw was protruding as ever, grimly set, as if attacking the final strides of a big race. He came forward, all thighs and shoulders, wearing a black fishnet T-shirt, shorts, and sandals.

Reporters, who had been standing a respectful distance

away, moved ahead two steps to meet him—British, German, Italian, French, Japanese, all of them. Evans seemed to be coming directly toward Jennings and me. Peter cleared his throat, smiled slightly, and began to lift his hand.

"Neil," said Evans. Somehow, he'd always dispensed with the "O'" in my name. "Neil, come with me."

Jennings dropped his hand. Astonished, I looked at Peter for a silent moment, then followed Evans inside. Yes, he knew me well enough, saw me at many meets. But we didn't have *this* kind of relationship.

We took an elevator, making small talk about the team's month in Europe and its collective craving for American fast food. Entering Evans's suite, I caught a breath. There they were, 18 of the world's finest athletes, flopped on beds, propped in corners, lying on the floor. Some were in track suits, others stripped to their shorts. Sweat clothes, socks, and ankle wraps lay all over the place. They were uniformly unsmiling, except for the nineteenth gentleman. It was Skinner, sitting at the foot of a bed. He winked at me. I began to understand.

Evans said, "Neil, can you type?"

"Sure, Lee. I can type."

"Good. You're gonna help us write our statement."

Using my walkie-talkie, I called back to the Broadcast Center for a portable typewriter and several carbon "books"—the kind used in newsrooms to produce ten carbon copies of each page.

For the next 30 minutes, Evans dictated his thoughts, sentence by sentence. I tried to sharpen them, offering a selection of phrases, then committing his final choices to paper. The others flipped through magazines or gazed outside, trying to ignore the gravity of the moment. There was conspicuously little talk. When Lee and I finished, he democratically offered his creation for criticism. The others approved it.

Turning back to me, he said, "Neil, I want you to take this downstairs and give it to the reporters."

"Me?" I reflexed.

"Yeah. You. We learned in Mexico City, Neil. If nobody's a spokesman, nobody gets in trouble. We'll walk if we have to, but we'll do it all together."

I wished them luck. Evans thanked me. Skinner winked again on my way out the door. I returned to the sidewalk and, giving new meaning to the phrase "participatory journalism," distributed the statement:

> In light of the Rhodesian acceptance into the Games, the United States' black athletes now in Olympic Park believe it imperative to take a stand concerning the issue. We denounce Rhodesia's participation and, if they are allowed to compete, we will take a united stand with our African brothers.

Apparently, it was just the turn of the screw that the Africans needed. Four days later, the International Olympic Committee again banned Rhodesia from the Games. The vote was heart-stoppingly close: 36 in favor, 31 opposed, 3 abstentions. IOC president Avery Brundage called it "naked political blackmail."

That was the start, the opening salvo, of the most embattled sports event in history. Not before, not since, has the world of sports produced such a continuous flow of hard news in a three-week period. Every day, it seemed, held a crisis.

In the opening round of boxing, unheralded Reggie Jones of Newark, New Jersey, knocked Soviet world champion Valery Tregubov all over the ring for three rounds but lost a decision. A *New York Times* headline the next day called it the "Biggest Steal Since the Brinks Job."

Jones's postfight comments were shamefully embarrassing for the IOC aristocracy. An intimidated ghetto youngster resigned himself to Olympic politics: "This ain't the first time or the last. . . . I knew this was not no dream. I knew I was not gonna get no medal. There was no sense startin' anything, gettin' mad. I just left the ring."

Within 24 hours, six boxing judges were fired and 18 others reprimanded.

Controversy raged also in the pole vault, where Bob Seagren, a handsome part-time actor from California, hoped to defend the title he'd won in 1968. Seagren sailed into Munich on the wings of a pending world record, 18-5¾, vaulted at the Olympic Trials. On arrival, however, he found that his record pole was suddenly declared illegal. It was called Catapole, a light, springy breakthrough of technology that he had mastered better than anyone in the world.

While Seagren ate dinner one evening, four Catapoles were confiscated from his room in the Village. American coaches charged conspiracy, an attempt by Europeans to deliver victory to East Germany's Wolfgang Nordwig, who still used the heavier, older model. Seagren was a gymnast at the top of his whippy pole, Nordwig a grunting muscleman.

But under new regulations, the East German prevailed. Seagren, finishing second, sarcastically "presented" his substitute pole to the international official who'd made the rule change. Then he retired on the spot, saying, "I don't want to deal with these imbeciles any longer."

The United States had no more luck in basketball. In the final game, two free throws by Doug Collins at 0:03 gave the United States a 50–49 lead over the USSR. When the Soviet inbounds pass went awry and the horn sounded, American players erupted in joy. But not so fast. An official ruled that the USSR had called timeout. Resetting, the Soviets botched another pass. The U.S. team celebrated again. But wait. This time, the officials ruled that the timer hadn't put all three seconds back on the clock.

On their third attempt, the Soviets threw a court-length pass to 6-foot-8 Alexander Belov, who bowled over

6-foot-7 Jim Forbes and 6-foot-3 Kevin Joyce, to sink the winning basket. Nobody could quite understand why 7-foot-4 Tommy Burleson remained on the U.S. bench for all three plays and the intervening arguments. Frank Gifford's call of Belov's layup: "And this time, it *is* over."

Despite Mark Spitz's seven-gold-medal *tour de force*, there was American disaster at the swimming pool as well. Rick De Mont of San Rafael, California, won the 400-meter freestyle and looked forward to the 1,500, actually his better race. But hours after the 400, he learned that his drug test had come up positive.

Since childhood, he'd taken Malax, a treatment for asthma. It contained ephedrine, a banned substance. This would have been okay if someone had warned the IOC medical staff in advance. But U.S. team doctors forgot. A tearful Rick De Mont had to return his gold medal from the 400 and was disqualified from the 1,500.

You get the idea. The American team was in chaos, reeling from one calamity to another. But this was not the worst of it. On the opening day of track and field, there came "The Case of the Empty Starting Blocks."

On the morning of August 31, Eddie Hart, Rey Robinson, and Robert Taylor of the USA ran their heats of the men's 100 meters. All three qualified easily to the quarter-finals. They had time to kill before their next race, so after lunch they stopped at a favorite spot, ABC's Broadcast Center. The entrance lounge had a large television that showed German coverage of the Games nonstop. This was a gathering place for our drivers and translators, as well as American athletes because their Village entrance gate was adjacent.

At about 4:15 P.M., the sprinters saw something very strange appear on the television monitor—100-meter sprints. Robinson thought it was a replay of the morning heats.

"This film or somethin'?" he asked.

"No," said a driver, "this is live."

The three sprinters turned to each other in horror.

"WHAT THE FUCK?!" screamed Robinson.

They leaped into an ABC car. Horn honking and tires squealing, they sped against traffic on one-way streets, through a German policeman's "Halt!" signal, along sidewalks and fresh landscaping to Olympic Stadium. The ride took seven minutes.

Dashing through the athletes' tunnel, Hart saw his race go off without him. Robinson's was the race they'd seen on television. Only Taylor made it on time. Without stretching or warming up, he jumped onto the track and qualified for the semifinals.

At that hour, Cosell was just returning from his bouts at the Boxhalle, due shortly at a dinner for ABC's Olympic sponsors. He turned the assignment over to me. All I had to do was find Hart, Robinson, and sprint coach Stan Wright—three men who wanted to crawl under a rock at that moment—and convince them to sit for interviews with Howard, well known even then as Mr. Congeniality.

Wright was at the stadium, filing a feeble protest. He seemed dazed, literally turning in circles, when I found him. Stan was near 50, heavy, jowly, with large ears and sad eyes so full of tears that the next blink was sure to start a deluge.

"Coach," I said, "I'm awfully sorry about what happened. I see you're busy with the protest, but I must ask when you can do an interview with ABC."

"I don't know. I have to talk to Bill Bowerman [head U.S. track and field coach]. Have you seen him?"

"No, I haven't."

"I have to find him before I say anything."

"Coach, there are going to be a lot of reporters wanting to hear your side. We understand that. But we can't be *beaten* on this story." I tried to fix solid contact with his moist eyes. "If you talk to anybody this evening, will you be sure to include us?"

He slumped, glanced at the ground for a moment, then looked up.

"Okay."

The search for Hart and Robinson took me back to Buildings 12 and 14 Nadistrasse. This time, the mood was ugly. Five reporters who wouldn't take no for an answer entered U.S. quarters without authorization. Coach Bowerman held forth on the top floor, a crusty, 61-year-old drill sergeant-type who cared not for the press and was accustomed to total control at the University of Oregon. He called Village security, demanding that his building be cleared of outsiders. German police evicted the five reporters, roughing up feisty Paul Zimmerman and Larry Merchant of the *New York Post*.

Bowerman's reprisal was to keep the media cooling its heels open-ended on the sidewalk: No explanation of the fiasco. No word of a forthcoming press conference. No sign of the two sprinters.

Other U.S. athletes came by. Their consensus: The start of the 100 quarterfinals was listed at 16:15. Stan Wright, unfamiliar with military time schedules, read that as 6:15.

We continued waiting. The pack grew hungry as its vigil stretched through dinner toward the five-hour mark. But no one dared leave. Bowerman might appear at any moment. Daylight turned to dusk turned to darkness. Newspapermen missed their deadlines. Merchant and Zimmerman retold their story to each new wave of arrivals.

Finally, there came word of a 10:30 P.M. press conference. I called Cosell. He met me in a large, stark room with 100 of the angriest sports reporters I've ever seen. The four principals sat up front—contemptuous, crew-cut Bowerman in the middle, hangdog Wright at his shoulder, the two sprinters on either side, positioned as far from the coaches as they could get.

Hart was the more mature, a 23-year-old graduate of Cal-Berkeley, now coaching at his alma mater. He wore a full Afro, mustache, patchy sideburns and chin whiskers. Eddie was among the most approachable athletes on the team, always very accommodating to me. His visage on this occasion spoke not anger or hostility but astounded disbelief.

Reynaud Robinson, on the other hand, was a comparative adolescent—20 years old, a junior at Florida A&M. He was extremely thin, 152 pounds stretched over more than 6 feet. He had prominent front teeth and showed his new world a skeptical, somewhat pinched, face even in the best of times. This was his first trip abroad. Indeed, he was unknown internationally until his speed-gift burst forth that summer.

Sprinting surprise of the U.S. Trials, Robinson had finished second to Hart in a world record-equaling 9.9 seconds. This was a double bonanza. Traditionally, the top four finishers at 100 meters comprised the USA's 4 × 100-meter relay team. Bowerman and Wright had confirmed Rey immediately on the first leg, despite his inexperience running the curve of the track as leadoff men do. After the Trials, he dutifully went to an optional Olympic training camp in Maine to improve his start, curve technique, and baton pass. His coaches were pleased.

But as the European tour began, Robinson faltered in Oslo, Norway. He ran fifth in an open 100 meters that included the American sprinters and a few Europeans.

Later that day, in the relay, Soviet Aleksandr Kornelyuk, a tiny 5-foot-5 demon, beat him out of the blocks. This should have been no embarrassment—Kornelyuk was the fastest starter in the world. But the finish of Robinson's leg was worse. Jostled by bigger men in the passing zone, he nearly dropped the baton.

Coach Wright panicked. From his perspective, world competition was tougher than ever. Jamaica had four sprinters trained at American colleges. The Soviets had superior stick-passing and Valery Borzov, the world's leading dashman, to anchor. At the U.S. Trials, this specter had prompted Wright to tell me, "We don't want to wait till the last leg to win the race."

Departing Oslo's Bislet Stadium, Wright reviewed his relay lineup. He decided that Robinson was inconsistent out of the blocks, risky with the baton, and too slight to withstand four rounds of the 100 plus three of the 4 × 100. He dumped him from the team and inserted Larry Black, a 200-meter man whose specialty was running the curve.

Robinson took it hard, knowing he was losing a sure gold medal. Only once since 1920 had the United States failed to win the Olympic 4 × 100, and that was a passing-zone disqualification of the dominant 1960 team in Rome. He protested, but Wright was intractable. Now as I watched Rey twist his chair another inch away from the coach, I knew he was seething with this recent history.

The press conference went badly. In a cacophony of foreign languages, broken English, and colloquial American, the journalists shouted. Their four victims, drained from an emotional day, had nothing to offer, especially in this atmosphere.

When four or five questions went nowhere, Cosell suddenly jumped to his feet and announced, "That's it. Terry, you take Eddie. I'll take Rey. Let's get the hell out of here."

Pandemonium. It was jailbreak for the foursome at the front. The room descended on Howard. American reporters were indignant. Non-Americans wondered who the hell he was, dismissing this press conference and having everyone obey.

I headed straight for Wright, intercepting him before he could rise from his chair. I attempted to redeem his earlier promise with nothing more than my eyes and the one word: "Coach?"

"I know," he sighed. "What do you want from me?"

"We'd like to walk back to the Broadcast Center and do it right now."

"Okay."

Hart, incredibly, was coming toward me. I must have been the lesser of many evils in this madhouse. Like a sergeant-at-arms, I escorted him to the door.

Outside, Paul Zimmerman jumped into my face: "You can't do this! What do you think you're doing?"

"Why don't you come with us," I suggested. But he stalked off.

Eddie and I walked in silence, Howard behind with Wright and Robinson. I couldn't think of a thing to say until we got just inside the Center, standing by the television where the sprinters had seen their Olympic hopes go flickering by just seven hours earlier.

"Eddie, would you like to call home?" I asked.

"Yeah. Thanks."

I left him 10 or 15 minutes in my research room until Roone said it was time to tape. Returning, I found Eddie Hart, college track coach, well-traveled man of the world, with big tears on his cheeks.

Cosell's interviews with the athletes were sympathetic. Then Wright sat down under the hot lights. And Howard blistered his ass:

"Now earlier, Stan, as you know, Rey Robinson said you were the culprit, you were the man to blame for their failure to show. Is this or is this not true? . . . I feel deeply sorry for you, but we all have to answer to the American public. Why in the world was America the only country to have the wrong information? . . . Final question: Do you believe that your young men can still have confidence in you as the coach in view of what happened?"

Wright ducked and fumpfed, mumbling about someone from a "higher echelon" who'd misinformed him. Not even Cosell could get him to be more specific. Roone stopped tape and sent one of his assistants into the studio to suggest a different line of questioning. Wright stepped away. After a moment, Cosell approached him, asking for another take. Stan burst into the violent sobs of a little child.

"I can't, Howard. I can't! I've said enough."

Pleadingly, he looked at me, a 23-year-old neophyte whom he knew was utterly without authority. Just then, some gear inside Cosell reversed. He said okay, threw a compassionate arm over Stan's shoulder, and led him to the door.

Back in the States, reaction to the interview was feverish. A Milwaukee headline named Cosell "Mr. Obnoxious." A Chicago columnist wrote that "the time has come, once and for all, for ABC to get rid of Cosell." A letter to the editor of *The New York Times* accused him of "trying to humiliate the man in front of millions of people. . . . The only conceivable reason for Cosell's further tasteless questioning could have been to get Wright to commit suicide in front of the TV cameras." *Sports Illustrated*, in an item headlined "The Hanging Judge," editorialized, "Cosell relentlessly badgered the obviously suffering Wright. . . . Cosell seems to think himself a crusading district attorney."

It was an ordeal personally devastating to the men involved. But on an institutional level, it was something else: apocalypse for a television form that later came to be known as "sports journalism." For the first time, a massive prime-time audience was getting its sports the way it got important, breaking news—the event, background, reaction, commentary—all immediately, before they could read it in their newspapers. Like a Presidential election or a space launch.

And the public didn't immediately accept it, didn't like swallowing its caramel-coated sports programs with a spoonful of castor oil. This was brutal, unvarnished truth, wrenched out of a man the way Mike Wallace did it on *60 Minutes*. As Cosell later wrote, "Hard news is often alien to sports coverage but it became an integral part of our Olympic coverage. This in itself was a shock to many."

Ten days after the 100-meter disaster came the 4 × 100 relay. As expected, Soviet leadoff man Kornelyuk was first out of the blocks, but Larry Black—Robinson's replacement—almost caught him at the baton pass. On the second leg, Robert Taylor opened the slimmest of leads on Jamaica and the Soviet Union. Running third, in his only Munich event, was Gerald Tinker. He scorched one of the fastest relay legs in Olympic history, nearly climbing up Eddie Hart's back with a three-meter advantage.

Now the scripted melodrama: Hart versus Borzov, anchoring head to head, for the gold medal. Having swept the 100 and 200, Borzov was in position to defeat the American sprint team single-handedly, sending them home empty and humiliated. Wright and Bowerman stood breathless at trackside. Rey Robinson watched from the grandstand.

In their first five strides, it became obvious that Hart's mishap in the 100 had left him the fresher athlete on this final day of competition. Borzov was running his eleventh race of the Games. He never closed Eddie's lead. Indeed, he watched it expand to five meters at the tape.

As Black, Taylor, and Tinker celebrated around him, Hart walked back up the track pensive and composed. But he couldn't stop an ironic grin from overspreading his pleasant face. Finally, he clenched a fist. You could read his lips: "*Damn.*"

Rey Robinson had seen enough, kept the cork in his bottle as long as he could.

"What about three years?" he exploded to the press. "What about torn ligaments, pulled muscles, a broken leg? What about all those fuckin' meets? All that bullshit at Tuskegee and Alabama State? . . .

"The man's a coach. He's supposed to get his sprinters on the blocks. What else he got more important to do? A man lives by his stopwatch. Two 9.9 sprinters out of the

Olympics. Do you dig that? Do you, man? Dig on that for a minute." In bitter cold anger, Robinson looked to the future: "He can go on bein' a coach. What can I go on bein'?"

When I spoke to Hart and Robinson in April 1988, it was nearly 16 years since Munich. We all agreed it seemed like yesterday.

Hart reconstructs: "I always figured I'd do my best at the Olympics and then, win or lose, I'd go on—have a family, get a job. But when I got home, I felt this void. Emptiness. Nothingness. Running the relay isn't the same as running the open 100. . . .

"Indirectly, I'd been preparing for the Olympics all my life. And directly, I'd lived and died with it for ten years. Then it came and I didn't even get a chance to compete. I spent the next year just wandering. I wasn't focused. But I was never, ever angry with Stan Wright. He just made a mistake. Eventually, I knew I had to deal with it."

When that year passed, the old Eddie Hart reappeared. In September 1973, he married his childhood sweetheart, Gwen Carter. He hustled several daytime jobs and finished his education at night. Today, the Harts live happily in Oakland, California, with their two children, Paris, 14, and Eddie, Jr., 10. Eddie, Sr., teaches health, physical education, and recreation at Laney Junior College in Oakland. About 1972, he confesses to a recurring dream.

"I dream about winning the 100 meters," he says, self-assured as ever. "I don't dream about Borzov so much. I just see the race—the start, hitting the tape, the victory stand, the accolades, the cheers. . . ." His voice softened as it trailed off.

Rey Robinson had a more severe reaction, tormented by the incident for many years. Olympic gold had been his obsession since age 12, when he watched television coverage of Bob Hayes, another Florida A&M sprinter, winning in Tokyo. Rey recalls:

"I told my mother, 'That's what I want to do.' Eight

years later, you get to the place where all your dreams can come true. You've tied the world record. You're at your best. You know the financial situation if you win—that was in the back of my mind. And then, you don't even get to run. For a long time, I thought, 'Why me?' "

Returning home, Robinson quit sprinting and tried football. He failed tryouts with the Miami Dolphins and two World Football League teams. He was in and out of school during this period, not making much progress toward a degree. Feeling isolated with his pain, he drifted to Rochester, New York, and Toronto, Canada, near his mother.

In the winter of '76, she took him to an indoor track meet where Robinson erupted in tears. His mother urged him to give the sport one more try. That spring, he won an all-comers meet in Toronto, then returned to Florida for serious training. He had less than three months before the '76 Olympic Trials in Eugene, Oregon.

There, Robinson was an extreme outsider—more an object of finger-pointing curiosity than a serious contender. The 100 meters is run in four rounds—heats, quarterfinals, semifinals, and final. In each of the first three rounds, the top four men advance from a field of eight. In Robinson's first three races, he finished fourth, fourth, and fourth, unexpectedly squeezing into the final. It seemed miraculous. Was Rey Robinson about to be compensated for 1972?

Not quite. In the Trials final, he finished sixth in :10.26. Fourth place, including a spot on the Olympic gold-medal relay team, went to Johnny "Lam" Jones in :10.23. Who knows if another month of training might have meant the difference? Robinson had missed redemption by just *three-hundredths* of a second.

This latest heartbreak doomed Rey to several years of near vagrancy. He wandered through various jobs—flipping burgers, cooking soul-food ribs, mopping and hauling as a janitor. Tired of being asked about Munich, he used pseudonyms and stopped mentioning track on his work applications. He now compares this period to the post-traumatic stress disorder that many Vietnam veterans suffered.

Robinson only dabbled in track during the late '70s. His last meet was the 1980 Olympic Trials, an event rendered meaningless by President Carter's boycott of the Moscow Games. Rey was eliminated in the 100-meter semifinals.

But this was a turning point. Returning from those Trials, he packed up and returned to college, finally earning his B.A. in 1983. That fall, he became women's track coach at Florida A&M and started work on a master's degree. Today, he teaches health education and coaches track and football at a high school near Clearwater, Florida.

Robinson's tone suggests that he's made an accommodation with Munich, though it rankles him still. He said he's never heard from Stan Wright, apart from a mumbled apology in our ABC studio that evening. Typically, Robinson and Hart were not included in Bill Bowerman's lengthy meeting, and Rey says Wright never sought him out in Olympic Village. It would have been so much easier, he believes, if he'd had a long talk with Wright.

I asked how often he thinks of 1972. After a pause, his voice dropped a notch. There were wide spaces between his words:

"All the time. Every time I see a track meet. Something like that, you never forget it."

In the final days of Munich, track and field offered one more controversy. Vince Matthews and Wayne Collett struck an unusual pose on the victory stand after running 1–2 for the United States at 400 meters. While "The Star Spangled Banner" played, they stood with hands on hips in a casual, almost petulant, manner. Matthews stroked his goatee. Collett shuffled about. They even turned and spoke to each other briefly.

31

This behavior contrasted sharply with the posture of Julius Sang, bronze medal winner from Kenya. A student at North Carolina Central University in Durham, he stood at attention upon hearing the familiar melody. When the ceremony ended, 80,000 fans showered the two Americans with a chorus of hoots and whistles.

In Collett's case, his body language bespoke disappointment in his second-place finish, disgust with seven weeks in Europe, and intense longing for Westwood, L.A., CA, USA. In Matthews's case, it was another unhappy tale of acrimony with the coaching staff.

Inactive in 1971, Vince began the '72 season a rank longshot to make the U.S. team. Collett, Lee Evans, and John Smith were overwhelming favorites. All three were from the West Coast, where training and competition were the best available. Matthews was from Brooklyn, of all places. He maintained a full-time job with the Neighborhood Youth Corps and supported a wife. Evenings, he scaled a 10-foot fence to train on a pitted, bumpy track that was locked up tight for security reasons. Matthews joked that climbing in wasn't hard; climbing out after an exhausting workout—that was hell.

But his effort paid off at the Trials in a third-place finish, just ahead of Evans, the great champion. West Coast coaches remained unconvinced. One predicted that Matthews wouldn't make the Olympic semifinals. Bowerman agreed, usurping U.S. Olympic Committee rules by effectively leaving the third spot open throughout the European training tour.

There, Vince proved himself over and over. Still, Bowerman held out. He decreed a match race just one week before the Games. Matthews defeated Evans again— by one yard, one-tenth of a second—finally confirming his position.

He later admitted that these were the thoughts in his mind as he slouched defiantly on the podium, twirling his gold medal. He was thinking of those fences in Brooklyn and the people who'd said he couldn't do it. But at the time, nobody knew. With the "Black Power" of Mexico City so unforgettable, our track and field commentator, Jim McKay, captured the prevailing confusion: "I can't really tell if this is some sort of protest or not, but it's certainly not standing at attention for the playing of the national anthem."

For me, it was *Mission: Impossible* once again. Convince them to sit for an interview with you-know-who.

"Cosell?" asked Collett. His tough exterior was barely thick enough to contain a boiling resentment. "Not me, man."

"Why not?" I asked.

"We won't get a fair shake."

"What do you mean?"

"He'll try to make it something more than it was."

"Wayne, that's just the point. Nobody *knows* what it was."

"That's fine. Let's just leave it that way."

"But it's not that simple. This is the Olympics. Millions of people saw you. They want to know, and they won't leave you alone till they find out."

"Well, maybe we'll tell somebody other than Cosell."

"Look, Wayne, you can think what you want about him, but remember Mexico City. He gave Carlos and Smith a platform to say whatever they wanted."

"Yeah, but what about what he did to Stan Wright?"

"What about it?"

"I hear he destroyed the poor bastard."

"Are you taking his side over Eddie and Rey?"

Collett almost cracked his angry face. "No, man. 'Course not."

"Look, he's as tired as everybody else around here. He's not gonna take advantage of you guys."

I turned to Matthews, reminding him that Cosell was a Brooklyn home-boy. Vince was exasperated, head tilted back, oblivious to his triumph in a moment that should have been the happiest of his life. We talked some more. When they agreed to have a drink with the feared ogre, I knew Howard would do the rest.

Collett wore a black and brown African dashiki to the interview and decided to make a social statement. He said his victory-stand posture mirrored White America's attitude toward blacks—uncaring, indifferent "as long as we're not embarrassing them," he said, looking straight into the lens.

Matthews was evasive. He wouldn't reveal his bitterness with Bowerman. As for political interpretations, he said, "Wayne and I have both seen protests. If we had meant to stage a protest, we could have done a better job than that."

Next morning, they got the same treatment as Smith and Carlos in '68. Without a hearing, without due process of any kind, the IOC banished them for life. This action, combined with an injury to John Smith, left the United States without four healthy, eligible men to run the 4×400-meter relay. Two days earlier, the Americans had looked certain to set a world record in the event. Now the team was scratched, meaning that Lee Evans never got to run in these Olympics. After all that.

Troubled as they were, however, Collett and Matthews —like Hart, Robinson, Wright, Seagren, De Mont, Reggie Jones, and the U.S. basketball team—turned out to be mere sports stories in the wider history of Munich, 1972.

Andrei Spitzer, Israeli fencing coach and a perceptive man of 45, had recognized these Olympics as once-in-a-lifetime. He thus insisted that his wife, Ankie, come along. They took a hotel room in downtown Munich.

When Spitzer's fencers were eliminated midway through the Games, he saw a chance to spend two days in the Netherlands, where Ankie was born and the couple had met four years earlier. All this time away, Andrei missed his beautiful, moon-faced 2-year-old, Anouk, who was staying with Ankie's parents in Amsterdam.

After the 48-hour furlough, he planned a return to Munich and his first stay in Olympic Village. Ankie and Anouk would follow in time for closing ceremonies. Perhaps the music and pageantry would leave the little girl some memory of her father's one glorious trip to the Games.

Monday evening, September 4, in Amsterdam, Andrei lingered too long over dinner with his family and in-laws. He could not let go of paternal bliss, feeding Anouk by the spoonful, bouncing her on his lap. Andrei was an adoring father. He had delayed marriage until his 40s, when full maturity was upon him, full appreciation of the divine gift who presently gurgled on his shirt.

Ankie looked at the clock and insisted they leave. She was a contemporary woman, brilliant and assertive in her late twenties, wearing long, straight brown hair to her shoulder and wire-frame glasses the way American women did in that period. Hers was the look of Gloria Steinem or counterculture Jane Fonda.

Andrei's appearance was more traditional: dark-edged glasses such as European men wore, a trim manly face, framed in bushy black sideburns. These two were not so much a match as a fine complement—her fire, his steadiness.

Andrei took the wheel of Ankie's father's car as they raced toward the Amsterdam railroad station. Traffic was heavy on this workday afternoon. Too heavy. They missed his departure.

From her youth, Ankie knew the rail schedules well. This train would stop twice more in the suburbs before rolling southeast toward Munich. They had two more chances.

She navigated from the passenger seat, pointing shortcuts through city streets. Andrei was enjoying the chase, laughing about her keen memory and refusal to be defeated. At the first suburban stop, they missed by seconds, watching the train pull out just as they parked. But they were gaining.

The coach fought his temptation to arrange another near miss. Much as he might have loved another night with his family, he could not disappoint his devoted fencers, even if their Olympics had ended. Andrei's heavy foot won the race by half a minute, time enough for a deep farewell kiss before he boarded and they waved good-bye.

He phoned about midnight from Munich.

"Well, I made it," he said. "I'm finally going to see what my bed in Olympic Village looks like. This will be different—staying with the boys."

"I love you," said Ankie.

"I love you, too, darling."

Within minutes, most of the Israeli delegation joined Spitzer in Building 31 Connollystrasse. German organizers had named their Village streets for Olympic heroes. Not many young athletes recognized the name of James Bernard Connolly, an American. In 1896, he was forced to choose between Harvard University and the first modern Olympic Games in Athens. Harvard's dean of studies refused to grant him leave of absence for this brand-new contrivance of an unknown French baron. So Connolly quit school and became the first athlete to mount a victory rostrum in the modern era after winning the hop, step, and jump.

Village streets were actually broad pedestrian malls, closed to vehicular traffic. They were lined with eclectic architecture: 10- to 12-story dormitories for huge delegations like the Americans and Soviets; pyramids of terraced, garden-style apartments for midsize groups like Poland or France; small, functional rectangles for the others to keep them from feeling overwhelmed. Building 31 was a three-story structure that housed Israel's 21-man delegation in apartments 1 through 6. (Two female athletes and a chaperone stayed separately in the women's

Village.) The units were duplexes, designed for conversion to middle-income housing after the Games.

It was a happy group that returned to these quarters shortly after midnight. They'd enjoyed a German production of *Fiddler on the Roof*. With the Games winding down in their final week, athletic tension was easing. The Israelis may have been gritty competitors, but they were not skilled to world class. None was a medal contender. In fact, only wrestler Mark Slavin was still competing at this point. Thus it was not irresponsible for the group to be bedding down at 12:30 A.M.

Slavin's coach, Moshe Weinberg, was the only man who didn't take the team bus back to Olympic Village. Veteran of three Olympic Games and collector of international friends, he'd stayed downtown in the Schwabing district, Munich's answer to New Orleans' French Quarter. There, he relived the '64 and '68 Olympics with wrestling confreres from around the world. They clapped and squeezed each other hard, as big men will do, swilling German beer and exaggerating their victories.

"Munya" Weinberg had a surprise. Reaching into his back pocket, he produced pictures of a baby son, Gur, born just four weeks earlier. The group gathered round. They tousled Weinberg's curly brown hair, patted his olive face. Gur was handsome, they said, showing no resemblance to his dad. He was the image of his mother, Mimi, who was fair in coloring with Mediterranean-blue eyes. Munya smiled a father's smile, counting the days until he'd see his son again.

Weinberg's reunion continued past 3 A.M. In that time, 50 or so ABC employees fed the satellite for Monday night's prime-time broadcast in the States. By the clock, this was a graveyard shift, but everybody on staff would have given a week's salary to work it. This was the only opportunity to admire the massive television mosaic in its completed form. Recording and editing during the day was piecemeal, confined to one sport or one venue. Only during the 1 to 4 A.M. feed could we observe the whole pattern of Arledge's format, appreciate his pacing, watch him integrate videotape with Schenkel's live lead-ins from the studio.

When we finished each night at 4, there was no reason to linger. We packed cars and minivans for a 15-minute ride back to the brand-new Munich Sheraton. Its kitchen stayed reluctantly open to serve us a limited menu of supper/breakfast. Some nights, I needed a bottle of wine or hot bath to descend from the anxiety of three hours' live television. My goal was to be asleep by 5 A.M.

The Arab fedayeen no doubt tracked the regularity of our 4:02 A.M. exodus. It was the last major activity of each night in Olympic Park.

At 4:10 on the morning of September 5, someone standing at ABC's front door would have seen six men, dressed as athletes, mounting the Village fence. This was not unusual. Entrance gates were locked at midnight. But athletes by the hundreds scaled the eight-foot fence every night after hours. The wire mesh provided good footing; there were no barbs or protrusions at the top. Security was conspicuously underplayed. Beyond any other goal, German organizers had wanted to erase the world memory of Adolf Hitler's 1936 "Nazi Olympics" in Berlin.

Two Village workmen, arriving for an early shift, saw these six hoist heavy equipment bags over the fence. Poking out the top were long rods wrapped in canvas. The "athletes" waved. The workmen waved back.

"Probably members of the rifle team," they said to each other and kept walking.

Once inside, the six moved to a grassy hillside, shucking their athletic suits in favor of other disguises—hoods and scarves, tropical hats. Some applied charcoal or colored cream to their faces and necks. They split into two groups, moving down either side of Connollystrasse. It was 4:30.

The group that walked the backside traveled an underground roadway. This was the route of bus traffic and truck deliveries, preserving the upper terrace as a shimmering, pulsating, insular village for the athletes of the world.

At the back entrance to Building 31, the threesome was joined by another pair similarly dressed. These two had been employed in the Village for more than a year, one as a cook, the other as a gardener. Ascending three steps from the underground roadway, they reached for a doorknob that should have been locked. It wasn't. Up another few steps, they were in the building lobby.

Their three fellows, walking the front side of Connollystrasse, were spotted in that moment by a shotputter from Uruguay. Unable to sleep with the disappointment of his nonqualifying performance the previous day, he was pacing at the window. Suddenly, here came three bizarre figures. In the dim outdoor lighting, it seemed they had weapons laced and strapped over their bodies, their faces painted black and red. But the Village was full of pranksters, practical jokers more intent on fun than competition. He dismissed them and returned to bed.

The eight gathered now in the lobby, outside the door to Apartment 1. It was the only Building 31 unit with an internal entrance, hidden from street view.

The cook handed a duplicate key to his leader, the one they called Issa. He was 30, very small and thin, dressed in a light blue-gray leisure suit with epaulets. He wore a white beach hat. Under the brim, his face was barely visible behind large, black sunglasses. He had darkened his skin all the way into his white cotton shirt. Later in the day, as his beach hat and diminutive form became prominent on television sets around the world, North American viewers would note a striking bodily resemblance to golfer Chi Chi Rodriguez.

The lock to Apartment 1 would not release immediately under Issa's twist. He struggled, jiggled, whispered a question to his locksmith-cook. Inside, their commotion awakened Josef Gutfreund, whose room was on the ground floor, closest to the door. Officially, Gutfreund, 41, was listed as a wrestling judge, but some insiders later claimed he was a government security official, dispatched to Munich specifically for this moment—a knock on the door in the middle of the night. He was well sized for either job: hulking, 280 pounds, brutishly strong.

If he suspected, climbing out of bed, that this might be Munya Weinberg returning from downtown, it was only a fleeting misimpression. Issa coaxed his key and the door slammed into Gutfreund's massive hands. He saw rifle stocks wedge through the crack and knew immediately.

"ARABS! TERRORISTS! COMRADES, GET OUT FAST!"

His roommate, stocky weightlifting coach Tuvia Sokolsky, popped out from under his thick German comforter. He later estimated that Gutfreund, fueled with fright, held a stalemate for 20 seconds. The door quivered like a living thing, buckling at its hinges.

The insurgents preferred not to shoot for fear of sounding a premature alarm. Instead, they butted like an eight-headed battering ram, finally overcoming Gutfreund, entering through the tangle of his muscular arms and legs.

Sokolsky reacted just in time. He crashed a chair through the glass of their French door on the back or garden side. Following behind it, he escaped in a hail of gunfire from the edgy attackers. The time was 4:35.

Issa went up the duplex's internal spiral staircase and greeted four others just awakening—track coach Amitzur Shapira; riflery coach Kehat Shorr; Yacov Springer, listed as weightlifting judge but also believed to be a member of Israeli security; and unlucky family man Andrei Spitzer, who'd caught the train outside Amsterdam and been in his Village bed just four hours. Issa took them downstairs to join Gutfreund and had the five tied up tightly, arms bound to their sides.

Down the flower-bedecked pedestrian mall rumbled Weinberg now, returning from Schwabing. He was counting on a few hours' sleep before taking Slavin to wrestling weigh-in. Munya was heavily muscled like a big, graceful cat. At 33, he may have been a coach, but plenty of ex-athlete still throbbed inside him. He bulged the beige slacks and royal blue jacket of his dress uniform, the one he would wear to closing ceremonies in five days before flying home to his family.

Weinberg encountered terrorist sentries posted outside Building 31. He landed a huge fist, swelling one commando's eye closed for the rest of this endless day, before a bullet ripped through his jaw. The Arabs bandaged him crudely, then dragged him along the face of Building 31, demanding to know where the delegation head slept.

At Apartment 2, peopled with little fencers and shooters, Weinberg said no. At Apartment 3, filled with weight-lifters and *his* wrestlers, Weinberg said yes, praying the team strongmen would resist.

But this time, the incursion was quick and soundless. On the first floor, two weightlifters were jolted upright in their beds—Zaaev Friedman and Josef Romano. In a bookend of Andrei Spitzer's story, Romano was scheduled to leave Munich the next day. He had injured knee ligaments and cartilage in competition. Surgery was set for end of the week in Tel Aviv.

Romano's Semitic appearance was dominated by thick, curly black hair, like sheep's wool, that grew low on his forehead and astride his face in wide, muttonchop side-burns. He was also 33, Libyan by birth, an interior decorator by profession, quiet among his garrulous teammates, and fiercely proud of his three daughters.

Back home, his wife, Elena, had looked forward to picking him up at Ben Gurion Airport the next morning, but she couldn't shake a sudden, stabbing fear:

"I felt something was going to happen. I can't describe it. A neighbor ran in to tell me the news and I went hysterical. I knew that even if Josi were outside this battle, he would go in to help his teammates. It was the Feast of the

New Year and I screamed, 'God in heaven, is this a holiday gift?' "

The terrorists made their first mistake at this point, sending only one man up the Apartment 3 stairwell to capture four Israeli athletes. In the front bedroom were Slavin and Eliazir Halfin, wrestlers and recent immigrants to the Promised Land. On the garden side were Gad Tsobari, a wiry 135-pound wrestler, and David Berger, weightlifter, native of Cleveland, Ohio.

The gunman took Slavin and Halfin first, then turned his back on them as he summoned Tsobari and Berger. This was the opportunity—four on one. Tsobari knew it. A veteran of the 1967 Six Days' War, he later told me, "We grow up anticipating this moment."

Tsobari signaled with his eyes and mouth. But Halfin had lived in Israel only three years, Slavin only three months. They did not understand.

So the fedayeen had taken another seven Israelis—six occupants of Apartment 3 plus Weinberg. They were cuffed and pistol-whipped into line, ready for marching toward a consolidated position in Apartment 1.

Berger, the American, screamed, "Let's attack. We're lost anyway." But a rifle butt subdued him. It was 4:40.

Filing onto Connollystrasse, Tsobari was at the front, Weinberg second. Slowly, they approached the lobby door —translucent glass framed in the same sky blue pastel that was everywhere during these "Games of Serenity."

A nightmare-come-to-life stood at the doorway. Its head was covered in canvas sack. Two cutouts showed wet, black eyes, bloodshot in the gray ovals where whites should be. "The face of death," Tsobari later described it to me.

The masked man held a submachine gun and motioned the little wrestler inside. Tsobari slowed almost to a stop. He felt Weinberg tapping him in the back. One, two, three. This was it.

Tsobari shoved the ghastly hood and ran, zigzagging to

avoid the shots. Weinberg sprang to cover him and landed another punch. Romano, on that damaged knee, hobbled back to the kitchen of Apartment 3 and grabbed a butcher knife. Weinberg followed, brandishing another.

Then, in an act of utter defiance, these two Sons of David appeared in the doorway of Apartment 1, armed only with kitchen knives against the terrorists' Kalashnikov automatic weapons.

Autopsy reports later showed that the knives indeed dug deep into Arab flesh. But in moments, the fedayeen rained a torrent of machine-gun fire on them. The commandos emptied so many rounds into Romano that when German stretcher-bearers came to take him away that night, his torso split in two at the waist.

It was 4:50. Issa knew that police would soon be arriving. There was no time to raid another Israeli apartment. He would have to be content with these preliminary results: Two escaped, two dead, nine taken hostage.

Tsobari, meanwhile, ran almost the same route out of the Village that the insurgents had taken coming in. He went over the fence at roughly the same spot and headed for the first building he saw, the ABC Center. American television personnel were gone. Only a German cleanup crew remained. In English, Tsobari told them:

"I sportsman from Israel. Five terrorists come to my house. Street Connolly number 31. They keep seven boys. I am running. They shoot after me. One wounded is Mr. Moshe Weinberg. He is wounded."

Together with Sokolsky's phone calls from South Korean headquarters, Tsobari's report set Village security in motion. At 5 A.M., an officer approached Building 31. He wore the sky blue Olympic uniform with white hat and carried only a walkie-talkie, no weapon. He saw a lanky young man in yellow turtleneck shirt and green camouflage hat, slouched against the door jamb, smoking a cigarette. A machine gun was slung over one shoulder and two hand grenades were affixed to his belt. This was Issa's younger brother, Tony, his second in command.

The security officer looked up to see Issa dropping a clip of paper from the second-floor window. It read: "The revolutionary organization Black September demands that by 9 A.M. the Israeli military regime free the 236 revolutionary prisoners whose names are listed herewith." The list covered two full sheets, in columns, single-spaced.

Black September is a violent appendage of the Palestine Liberation Organization. It was formed in September 1970 from the remnant of an Arab force routed in Jordan. Its clearly stated purpose: to drive Jews from Israel with terrorist action like this.

At 5:20, a dark-uniformed officer of the city of Munich police department arrived. He and Issa argued for a moment at the front door. The small man lost his temper: "If you don't believe us, we'll show you we're not talking to hear ourselves talk!"

With that, he leaned inside and shouted in Arabic. Two commandos dragged Weinberg's corpse by the armholes of his dress blue blazer and sent it thudding headfirst onto the pavement of Connollystrasse.

By 6:15, Roone Arledge was awakened. He'd barely gotten to sleep. Peter Jennings, who knew Black September well from his Middle East coverage, took up a superb position with walkie-talkie in Italy's team building, just across from the action. Respecting my nocturnal schedule, Dick Ebersol—Roone's assistant and my predecessor as Olympic researcher—waited until 8 o'clock before phoning my room. He knew there was nothing in my fat research books to apply to this ghoulish situation.

In plain truth, it was a day without much to report. German army tanks rolled in to seal off the area. Police sharpshooters, thinly disguised as athletes, took up rooftop positions along Connollystrasse. The fedayeen's deadlines came and went. Israeli prime minister Golda Meir flatly refused to negotiate.

Caught in between was the German crisis committee, headed by Manfred Schreiber, Munich police chief, and Hans Dietrich Genscher, federal minister of the interior. What shudders must have gone through them, awakening to the news that Jewish blood had again been spilled in Germany. But what could they do? Surely not storm the building and risk massacre. No, they would hope for a break while trying to keep Issa's mercurial moods in check.

To that end, they enlisted policewoman Anneliese Gräs, who did something very good to the official Olympic uniform. On her blonde wavy hair, the white hat looked nicely prim. Her blue skirt was hemmed just above the knee, revealing fine, shapely legs. Issa preferred her to any of the male negotiators, so she made regular visits to the front door. Three years later, giving her first interview on the subject, she told me:

"The one he told me was his brother [Tony, from a second-floor window], he kept waving to people over on the other side, shouting things to them. He spoke only in English. I said to [Issa], 'You seem to be in a good mood.' And he said, 'Well, in a few hours, everything will be done and we'll be going home.' They really thought everything would be all right. And I said, 'You shot somebody.' He said, 'Well, that was his own fault. He was getting at me with a knife.' And he showed me the cut in his jacket.

"So I asked him where he did come from. He said he was born in Nazareth and his mother was Jewish and his father Jordanian. He said he'd led a good life—plenty of women, plenty of money. But he said he didn't like that anymore since he'd seen what happened over in Palestine. Then he told me he had two brothers in prison in Israel, one 18, one 28 [two of the 236 whose freedom Issa demanded]. He thought that things must be done now and people should see. That's why he was here."

At ABC, the control room monitors showed a Felliniesque film of bewildering contradiction. On one screen

45

were Issa and Officer Gräs outlined against the gray concrete of Building 31, on another monitor volleyball, on another boxing, on another a mass demonstration in Olympic Park to halt the Games. Incredibly, the IOC allowed competition to continue into late afternoon. It was 3 P.M. when Cuban heavyweight Teofilo Stevenson knocked out American hopeful Duane Bobick.

Minutes later, Issa told Officer Gräs that he wanted to take the hostages to Cairo, Egypt. She summoned Genscher and Schreiber to the scene.

Genscher asked, "Are they still alive? We want to see them."

Issa turned to Tony, who produced a haggard-looking man in the second-floor window. He had dark frame glasses, dark hair, sideburns, and a white undershirt. It was Andrei Spitzer. Ankie watched, spellbound, on her parents' television in Amsterdam.

Spitzer told Genscher that the hostages were fine, just sitting on the floor quietly. He volunteered an opinion that Israel would not trade prisoners. Yes, it was true, he said, the hostages wanted to go to Cairo with their captors.

After conferring with Prime Minister Meir, Genscher decided not to let the group leave German soil. Extradition to Cairo, they agreed, was a death sentence. But the flight was a fine pretext to get the commandos out of their fortress, into some venue where a firefight wouldn't endanger bystanders.

Schreiber planned to attack in one of three places—along the underground roadway as the group boarded buses; at a grassy, makeshift helicopter pad along the Village fence; or on the tarmac of Fürstenfeldbrück Airport, an isolated military airfield located 15 miles from Munich.

At 9 P.M., the nine Israelis—bound hand and foot, roped together, and blindfolded—were led downstairs to the back door of Building 31. Attack option #1 dissolved immediately when Schreiber saw the Arabs packed in tightly with their hostages. Worse, he was stunned to count eight terrorists for the first time, not five as he presumed from Tsobari's account and his own observation.

At the helicopter pad, option #2 also faded quickly. The revving Bell Iroquois drew hundreds of spectators. One of them was Jim McKay's teenage daughter, Mary. She later told me, "The Israelis were so close, you felt you could almost touch them. But nobody in the whole world could help."

Schreiber's ambush was now destined for the airfield. It showed a small, three-story control tower and ample floodlighting from latticed steel girders. But the Germans would face disadvantages. Having miscalculated enemy strength and spread his force to cover three potential battle sites, Schreiber was thin of men. He had only five sharpshooters at the airport. And by an oversight, they had neither infrared rifle scopes to combat the darkness nor walkie-talkies to discuss target selection.

The two helicopters touched down at one side of the terminal building. Hostages and commandos were distributed in each. On the opposite side of the tarmac, perhaps 130 meters away, a Lufthansa 727 jet sat fully lighted with motors turning. Three of Schreiber's five marksmen were aligned on a second-story ledge of the terminal building, behind bowl-shaped floodlamps. Two more knelt in darkness across the field.

Issa left Tony in charge of the helicopters and took a compatriot named Paolo to inspect the 727. Weapons in hand, they walked briskly at a slight crouch, panning left and right. Issa's white beach hat gleamed in the harsh lights.

The airplane's front left passenger door was open. A conventional stairway led up from the tarmac. But upon entering, Issa and Paolo found no one. A regular Lufthansa crew had been instructed to stay in place, promised that the terrorists would not be engaged in the airplane. But at the last minute, helicopters buzzing into view, the seven civilians panicked and dashed away. We will never know Issa's and Paolo's reactions to seeing an empty airplane.

Back across the airfield they started. Marksmen had been ordered by Schreiber to fire when ready. As the pair came even with the terminal building, five Germans knew this was their best chance.

Crack! The first shot rang out, dropping Paolo. Issa ran a weaving path, 70 or 80 meters, through lighted, open space. Amazingly, the sharpshooters missed him.

He scrambled under a helicopter and began shooting out the lights. The four German helicopter pilots bolted from their seats. Two were shot to the ground.

For the next 90 minutes, gunfire was only sporadic. The Germans dared not fire on the helicopters for fear of hitting hostages. The terrorists couldn't see anything to shoot.

At 11 P.M., there came an offer via loudspeaker, repeated in German and Arabic: "Throw your weapons away and give yourselves up. In the name of the German Federal Republic, we promise your lives will be spared. Give us your answer vocally."

No reply.

Within 10 minutes, the cease-fire triggered false reports that the hostages were safe. At ABC headquarters, Conrad Ahlers, German press secretary, swept past me along a hallway and entered the studio to sit with Jim McKay. He was a smooth, reassuring presence in white hair and dark suit.

Ahlers told U.S. viewers, "I'm very glad that, as far as we can see right now, this police action was successful. Of course, it's an unfortunate interruption of the Olympic Games. But if all comes out as we hope it will come out, or *has* come out, I think it will be forgotten after a few weeks."

The same message reached Golda Meir in Jerusalem. Her crisis room erupted in joy. Cabinet ministers opened bottles of cognac and champagne.

Back at Fürstenfeldbrück, Schreiber sat in darkness and stalemate with Issa. It was not, however, the same condition they'd known on Connollystrasse. Issa had now involved German nationals—the two helicopter pilots lying wounded. Looking down from the control tower, Schreiber still wanted a safe result for the Israelis. But he determined to rescue his two countrymen.

At 11:55, long-awaited German reinforcements arrived —six impregnable armored cars. Schreiber rolled them onto the tarmac. The fedayeen responded with automatic blasts, a futile waste of ammunition. As the steel mastodons encircled, closing to within 30 meters, Issa jumped up from between the skids of one helicopter. He pulled the pin of a grenade and lobbed it squarely into the center of the fuselage.

Inferno. Huge flames sprang 40 meters high. In the other helicopter, Tony understood. He squeezed his automatic trigger, raking back and forth over the hostages until his ammo clip was empty.

Issa dashed toward him, zigzagging once again in exposed terrain. Searchlights atop the armored cars caught him. This time, German marksmen did not miss.

Without their leader, three commandos were broken. They played dead among the Israeli corpses until police discovered them. Brother Tony somehow escaped among the steel cars and led his pursuers—for 60 outrageous minutes—on a fantastic chase across runways and past fuel tanks to an airport parking lot. There, at approximately 1 A.M., he was killed.

Unofficial but accurate word of the Israelis' deaths reached ABC almost immediately. I stood behind Roone as he fed the news to McKay via his earpiece. It seemed an awful burden, knowing that Jim would have to carry this tragic secret for many minutes until confirmation came. But Arledge knew him well. The former Baltimore newspaperman was a rock.

Roone had summoned him from our hotel swimming

pool at 8:30 A.M., sensing his correctness as studio host this day. It was like McKay not to have taken five minutes to change clothes. Now, 16 hours later, he remained crisp and authoritative, anchoring between Peter Jennings and Lou Cioffi of ABC News—still wearing swim trunks under his slacks.

Returning to the Olympic press center about 2:30 A.M., Genscher and Schreiber addressed an auditorium overflowing with journalists. They listed five terrorists dead, three captured; one helicopter pilot critically wounded, the others safe; one German policeman killed, and all 11 Israelis dead.

As Camera 2 pushed into a head-and-shoulders framing of McKay, his summer tan seemed faded. His blue eyes had never looked so deep-set. At Arledge's cue, he reported:

"They've now said there were eleven hostages. Two were killed in their rooms this—ah, yesterday morning. Nine were killed at the airport tonight. They're all gone."

I have never been in a place that everyone was so universally desperate to abandon as Munich on the day after closing ceremonies. Your bones hurt. Your soul ached.

Beyond that, I don't believe Arledge, McKay, Jennings, or any of us felt another emotion. We were numb. It was surreal.

In November 1975, Roone assigned me to produce and write a reconstruction of the "worst day in the history of sport," according to McKay's ominously accurate phrase. I was privileged to interview many of the surviving principals, in both Germany and Israel. Only then did I begin to understand.

I saw rocket shells and overturned tanks on the Golan Heights, feeling the ever-present trauma of Israel. I interviewed Golda Meir, the former schoolteacher from Milwaukee, beheld the supreme dignity in that craggy, weary face. Of the Munich terrorists' demands, she told me:

"Our immediate reaction is negative. If we should give in, then no Israeli anywhere in the world can feel that his life is safe. It's blackmail of the worst kind."

I sensed the extended family atmosphere, Israel having been galvanized by centuries of persecution. Its people cling so closely that Tel Aviv, population 330,000, feels like a small town.

I heard stories of the Six Days' War, with air battles in the skies directly overhead. Israeli fighter pilots juked and dodged wildly to avoid the Egyptians' heat-seeking missiles. But if they failed and the heavens burst into flame, everybody aground knew from the airplane tail number whose sons had been killed.

I met the Munich widows. Elena Romano's face contorted as she re-created the horror of September 5: *"God in heaven, is this a holiday gift?"*

Ankie Spitzer was more composed as she told of chasing that fateful train through Amsterdam. Her wedding picture stood eerily on an end table—she and Andrei passing under the crossed swords of his fencers. Meanwhile, 5-year-old Anouk drew me a picture. She was beautiful— still moon-faced, wearing bangs and a long, dark braid. Her picture was sunshine and flowers.

We had to stop our interview with Mimi Weinberg after just a few minutes. She dissolved into tears at the mention of Munya's name. To compose herself, she went into the kitchen and prepared lunch for my crew. I rolled a ball across the carpet with 3-year-old Gur, the little towhead. Mimi looked at us through the doorway and said, "As he gets older, more and more he asks about his father."

2

Part I: Sports Journalism

RETURNING to New York in 1972, I found that Roger
Valdiserri was correct. Columbia was still there. I did my
master's in one wonderful year, aided no little by ABC
Sports.

In October 1972, I became statistician for *NCAA College Football* and *ABC's NFL Monday Night Football.* This
was another of the best jobs in TV sports. I got to sit in the
broadcast booth beside Schenkel on Saturdays, Gifford on
Monday nights. For this, they overpaid me $125 a game,
plus all the airline food and room service I could eat.

All I had to do was secure approval from Columbia
professors, who nicknamed me "Peripatetic O'Neil." I left
New York after Friday classes for the college game, returning Saturday night to spend all day Sunday in the
library. Mondays, I was finished on campus at 12:30 and
could make it into an NFL booth anywhere in the country
by 8 P.M., an hour before kickoff.

Returning for my Tuesday 9 A.M. class was simply a
matter of using every "red-eye" overnight flight in the air.
Monday nights in Denver and Kansas City were trickiest,
making for weird connections through Dallas or Atlanta.
But I made every class, determined not to disappoint my
faculty adviser. He'd been skeptical of this plan. No football fan, he shook his head and asked, "You mean they're

playing football on Monday nights now?" It was the fourth year of prime-time games.

Graduating in the spring of 1974, I headed to Richmond/Petersburg, Virginia, and an on-air assignment with the ABC affiliate there, WXEX. This was an audition. Arledge and his college football producer, Chuck Howard, had decided they would try a young sideline reporter on games that fall. I was one of five finalists to be considered.

It was a great time to call oneself a journalist, this being the summer of Richard Nixon's impeachment hearings and eventual resignation. Feeling proximate to the capital and imbued with the spirit of *Washington Post* reporters Bob Woodward and Carl Bernstein, I seized a juicy Virginia story that nobody was covering—not the locals, not the national sports press, though it surely was worthy of attention.

Seventeen-year-old Moses Malone of Petersburg High School was under siege—the most heavily recruited schoolboy basketball player ever to that point. WXEX let me produce and host a special, *The Courtship of Moses Malone,* that accused five schools—New Mexico, Clemson, Maryland, Kentucky, and Detroit—of NCAA recruiting violations.

Kentucky and Detroit allegedly supplied Malone female companionship at high school all-star games. Clemson, soon to earn a three-year probation (1975–77) for abuses in its basketball program, reportedly offered cash and a car.

New Mexico was the most arrogant. Its assistant coach, John Whisenant, took up residence in a Petersburg motel for three months, playing daily pickup games with Mo. Afterward, they'd inspect floor plans for the apartment, complete with billiards room, that awaited in Albuquerque, or maybe discuss Mo's new wardrobe. Recognizing that 7-footers wear only custom clothes, Whisenant had a campus tailor ship an assortment of slacks and jackets for the player's approval.

Maryland was under a regional microscope, situated just 110 miles north of Petersburg. On Malone's campus visit to College Park, he fell hard for the coed assigned as his weekend escort. This was not recommended in the NCAA handbook, but it certainly was not illegal. Problem was that Mo wanted to continue seeing the young lady. What a break for the Terrapins. Assistant coach Joe Harrington allegedly shuttled her to Petersburg for periodic visits as her class schedule allowed.

How we agonized about running that story. It came not from Maryland's recruiting competition but from Malone's playground buddies. We confirmed it twice over. I spent three days trying unsuccessfully to get Head Coach Charles "Lefty" Driesell on the phone. Finally, on the night before air, I told his secretary the substance of our information, asking for his comment. Within five minutes, Driesell's outrage was booming through my telephone:

"You mother-fucker. You cock-sucker. If you bastards say that on the air, don't you ever come near this campus again. Don't you *dare* think about getting into our gym as long as I'm here."

"Coach, is that a denial?" I asked.

"You mother-fucker. You cock-sucker. . . ."

We ran the story. Mo committed to Maryland soon thereafter but before enrollment signed with the American Basketball Association. The NCAA figured "no harm, no foul" and never pursued alleged violations in "The Courtship of Moses Malone."

Despite this splash, I didn't get the sideline football job. It went to Jim Lampley, and the minute I saw him on camera, I understood why. He was a smooth, polished performer. To my delight, I found he was also a soulmate. Call it generational if you like, we saw sports television identically.

When I returned to ABC as an associate producer in October 1975, Lampley and I set to work. At the '76 Innsbruck Winter Olympics, we had the reporting role all to ourselves, Cosell being uninvited. ("I don't know if America is ready for the sight of Howard in stretch pants" was Arledge's whimsical explanation.)

Lampley narrated and I produced a monstrous seven-minute backgrounder on under-the-table payments to Alpine skiers. Franz Klammer of Austria was the biggest of them. He'd switched between Austrian ski manufacturers that season, from Kneissl to Fischer. A Kneissl representative came on camera to charge that Klammer knew his new skis were slower but figured he could still beat the competition. Besides, the deal was worth more than $1 million. Fischer people denied the part about their skis being slower but wouldn't comment on payments to their new client.

This kind of story was freely bantered in Innsbruck, fireside over a glass of schnapps. But absolutely nobody was doing it on television, just one Olympics after Austria's Karl Schranz was banned from the '72 Games for accepting money.

If athletes maintained hypocritical "amateurism" for the sake of the IOC, Lampley and I agreed that was fine. What we couldn't understand was complicity by journalists who knew better. Arledge saw it our way, overruling internal arguments that the piece would sabotage the "fantasyland" appeal of these Games. Klammer won the downhill with a thrilling plunge, and American viewers had a fuller understanding of him thanks to Roone's conviction.

Lampley and I did not always prevail, however. In 1977, I was assigned to produce a one-hour prime-time preview of the upcoming college football season. This was part of ABC's contract with the NCAA.

I plotted the normal quota of touchdown runs and cheerleader wiggles, plus some predictable features—

Johnny Majors "comes marching home" to Tennessee, Darrell Royal and Frank Broyles play golf and reminisce after retirement from Texas and Arkansas, respectively. The kind of stuff you'd expect.

But I added this pitch in my advance memo to ABC Sports management: " . . . a piece on recruiting, which begins with Oklahoma's recent problems, namely, the ticket scalping matter. Billy Brooks, their WR of two years ago, recently told the Associated Press a lengthy tale of Oklahoma violations—clothing, cars and ticket scalping. Steve Davis also has confirmed this to me. If we could get one of them to do it on camera . . . and then get [Coach Barry] Switzer's reaction, we might have a piece."

No response from my bosses. So Lampley and I jumped on a plane to Norman, Oklahoma. There, in the shadow of Owen Field, we interviewed Davis, the Sooners' wildly successful quarterback from '73 through '75.

Davis had an astounding three-year record of 32–1–1, leading Oklahoma to three Big Eight and two National championships. But his group was known as the "best team nobody ever saw." They were on NCAA probation all three years, barred from television appearance most of that time. An assistant coach, long since departed, had been caught altering the academic transcripts of two players.

Apart from his on-field talent, Davis was a square-jawed, look-you-in-the-eye Okie. He had studied as a Baptist minister and spent his Sundays giving sermons around the state. Lampley and I had gotten to know him in '76 when he did commentary on a handful of ABC regional games. Taking seats on the grass outside Owen Field, we knew his word was 24-karat.

Steve told a story that was at once startling but also highly understandable: In 1973, a local auto dealer approached him, saying he needed OU football tickets for his top customers—75 season books for games in Norman, 100 seats for the annual war with Texas on State Fair

Weekend in Dallas. Would Davis kindly gather up the university-supplied tickets of his teammates? There'd be reasonable profit for them and for him.

Davis mulled. His teammates, mostly from middle- and low-income families, subsisted on campus without much money. Some couldn't afford a Saturday night date. Others couldn't afford to dress well for road games as they'd been instructed. Hell, Sunday nights, when training table was closed, a few couldn't afford dinner.

Davis also weighed the legendary Sooner permissiveness about ticket scalping. Switzer reportedly knew and joked about it among his coaches. He wasn't alone. Freshman year after the Texas game, Davis stood in the Cotton Bowl tunnel and listened to opposing players brag about getting $200 and more for their precious seats. Why not? The two universities were making plenty on this spectacle. To the preaching quarterback, this ticket-selling plan sounded like old-fashioned, Old Testament justice.

Labor Day weekend 1973, the auto dealer's bagman handed Davis $56,000 in cold, green cash. Some of those bills had Presidents he'd never seen.

Steve took a partner, halfback Grant Burget. The line at their checkout counter was 30 or 40 athletes long, stretching down a corridor of the athletic dorm. Davis negotiated; Burget wrote the checks. On average, they paid four times the $120 face value for season books.

Less than three hours later, the commerce done, there was $12,000 left on the table. With his half, Burget bought a brand-new '73 Camaro. Paid cash in full. Never mind the fact that his sudden wealth had been provided by the local Oldsmobile dealer.

Davis banked his share, later using it for clothes and for autographed photos that he mailed to beseeching fans. His teammates also benefited. Their athletic dorm sounded very good that year—there were a lot of new stereos.

Leaving Davis that summer day in 1977, Lampley and I went to see Grant Burget, who was now a stockbroker trainee in Oklahoma City. Burget's upper lip quavered—maybe vibrated is the word—when he heard Davis's tale. But he would not confirm it.

Lampley and I returned to New York, wanting to transcribe the interviews and assemble them coherently for comment by Switzer. But our airplane was no match for the speed of two mortified Sooners. Burget phoned his former coach. Switzer then phoned Jim Spence, vice president of ABC Sports. These two had recently been on a junket together and become friendly. Switzer said his program and his university could not tolerate the airing of this material. Spence allegedly said he'd handle it.

Jim Spence was a plain-looking, dark-haired man. He walked ABC's hallways with an aggressive forward lean, often pursing his lips as if readying for corporate combat. "The feisty little battler," we called him.

Outside the executive circle, he rarely appeared, remaining bunkered in his office behind great mounds of paper. "He thinks he's running the CIA" was the office joke, even among his closest allies.

Spence's view of television could not have been more different from Lampley's and mine. He was hired in 1960 by the organization that became ABC Sports. Watching Arledge scrap for events in those early days against powerful NBC and CBS, he must have decided that programming properties were everything. Indeed, taking charge of event acquisition several years later, his approach was to nurture and protect major rights holders above all else.

This strategy was sometimes dangerous. In 1977, Spence and boxing promoter Don King staged the "United States Boxing Championships." Avowed purpose: to crown American champions in all weight divisions. Real purpose: hot programming, big ratings.

A street-smart ABC Sports associate producer, Alex Wallau, warned Spence in several memos that the tournament was riddled with unqualified fighters from King's stable, some listing phony records. Spence ignored him, later admitting he hadn't fully read Wallau's memos.

The tournament crashed in major embarrassment, prompting a congressional investigation. The hearings in Washington produced several classic lines. Congressman Marty Russo of Illinois asked Spence, "Is it your policy to request of an employee of yours to prepare a memorandum and then not read it?"

Later, during a recess, someone in the men's room asked Howard Cosell why he didn't come to Spence's rescue.

Cosell, shaking himself off at the urinal, replied, "The guy makes $100,000 a year and doesn't read his memos? Fuck'm."

I had never trusted Spence since a moment in September 1971 when I saw him producing the *College Football Scoreboard*. In those precomputer days, game results were manually displayed by a technician on a scoreboard with flipping numbers. Just before air, Spence would instruct his board operators to withhold changes in one or two critical scores. Then during the program, when a camera panned to those games, technicians would post the scoring changes on Spence's cue. The commentator would marvel, "Oh, look here, late-breaking developments! XYZ State has just scored a touchdown."

It was no surprise, then, that Jim Spence told Lampley and me our Oklahoma piece was inappropriate for the preseason show. He said the program was an "NCAA promotional vehicle." When we suggested halftime exposure in an important telecast, Spence said we couldn't air it without Switzer's reply. And Switzer wouldn't reply. Later, he said that ticket scalping was old hat, really not newsworthy anyway.

"I think he tried a little bit of everything," Lampley now remembers.

When Spence told us to abandon the piece, the lesson to Lampley and me was clear. There was no commitment to "sports journalism," no consistent guideline about what did and didn't air. There was only expediency. Oh, and one other thing we learned: It helped to have Cosell on our side.

Howard was a steamroller, a cement mixer in those days, crushing objections every direction he turned. Less than a year after the Oklahoma fizzle, I produced Lampley and him on a series called the *ABC Sports Magazine.* We tackled another touchy college football story—this time, with far better results.

On November 19, 1977, a freshman fullback from Irvington, New Jersey, named Bob Vorhies made the only carry of his life for Virginia Tech. He gained 12 yards against Wake Forest.

Vorhies was huge for a running back, 6-foot-2, 242 pounds, and athletic. A year earlier, he had been the nation's number five indoor high school shotputter. New coach Jimmy Sharpe marked him a foundation stone in Tech's rebuilding program.

Hours after the Wake Forest victory, Vorhies was in the dormitory, grinning about his 12-yard carry. Offering a replay to his buddies, Bob lined up in a three-point stance and went hurtling into a closet door. He hit the flimsy wooden panel with his muscular shoulder and curly brown head, leaving splinters in the hallway. A dorm adviser heard the commotion and had a laugh with the celebrating players but informed Vorhies that he'd earned punishment drill.

Two days later, the Gobblers had a normal Monday practice, concluding with ten 100-yard sprints, or "gassers." Then Vorhies faced his punishment:

- Ten 50-yard dashes at 0:15 each, including recovery to the start line
- Ten 100-yard dashes at 0:30 each, including recovery
- Two 100-yard bear crawls
- 50 pushups

- 50 situps
- Four other 100-yard drill

Under the supervision and urging of an assistant coach, Vorhies finished panting and exhausted. Too tired to shower, too weak to cut the tape off his ankles, he walked back to Hill Crest Dormitory in soaking sweat clothes. He then left a note for teammates Steve Wirt and Jeff Bowling, canceling plans to see a movie with them.

Wirt came back from dinner to find Vorhies's massive body perched on the toilet.

"How you feelin'?" he asked.

"Tired. Real tired," Bob groaned. "And I got diarrhea."

"What was runnin' like?"

"I got double duty."

Bowling joined them. "Did you puke any?" he asked.

"Yeah, I puked some blood."

Wirt and Bowling went to their movie. Bob Vorhies was too tired even to manage a short walk to the dining hall. Still wearing his ankle wraps, still not showered, he wobbled back to Room 227 and climbed into bed.

Wirt and Bowling returned from the theater at 11:04. In Vorhies's room, they heard an alarm clock ringing. It had been set for 9:45. Their teammate was lying naked on the floor. Dead.

Cosell wasn't required to make trips like Blacksburg, Virginia. But Lampley and I went. We learned there were three witnesses to the punishment drill. Two of them, Tech professor Jim Richardson and his wife, Kathie, wouldn't speak to us on advice of their attorneys. Without them, we didn't have much.

But on the district attorney's desk, our associate producer, Joe Valerio, spotted the Richardsons' testimony to a special grand jury. Reading upside down faster than most people read right side up, Valerio twigged instantly.

"Do you mind if we 'white-balance' the camera for a

moment?" he asked the D.A., sounding ever so sincere. With that, he held two precious pages to the lens.

The Richardsons had testified, "The player was extremely fatigued. . . . We could hear heavy breathing for a distance of over 70 yards. . . . It appeared he could hardly lift his feet. . . . Once the coach said something to the effect, after looking at his stopwatch, 'Eleven seconds late—let's go again.' "

The third witness, janitor Robert Wingo, was not called before the grand jury. But he told us, "They made him crawl. He fell down and they made him do it again. He was crawling and he dropped down and the coach made him get back up. The coach said, 'Get back up.' He said he couldn't. And the coach made him get back up."

The telling word, however, came from chief medical examiner Dr. David Oxley:

> OXLEY: As we stated in our report, the temporal relationship between the drills and the time of death suggest there may be some relationship between the drills and Mr. Vorhies' death. However, there is no anatomic connection and the physiological connection remains obscure. . . .

> LAMPLEY: So while it might be easy for the layman to look at this situation and say, "This guy had to undergo a very strenuous set of exercises after football practice and maybe they had something to do with the fact that he dropped dead," from a scientific standpoint, the bottom line is that a young, very healthy athlete dropped dead and you don't know why.

> OXLEY: That's true.

The scene in Irvington, where Cosell and I went to interview the player's father, was sheer anguish. Bob was Jerome Vorhies's pride, his only child, now dead at 18. Jerome broke down on camera as he vowed to sue Virginia Tech.

The university probably made a mistake in holding its own memorial service on campus, rather than traveling the team to New Jersey. The Vorhies family felt abandoned, its grief never shared nor adequately buried.

As we tried to leave, Jerome refused to turn loose the sleeve of Cosell's coat.

"Please," he sobbed, "please help me. You're a powerful man. People will listen to you. I have to know what happened to my son. A boy like that doesn't just die."

We went outside for Howard's on-camera wrap: "Every parent in the nation has to have a vital concern. . . . It is time, forevermore, to eliminate punishment drills for athletes in this nation."

The story of Jerome Vorhies continued long after our program left the air. Never satisfied with the university's or the grand jury's explanation, never purged of his bitterness, Jerome suffered a fatal heart attack at the gravesite on the third anniversary of his son's death.

At ABC Sports, executive row swelled only slightly when *Death of a Football Player* was nominated for an Alfred I. du Pont Award, Columbia University's prize for excellence in broadcast journalism. Mostly, however, our leaders seemed relieved that the NCAA took no offense.

Their paranoia was without foundation. In my 15-year network career, I never knew of a single instance where rights holders issued reprisals for honest, accurate journalism. Major contract negotiations were constantly underway, and in nearly every case, the issues were simply how much money and how much exposure.

Cosell, Lampley, and I were aberrant, never able to convince our colleagues that, when warranted, the reason for tough reporting was merely to present a balanced view of sport. This wasn't a Walt Disney movie. It was a mirror of real life. Athletes sometimes cheated, sometimes lied, scalped tickets, took money under the table, missed their races, dishonored the flag, got taken hostage, and died. The human reason to report this was simple—it was the truth. The television reason was also simple—it was riveting, the stuff of big ratings. What did Daniel Webster say? "There is nothing so powerful as truth."

It occurs to me that my introduction to sports television was most unusual. For the first 15 months, I had no exposure to cameras or videotape machines, the conventional starting point in a visual medium. I had only my Olympic research—people and their stories. Funny how Cosell and Lampley didn't start with pictures, either. They began in radio.

What an unlikely trio we were. Unlikely, yet collectively distinct from our colleagues. Mondays after we'd slipped some good reporting past executive corner, Cosell could be heard to say, "Goddamnit, we're the only ones who recognize a fucking story around here."

Part II: Cosell: Superstar or Journalist?

NO MISTAKING, this was the big time—riding to Schaefer Stadium in a stretch limousine with Chet Forte, the legendary director of ABC Sports. Security guards waved us past their barricades without question. Pedestrians craned to see the "celebrities" behind tinted-glass windows.

Forte was the only celebrity. At 5-feet-8, he had beaten the odds and become an All-America basketball player at Columbia University. It was the late '50s. His two-hand set shot was deadly from long range.

Next stop for Forte was CBS, where he worked in the associate director pool and organized nonstop card games. In 1963, he departed for ABC Sports, a move that looked foolish to the colleagues he left behind. After all, CBS was the "Tiffany's of network television" and ABC, saddled with the weakest affiliates, was ridiculed as the "Almost Broadcasting Company."

But those who doubted Chet's judgment didn't know Roone Arledge and his plans for ABC Sports. More to the point, they hadn't realized that Roone was a producer, and his two senior aides, Jim Spence and Chuck Howard, were also producer-types. Swallowing up major events at a furious pace, Roone badly needed a top director. Enter, Chester, and sign in please.

By the time he stepped into this limousine on August

24, 1980, Chet had done it all—seven Olympic Games, all ten years of *Monday Night Football*, countless championship fights, the World Series, Baseball All-Star Game, Indianapolis 500, Kentucky Derby, NBA basketball, even the Bobby Fischer–Boris Spassky world championship of chess from Reykjavík, Iceland.

He was the preeminent director in sports television. Yet he did not indulge in self-congratulation, disdaining the tag that concluded ABC Sports broadcasts: "recognized around the world as the leader in sports television."

About this time, Chet offered an opinion on *Monday Night Football*, the series that made him famous and drove his salary beyond $500,000 annually: "The worst thing you can do is sit on your success. And for the last two or three years, I think that's what we've been doing. We've gotten blasé, and the show's gotten a little tired and stale. It's so damn easy for me to do this show now. You've got to have something to keep you up."

As we rode, it was actually the starting pitchers of major league baseball who were keeping Forte's interest. His swarthy Italian face narrowed as he hunched over the *Boston Globe*'s baseball page. He winced behind reading glasses, mumbled about Tom Seaver's last outing, made his selections, and marked them with a ballpoint pen. When we arrived at the truck, Chet's first move would be to call his bookie.

Our game was football. It was still two-and-a-half hours to kickoff of an NFL preseason game between the Philadelphia Eagles and the New England Patriots. It was my third telecast as producer of the most celebrated series in our business, *Monday Night Football*.

Only three years a producer, I hadn't earned this seat in Forte's limousine on lengthy experience. Sure, I'd produced college football, *Monday Night Baseball*, *Wide World of Sports* events, prime-time boxing, tennis, studio scoreboard programs, even a live entertainment special at the Kentucky Derby. But having just turned 31, I was one of the youngest producers on the ABC Sports staff. My distinguishing feature was a reputation for working effectively with Cosell.

Howard was at the depths of impossibility in 1980. His fame and influence were so overwhelming that he'd lost all pretense of civility to underlings. His work load, meanwhile, had become so enormous that life seemed joyless— a forced march from one broadcast to the next, one airport to the next, one tantrum to the next.

In this ill humor, no one dared cross him—not athletes, not coaches, not coworkers. Producers and directors were ridiculously overmatched. Cosell dressed them down in public for mere sport. Even Arledge kept his distance, maintaining only the faintest of relationships. But *somebody* had to work with him on *Monday Night Football.*

Ever since Munich, Howard had treated me just slightly different from the others—not with esteem, mind you, but with a certain accommodation. Among colleagues who saw themselves as being in the entertainment business, Cosell and I were self-described journalists.

Our collaborations tended to be news-style reports—the U.S. boxing team's fatal airline crash in Poland, or the first interview with Renée Richards after her sex-change operation. Howard praised a 1977 minidocumentary I did with Arthur Ashe on racism in South African sport. It was this kind of work that had won me a seat beside Chet Forte in August 1980.

Our limo came to a halt in the middle of the ABC Sports compound, $8 million worth of house trailers, television mobile units, and sophisticated electronics. Forte waited for the driver to get his door. I, meanwhile, yanked my own door handle and jumped out to meet a dozen milling technicians.

It was hot, nearly 90 degrees in the noonday sun, and their pace was slow. They stopped to study us, mostly me. Their collective gaze said: "Well, here he is, the kid producer. How old is he? Boy, he'll be a *hundred* and thirty-one when he gets done with this season. Do you think he has any idea what he's in for?"

This was part of the technicians' compensation. Yes, their jobs often meant holidays away from home. And yes, there was grunt work, anticlimactic "knockdowns," long after the stadium lights had dimmed and the production people had swept away. But there was the sanctuary of union protection. And there was this kind of payback, too —proximity to observe the game behind the game, to wonder how the new kid would work out as fourth producer of a series Don Meredith had nicknamed "Mother Love's Monday Night Traveling Freak Show."

Could it have been only five months since that rainy night in late March when Roone Arledge summoned me to his office at ABC News? It wasn't often that one saw the great man. Indeed, since he'd added the presidency of the News division in 1977, the joke went, "Now there are *two* offices where Roone can't be found."

He worked a later shift than most, often arriving in the office at lunch hour. But in the evening, when others were having dinner with their families, Roone would watch both feeds of *World News Tonight* and go roaring toward 10 P.M. with a full round of meetings. We weren't surprised to be summoned in the late afternoon, when it was already dark. This was the time when Roone did his best work.

Forte sat beside me on a sofa, facing Arledge's desk. With us were Chuck Howard, Jim Spence, and John Martin, three vice presidents of ABC Sports. On 95 percent of the division's business, these three *were* the management. But they got few lines in this performance. This, clearly, was Roone's show.

A desktop lamp illuminated the right side of his pinkish face. There was never any harsh, overhead neon to be seen in Arledge's office. It was forever calm, sedating staff and visitors alike. Roone's manner was purposeful, businesslike.

"We just have to make a change on *Monday Night Football*," he said evenly, without drama. "It's out of hand. I spend half my time listening to the announcers bitch about each other.

"The biggest problem is Howard. He's out of control. If you ask him, he thinks he can produce, direct, do all the commentary, and play quarterback for both teams. We picked you because we think Howard respects you. You've worked well with him in the past."

Forte sat forward to interject. "But *you* have to be the producer," he said to me. "Not Howard. *You*. It doesn't work the other way. We've found that out."

I looked back at Roone. He nodded.

The assignment was thrilling beyond description, but it was hardly news. As early as the prior football season, Forte had phoned me from the truck in the hour before a Monday night game: The series was chaos, he said. The current producer held nobody's respect. Cosell was a loose cannon. I should be sure to watch each game and begin thinking about how I'd change things. He and Howard had talked about my taking over in 1980.

After confirmation by Arledge, the natural starting point seemed a separate conversation with each of the three commentators. What a rude comeuppance for the eager-beaver kid producer.

In the bar of the Dorset Hotel, around the corner from ABC, Meredith was barely able to speak about Cosell. At the mention of his name, Don's face wrinkled, the lines near his mouth deepening. He looked off to the ceiling and said things like, "bitter old man" and "vindictive." I tried redirecting him. How might their relationship be different, both on and off the air? Don just shook his head. It was way beyond that stage, he sighed. His look said, "Don't you understand? Haven't you heard?"

The next meeting left me stunned and genuinely concerned. I barely knew Meredith, but Gifford was a friend. I'd known him for nine years. He was a compassionate, reasonable man; he'd want to help me. When the same look crossed his face, I knew this was trouble.

Frank had taken a lot from Howard. Tuesday mornings after his radio show, Cosell could often be found in the ABC lobby, cataloging Gifford's mistakes of the previous night. It was a shocking scene. Cigar in hand, Howard would stop various executives on their way to the elevator, asking, "Did you hear what the 'mannequin' said last night?" In public, he still called his colleague "Faultless Frank," but the sarcasm he intended was evident in his private nickname for Gifford, "The Male Mannequin."

Howard could do a whole litany for you. He'd start with the night Frank had Mike Eischeid punting for both teams. And there was the "Great Escape" game: Frank had Oakland's Warren Wells split to the top of the screen when, at that very minute, he was serving time in a federal prison. Then there was the time Gifford confused Raider receivers Cliff Branch and Fred Biletnikoff.

"Perfectly understandable," said Howard. "One's number 21, the other's 25. One's a black man, the other has blond hair flowing out the back of his helmet."

This had been going on for years. In 1973, when I was a statistician on the series, Frank had erred in the opening minutes of a telecast from Pittsburgh. Terry Hanratty was starting at quarterback for the Steelers, and Gifford, apparently thinking of Terry's All-America past, said he'd be throwing to Jim Seymour. Actually, Seymour had been his top receiver at Notre Dame but was now out of football.

As the three announcers were leaving their on-camera stools, switching to the commentary desk, Howard took my shoulder and asked, "Did you hear that?" I grimaced and kept shuffling toward my position at Frank's side. *"No,"* he demanded, pulling me around to face him, "did you *hear* that?"

Believe it or not, Howard's complaint was probably more institutional than personal. He was angry with a system that had denied him success until his fifties. He'd started late, a 37-year-old rookie radio commentator in 1957. But he did good work, hauling a 35-pound tape recorder on his back, dugout to dugout, in search of precious "actualities" from the New York baseball stars. The system ignored him.

He kept working, interviewing Cassius Clay on radio the night he took the title from Sonny Liston, breaking into television on Saturday afternoon baseball. The system barely noticed.

Finally, he took the viewing public by its shoulders, as he had me, and *demanded* recognition with his campaign for Muhammad Ali, the Islam convert and symbol of rebellion who emerged from the persona of Cassius Clay. This was not yet a popular stance in the mid-1960s. Defending Ali's resistance to the Vietnam War, Howard was utterly alone, beached. But along came a national tide, the antiwar movement of the late '60s. Suddenly, Howard was swept into the mainstream, invited to speak on college campuses, hailed as a courageous journalist.

The system is nothing if not responsive to such capricious popularity. It instantly gave Cosell all the exposure, all the fame, all the money he could ever want. But Howard would not forgive. He would not forget the television executives who'd shunned him earlier, denied him promotion, kept him "day in and day out, on the precipice of being fired," as he once told me.

Whom did these executives prefer on their sports broadcasts? Ex-athletes, virile-looking men with straight teeth, pleasant manner, and Christian-sounding names, men like Gifford and Meredith—in Cosell's words, "men without intellect, without training, without my background at law, without the spontaneity of articulation that I possess. In other words, the 'jockocracy.'"

In other words, institutional. Not personal. Gifford and Meredith could have been "Red" Grange and "Bronko" Nagurski. Howard's reaction would have been the same. His argument was with a process that elevated, worshiped, and lavished such men, to the exclusion of himself, the more deserving one.

While Howard smoldered with this resentment, it was simply Frank's and Don's bad luck to draw the seats on either side of him. Gifford had become an American icon while occasionally confusing the yard stripes. And Meredith had done in 14 weeks what Howard could not do in 24 hump-busting years—win an Emmy Award. But whose fault was that? Again, it was "the system" that passed out Emmy Awards.

My meeting with Cosell, in his office, was much like the prior two, except more theatrical. There was actually a rattle to his voice, venomous, as he ripped his colleagues. I departed wondering how serious he was. After all, I'd seen Howard refuse in production meetings to promote college football: "Oh, no. Not me. I'll have no part of the lying, fraudulent NCAA, the sick hypocrisy of football mercenaries posing as students on the nation's campuses. Not me. You can get someone else."

But when the moment arrived in the telecast, he'd come on like gangbusters: "Don't forget, Saturday afternoon, here on ABC, it's the number one Oklahoma Sooners, led by Coach Barry Switzer . . . " So this was no time to draw conclusions.

At our first preseason telecast, the Hall of Fame Game in Canton, Ohio, I began to see the problem more clearly. These men were missing the common pleasure, the bonding experience of preparing for a game together. Frank got ready by watching film at the NFL office in New York. Howard and Chet seemed to prepare by sitting at the hotel swimming pool, reading the local newspapers. About Meredith, I wasn't sure; he wouldn't be joining us until the regular season.

But it was no wonder the telecasts had begun to look "tired and stale," in Forte's phrase. There was no fresh information being injected each week. How ironic this was for Cosell, the reporter's reporter, the man who'd grown broad-shouldered with that old radio tape recorder. Had he gone soft, lost his hustle now that he was a star?

No wonder there was so much time to bitch about each other. No wonder the comedy of the early '70s had dissolved into on-air cattiness. Everybody was ignoring the most obvious "distraction" for the sniping commentators —the goddamn football game.

In Canton, I asked if anybody would like to accompany me across town to meet Joe Gibbs, then offensive coordinator of the San Diego Chargers. Together with Head Coach Don Coryell, he'd developed "Air Coryell," the most exciting pass offense in pro football. Gibbs was offering to give us a brief clinic in advance of the next day's game.

Chet replied, "Terry, if that's the way you get ready for a game, you go ahead and go." So I did. Alone.

The next week was a little better. At least I coaxed my colleagues into the Pittsburgh Steelers' hotel on the night before their game with the Atlanta Falcons. But what transpired there was the best evidence yet of the dichotomy between Cosell and me.

I was sitting with Dick Hoak and George Perles, Steeler offensive and defensive coordinators, taking advantage of a pipeline to the defending world champions. A few years earlier, I'd coauthored a book, *Fighting Back*, with Rocky Bleier about his comeback from Vietnam War wounds to four Super Bowl rings in Pittsburgh. The experience left me with solid contacts who delivered this night. Hoak and Perles went through their starters one by one, offering inside information that was beyond candid.

Cosell, meanwhile, was sitting an arm's length away. His reaction was described in an *Inside Sports* magazine article by free-lance writer Robert Friedman:

> Three hours and as many martinis later, I was sitting alone with Cosell in the Windjammer Lounge of the Marriott Hotel. In the next booth, Terry O'Neil, the rookie

producer of *Monday Night Football*, was talking with two Pittsburgh assistant coaches, hoping to learn something about the Steeler game plan.

"Jock talk," Cosell sniffed. That was not his way to prepare for this game. He had come to the Marriott, where the Steelers were encamped, to pay a late-night call on Lynn Swann and Franco Harris. His audience cared more about these two stars than all the X's and O's in the Steeler playbook. Much to Cosell's dismay, both men sent word that they had retired for the evening.

Nonetheless, it was an excellent telecast by all accounts. On the postmidnight charter flight back to New York, Gifford raved about the surprising smoothness between booth and control truck. He and Cosell shared a cocktail and bantered easily, proving once again that nothing heals like the afterglow of a good broadcast. Forte groused that an official's call had cost him a sizable bet on the favored Steelers but approved of the evening otherwise.

I took advantage of the mood to engage Cosell in a discussion of our final preseason game, Philadelphia–New England. The Eagles, curiously, were on their way to the Super Bowl that year. But at this point in preseason, they were a team without national profile, struggling for visibility in a division dominated by "America's Team," the Dallas Cowboys.

New England, on the other hand, was aflame in controversy. Four Patriots—Mike Haynes, Sam Cunningham, Richard Bishop, and Tom Owen—all represented by the notorious attorney-agent Howard Slusher, were being held out of camp in contract disputes. Cornerback Haynes was All-Pro, simply the best in football at his position. Fullback Cunningham was hugely productive, a Pro Bowl selection in '78 and the team's unquestioned spiritual leader. Nose tackle Bishop was tough and quick, a helluva bargain at $70,000 per year. Quarterback Owen was a backup.

Adding intrigue was Slusher's recent history with the Pats. In 1977, while thousands of New Englanders were making Super Bowl reservations, Slusher had pulled clients John Hannah and Leon Gray off the team in a bitter salary hassle.

Cut in Miami, Gray had come to New England as a free agent. He signed for very little but extracted from Coach Chuck Fairbanks a promise of renegotiation if he ever had an "All-Pro-type year," as Gray quoted him. He made the Pro Bowl in 1976, learned that he was the lowest-paid all-star on either squad at $30,000 annually, then attempted to redeem Fairbanks's guarantee.

"I said 'an All-Pro year,'" the coach advised him.

Gray exploded in an accusation of bad faith. The Pro Bowl took two players at each position, the All-Pro team just one. Whether by performance or reputation, Gray still ranked behind Art Shell, Oakland's left tackle who was en route to the Hall of Fame. New England held firm against renegotiation.

Hannah's case was different. The Patriots' first-round draft choice in 1973, he was outstanding as a rookie and looked to be a fixture at left guard for the next 15 years. In 1974, he found religion and was persuaded to make a large contribution to a Christian boys' camp in his native Alabama. But Hannah didn't have the cash. So he went to New England owner Billy Sullivan and asked for a salary advance or conversion of his deferred payments.

Sullivan agreed in return for a contract extension of several years with very modest salary increases. Hannah seemed pleased at first, then realized that he'd stripped the earning power out of a promising career. Within days, he was back in Sullivan's office, eliciting the owner's pledge: "I will always take care of you." By 1977, after four excellent seasons, he, too, was eager to convert his "promissory note" into legal tender. Like Gray, he phoned Slusher for advice.

Slusher suggested that they remain in tandem, shoulder

to shoulder, the way a left guard and left tackle always line up. Two days before New England's hotly anticipated '77 season opener, Hannah and Gray walked out. Slusher, meanwhile, filed a grievance with the NFL's Player/Club Relations Committee.

Scheduled at the players' union headquarters in Washington, D.C., the hearing was a stomach-twisting confrontation, with hostility in the air and personal integrity being challenged on all sides. Moments before it began, Hannah raced to the men's room and threw up. Once inside the hearing room, he quickly broke into tears. Billy Sullivan cried, too, as he explained his fight to avoid bankruptcy and keep a competitive team on the field.

Ultimately, Slusher was slapped on the wrist for inducing two players to act together in violation of their contracts. Hannah and Gray were instructed to complete the 1977 season under their existing agreements, while the Sullivans agreed to renegotiate better terms at the end of the year.

Even though the pair returned after missing just three games, their walkout was divisive. New England failed to make the playoffs, and from Maine to Connecticut, fans railed at "Agent Orange," the red-haired Slusher who'd made team management blink.

Now three years later, Slusher squared off with Billy Sullivan's son, Chuck, operational head of the club as executive vice president. Their four-player impasse seemed natural to me as the dominant theme of our telecast and the subject of an extended halftime report. It was potentially great confrontational television. Besides, it offered a chance to showcase Cosell in the distinctive role that he'd carved out for himself—the People's Investigator, Prosecuting Attorney of Sports.

Howard liked the idea. It was his kind of stuff. Now to the logistics: Sullivan, luckily, had a law practice in New York. We would interview him Monday, Cosell's only planned workday in a vacation week. The Slusher interview was to be scheduled later.

Our session with Sullivan was perfunctory. He identified All-Pro cornerback Haynes as the "key man," theorized that Slusher was trying to provoke his trade to another team, but vowed not to trade him "under any circumstances." As for the others, Sullivan said he was trying to meet Owen's desire for a trade, was close to agreement on Bishop, and miles apart on Cunningham.

I bade Cosell safe trip to his summer home in Westhampton, Long Island, and began my telephone search for Howard Slusher. When I finally reached him Monday night, he was most accommodating.

Why not? If, as Sullivan alleged that afternoon, he was engaged in a "desperate effort to mobilize public opinion against the Patriots," what better forum? Slusher volunteered to fly to New York Wednesday night for a Thursday morning taping.

The next day, Tuesday morning, I phoned Cosell in Westhampton.

"Yes, kid. What'dya want?" he droned in a mix of fatigue and disgust that I'd come to know over nine years. The incandescent feeling of Friday's flight from Atlanta was nowhere to be found in his voice.

Sometimes it was just smoke. Sometimes, if you sold him well on your concept of a story or program, he could break into genuine enthusiasm for the task. But those times were fewer now. Lately, if you caught him wrong, it could mean an earful.

"Jesus Christ, kid," he ranted, "do you have any idea what my schedule is? I sustain this whole fucking department all by myself. I get a couple of fucking days off in the summer with my family and you want me to do some fucking halftime piece. Why don't you get Gifford to do it? What's he doing this week?"

One didn't persuade Howard on these occasions when, as his wife Emmy would say, he was "launched." One simply listened, endured, until he finally offered a tiny opening with a remark like, "I'm not going to go schlepping all over the country after these bastards."

That was the moment to say, "Howard, you won't have to. I spoke to Slusher last night. He's willing to fly in from California tomorrow. He'll meet you here in the conference room Thursday morning. If you let me send a helicopter for you, we can do the interview at nine or nine-thirty and have you back on the beach before noon."

It was important to allow Cosell the last word, something about how he'd bail your ass out again, or nobody else in the fucking industry could do this kind of piece, convincing these people to sit for interviews. Then, when it was nearly clinched, you had to grant him the final *final* word: "Just make sure that fucking helicopter is on time. And have a limousine waiting for me at the heliport."

Ultimately, it was worth the effort. Slusher arrived on time, stunning Cosell and me with his physical resemblance to Arledge. He had the same stocky build, red hair, freckled complexion, gold-rimmed glasses, even a similarly thoughtful pose with his pipe. He dressed in a way that Roone often favored: navy blazer, powder blue oxford shirt, wine red tie striped in off-white. I guessed that his blue eyes were not more than a shade or two deeper than Roone's.

Cosell, by contrast, gave the impression that his Long Island closet was mostly full of swimsuits and Bermuda shorts. His combination of gray suit, tan shirt, and iridescent blue tie was ghastly. But no harm. He knew he wouldn't be appearing on camera.

The two Howards had never met, despite their notoriety in the sports business. After a few minutes of circling, they came to enjoy each other and the match of wits. More important to me, they put some real sparks on videotape.

Cosell began with the 1977 incident, inducing Slusher to reveal an agreement negotiated by Coach Chuck Fairbanks with Hannah and Gray. But the Sullivans repudiated it, saying their coach had no authority in management affairs. This misstep deepened resentment on all sides.

Raising his hand to halt the interview, Cosell glanced over his shoulder at me and said proudly, "You didn't know that, did you, Terry?"

"I didn't, no."

"He's handling himself very well," Cosell continued off camera. "It'll play off very well against Sullivan."

"Yeah, it will."

When we resumed, Slusher charged conflict of interest by Sullivan in his new role as chairman of the NFL Management Council. This is the owners' policymaking board, the group whose most visible responsibility is to negotiate with the players' union:

SLUSHER: I think Chuck Sullivan has come to the game late. He has come to it in his father's shadow. I think Chuck Sullivan would very much want to say, "Look, I handled a tough situation. I bit the bullet on Sam Cunningham and Mike Haynes and Richard Bishop and my backup quarterback." I think he would like to beat his chest by saying, "Yeah, I destroyed those people and I handled the tough Howard Slusher"—and I certainly don't think I'm that tough. If he says that, he—in his own self and his own ego—has a great feeling that he's accomplished something. The only problem is that he perhaps is destroying the fans of New England and the New England Patriots, because people in this game will tell you that they have personnel that is second only to the Steelers and perhaps one or two other clubs in the league. And for that club not to be in the playoffs last year, and for that club not to be in the Super Bowl one of the last four years, is simply a crime. So I think it's Chuck Sullivan—in his attempt to do what he thinks is important, to go beyond his present position with the Patriots and to solidify his position as chairman of the Management Council . . .

We took another break, Slusher relighting his pipe, but videotape continued to roll on an unguarded exchange:

COSELL (*to me*): His answer's very good. I don't think you have to take all of it. I think you can get the nub of it. But that's *critical*.

O'NEIL: You're right.

SLUSHER (*to Cosell*): You think it's correct?

COSELL: I happen to believe that that's the *real* story.

SLUSHER (*flipping a match defiantly into the ashtray*): That's the story. There's no question.

COSELL (*referring to Sullivan*): I believe that he's really working for the NFL, not the Patriots.

At that point, Slusher quoted exact salary figures and permitted us to shoot letters of negotiation from the Patriots. Keep in mind this was 1980, before every player's salary was a matter of public record. Dollar figures for the four New England players had never been more than newspaper speculation. But here was a newsbreak and a richness of detail that sports television often missed.

In Cunningham's situation, Slusher estimated his total compensation package from the prior year—signing bonus, annuity, performance clauses, and base salary—at $250,000. New England's current offer was $181,500, all cash.

Slusher finished his presentation with the case of Haynes, who'd made the Pro Bowl in each of his first four years—a feat not equaled by O. J. Simpson, Roger Staubach, Johnny Unitas, or many other stars, he pointed out—yet earned only $85,000 in 1979.

Cosell exited toward his waiting limousine with a hurried "Good-bye, so long." But even as I watched him disappear, I knew we would have to interview Chuck Sullivan again. Slusher's presentation had been so devastating, so convincingly stated, that we must give his adversary another chance to speak. In particular, Cosell's assent to the Slusher thesis on conflict of interest had made this imperative.

Phoning Long Island the next morning, I obtained Howard's agreement easily. We set the second Sullivan interview for Saturday morning in Foxboro, the day before our game. I would review the Slusher interview and summarize his allegations one by one so that Cosell could offer them for rebuttal.

"We're going to have a superb piece," Howard insisted, having returned, chameleonlike, to a spirit of enthusiasm.

Chuck Sullivan's second interview was only marginally better than his first. Substantive issues aside, the television camera has a ruthless way of exposing personality differences. Sullivan is a truly nice man but, juxtaposed with Slusher, not a compelling figure. Squinty-eyed behind contact lenses and vague about the negotiations, he was no match for his buttoned-up rival.

Nonetheless, Cosell emerged from this final interview even more buoyant about the hard, balanced journalistic effort he would present the next afternoon. No sportswriter could get this information, he said. Not even the goddamn beat writers for the Pats, the "ribbonclerks" who supposedly cover this team every day. No, it took Cosell to come to town and break this story, Cosell to frame the issues and make it understandable.

"Goddamn it, he's right," I thought, as his monologue soared on. "Sure, he put you through hell in getting to this point, but nobody else in sports television was doing this kind of journalism."

In the Schaefer Stadium parking lot, vast and empty the day before the game, he gave me a we-got-'em smile. Howard had accepted an invitation to spend this afternoon at the Sullivans' Cape Cod beach house. As we parted, he said, "I've given you great stuff there. Now remember, just edit to the story *line*."

I grinned, tempted to recite that last sentence in unison with him. This was ritual. Whenever you finished gathering solid material with Howard, he'd send you into the editing bay by chirping, "Remember, kid, just edit to the story *line*."

Stepping into the videotape truck, I imagined Monday morning's newspapers, AP and UPI dispatches from Foxboro: "Howard Cosell reported yesterday . . ."

How he loved that. Because our subject was pro football, this would be bigger than Bob Vorhies and Renée Richards. Maybe it wouldn't have the prominence of Olympic controversies like Stan Wright or Collett and Matthews, but our reporting was every bit as solid. This was going to be another bull's-eye for Cosell and the kid from journalism school.

The next day, game day, Howard arrived at the trucks 30 minutes after Forte and me. Emerging from his limousine, he caught sight of Chet first.

"Ah, da little Chester. Ha, ha, ho, ho," he chortled, playfully patting Forte about the face. "The little tiny Chester."

This was another Cosell ritual, one that celebrated his height and reach advantage. He jabbed at Forte and circled, like Ali dealing with Joe Frazier. Seeing me a few steps away, Howard turned suddenly brusque.

"How's that halftime piece?" he demanded.

"It's good, Howard," I said. "I think you'll like it."

"When can I see it?"

"As soon as the crew gets back from lunch. We can put your narration on it right away."

He harrumphed grandly. "If you had better control of this crew, we could do it now." And he marched away.

These were the turns of mood with Cosell. They blew through like tropical weather fronts, sudden and without forecast. Times like this, I was sure that nineteenth-century Swiss author Henri F. Amiel had Howard in mind when he wrote, "Respect in yourself the oscillations of feeling: they are your life and your nature; a wiser one than you made them."

Shortly, Cosell was standing in the broadcast booth, commentator headset on, overlooking a virtually empty stadium, still 90 minutes to kickoff. Gifford stood nearby, listening on his headset.

Down in the control truck, three of us sat facing a wall of 25 or more monitors. Technical director Joe Schiavo, the man who punched buttons and pulled levers at Forte's command, sat to the left. I sat to the right. In between, Chet called, "Roll 'X.' " And our monitors lit up with the Sullivan-Slusher piece for first viewing.

When it ended seven minutes later, there was silence. Silence in the videotape truck where an operator hit the stop button. Silence in the house trailer where our production assistants sat ready with graphics of the principals. Silence in the broadcast booth where Gifford looked at Cosell for a reaction.

Schiavo, Forte, and I stared straight ahead at the monitor wall, now gone blank. Chet said nothing. He neither acknowledged me nor the piece in any way. I waited, touching Cosell's headset controls with my fingertips but not pressing.

We heard breathing from his mike. It started softly, indistinguishable in temper. Now louder, a kind of fuming or exasperation. He sighed, then stopped, as if collecting himself. Thirty seconds had passed since the finish of the tape.

"Ter-reeee," he hissed.

"Yes, Howard."

"Ter-reeee. I want you to listen to me."

"What is it, Howard?"

"Terry, I've spent a lifetime in this business. I've probably been in this business more years than you've lived." He paused again. "In that time, I've formed some relationships that are more important to me than any of your

goddamn halftime pieces or your goddamn friend, Howard Slusher."

"My *friend*, Howard?" I couldn't help myself.

"That's right. Your friend. And I'll tell you who my
friends are. I've known the Sullivans since they came into
football in 1959. I remember when they barely scraped
together the $25,000 that got them into the old AFL. I've
seen them worry and sweat and almost lose this team a
couple of times. The banks were going to foreclose them.
But they've survived—against Howard Slusher and all the
others. And I'm not going to put my voice on something
that's so biased and unfair to them. I'm just not going to
be party to it. You can get someone else."

My body flushed, then chilled in the truck's extreme air
conditioning. Chuck Sullivan and his father had spent the
previous afternoon feeding Cosell vodka tonics and the
Patriots' party line under a warm Cape Cod sun. Certainly, that was their prerogative. But they'd made this
matter personal and created a helluva mess for us.

I tried going over the elements of the piece with Cosell
to assess their merit. How would he suggest we change
them? We still had all the original recordings. There was
time to reedit if he had another format in mind.

He didn't. All that Howard had in mind was being difficult. When he spoke again, his hiss was metal-coated.

"Terry," he said. "We're going to have to decide one
thing on this series. We're going to have to decide whose
opinion we're following here—yours or mine."

Uh-oh. The gauntlet. And so soon. Since that March
afternoon in Arledge's office, I'd known this was coming.
From the moment Roone said he wanted a producer, not a
caretaker, this confrontation was inevitable.

One couldn't blame Howard. He was in his eleventh
season of the most prominent sports series ever, then and
still ABC's longest-running prime-time show. He was one
of the most recognized figures—not in sports, not in televi-

sion—in America, better known to certain millions than the President of the United States.

Monday Night Football had become his pulpit, his forum to anoint favorite players "All-World," to name-drop the afternoon's luncheon companion, to excoriate fan violence, to ribbon-cut a city's urban renewal program, to denounce the "jockocracy," to leave the booth for a phone call from an imposter posing as Muhammad Ali in Zaire, to tempt New York State Democrats seeking a candidate for the U.S. Senate, to eulogize a passing friend, to confer, to legitimize, to lay hands on, to bestow the sacred Cosellian blessing.

For ten years, it had been this way, Howard practicing free association with any thought that occurred to him. At any time. Nobody was safe from interruption, not even play-by-play man Gifford with a 50-yard pass hanging in the air. Yet now, after a decade of total control, he was being asked to work with a real producer?

Despite my optimism, I had known enough to fear this moment. I had just hoped it might come later, after I'd built some nonthreatening goodwill. But it was here and I had to respond.

"Howard," I said, "I think we should talk about that— but back in New York. Next week. We have to make a decision here."

I left him a pause. He said nothing.

"We can extend halftime," I continued. "We can get an extra minute. How 'bout if we leave you a minute at the end to say anything you want about the Sullivans. We'll even matte [superimpose] 'commentary' if you like."

I released the spring-loaded key that put my voice into his ear. Again, Schiavo, Forte, and I sat mute, staring ahead at the wall of monitors. I tilted my head upward, as if to *see* Howard through the sheet metal of the truck and the concrete of the stadium. Still he said nothing.

Then a sigh. "All right. Let's roll it. Let's do this fuckin' thing."

The piece began with exposition of the four players, highlight video with Cosell's voice-over. Then came a series of sound bites from Slusher and Sullivan, the two antagonists. It was simple, direct point-counterpoint material that Howard and I both relished. We had done dozens of reports like this over the years.

If Cosell was frothing with a defense for the Sullivans, he must have swallowed it sometime in the first half. His live tag at halftime was just as balanced as the videotape:

COSELL: So within the limited time we had—because I spoke to each man for a half hour or more—there's the impasse, the nub of it. I want to say this: What Chuck Sullivan says about what his family went through to reacquire the franchise, and the years of struggle and turmoil that he suffered through, is absolutely true. But co-equally, I want to say that Howard Slusher is a very effective attorney and agent who is doing his job as he sees it. And he can be effective only as long as his clients stick with him. The real sadness is that the fans of New England, who have now come to love their team and who understand its potency in terms of the quality of personnel on the team, have to stand by without Mike Haynes, who may be the best cornerback in football—certainly now today as good as Louie Wright. And without Sam "Bam" Cunningham, one of the most effective fullbacks in football. And I've already characterized Bishop as a slashing noseguard who's very critical to the 3-4 defense of the Patriots. There it is, and the Patriots can't win without them.

When we got back to New York, the death watch began. We had no game the coming weekend, Labor Day weekend, but I called Gifford on Tuesday, just to get a news bulletin. He warned:

"They're after you, my man. Howard and Chet. They want you out."

"Chet, too?" I asked.

"Oh, yeah."

"But he's been acting so supportive."

"He's a very talented director," said Gifford, "but I wouldn't trust him as far as I could throw him."

My memory spun back. But instead of hearing Forte's encouragement from that rainy afternoon in March, I listened to Sunday in Foxboro. Those deathly silences. There was plenty of time for Chet to say something, even something critical. But he waited for Howard's cue. Suddenly, I understood how he'd outlived everybody through ten years of Monday nights: Let the producer make his call, but don't react until hearing from the real power, Cosell.

Wednesday, I phoned Sullivan and Slusher, thinking I might need them as witnesses if this "crime" ever came to trial. Both went to great lengths to say that they'd been treated fairly and judged the final product balanced. Sullivan was my primary concern, given ABC's relationship with the league, but he could not have been more positive.

"I've heard something about this," he said. "I've heard some people are trying to get you. I just hope you survive it."

Thursday, I phoned Forte, ostensibly to consult on our tease for the season opener, Dallas at Washington, ten days away. He barely responded, growling, "Whatever you want to do is okay with me," and hung up. Gifford was right.

I avoided Cosell, feeling sure that he'd concoct another dispute, then take it to management and insist, "You see? I just can't get along with him."

Friday afternoon, I was having a late lunch when the call came to my office. Jim Spence and John Martin wanted to see me. I gulped when my secretary told me. If there was an execution in the offing, these two would be assigned to switch on the electricity.

They were a disparate pair. Spence was short and pugnacious; Martin, lean and elegant. "Suits" was Martin's nickname, celebrating his sartorial splendor. A 2-handicapper and former club champion at the famous Winged Foot Golf Club, he'd spent his Navy hitch teaching officers to play the game. In describing his savvy with fickle rights holders, it was said, "He meets people well." Much more than anyone in the organization, he was Roone's confidant.

Spence, gathering us in his office, characteristically got right to the point: "This is a tough meeting for you, a tough meeting for us. We're going to make a change in the producer's position on *Monday Night Football*."

My brain surged hot and a concussion flashed through my body, top to bottom. I gripped the armrest of Spence's sofa tightly, trying very hard to look composed. My heart thumped so heavily that, in the midst of this cataclysm, I actually wondered if they could hear it or if my shirt was vibrating.

Spence said the expected, that it was management's mistake in assigning me, that there hadn't been one single incident, but that the Sullivan-Slusher report was poorly done—the final straw.

"Let's call the two of them," I suggested, gesturing to the phone. "Let's ask *them* if they were unfairly treated."

I implored Martin. He looked away, avoiding me. I whip-panned desperately to Spence. He dropped his gaze to the papers on his desk.

"I *mean* it. If they say the piece was unfair, then I'll understand this. But I think it's one of the best, most balanced things that Howard and I have ever done."

I was reeling, panicky. Cosell, I pointed out, was in the impossible position of calling my work biased against the Patriots after he'd endorsed Slusher's major allegation against Sullivan. It was on tape.

"Let's screen the raw interviews," I suggested. "I'd feel better if you'd screen the tapes and then tell me where it's unfair."

Spence realized his mistake and turned the discussion back to generalities. I was left groping, struggling to square him up for a debate. In retrospect, it seems so pathetic. I was trying to argue facts; he was arguing pragmatic reality.

Howard and Chet didn't want me on the series. In Spence's world, it didn't matter why. This meeting might have been easier if they'd chosen their issue more carefully, but the only remaining charter members of *Monday Night Football* didn't need to apologize or explain.

Returning to my office 12 floors below, I found everyone gone. It was 5 P.M. on the eve of a three-day holiday. All the lights were out. I wanted to scream. I phoned Arledge's office. His secretary said he was in a meeting.

Frantic to confront somebody, anybody, I took an elevator back to the twenty-eighth floor. Racing through the deserted hallways, wheeling around a corner, I surprised Martin and Spence standing near a secretarial desk. Their embarrassed faces showed they'd been debriefing.

"I want out of my contract," I said. "It only has three months to go. Surely, you can do that for me."

Spence said no, they wanted to keep me. I couldn't look at him another minute. I fled.

Labor Day weekend, I assaulted Arledge's Long Island summer home as directly as I dared. I phoned twice a day, leaving messages with his wife. I considered showing up unannounced at his front door, then rejected the idea as undignified. By messenger, I sent him an aggrieved, handwritten letter. No reply. This was Roone. Two decades in network television had taught him not to take on every available crisis.

Despairingly, I awaited his callback, alternately lying on my bed and wandering in a pensive daze. A newspaper reporter had observed that I didn't seem awed about winning the *Monday Night* producership but I certainly was devastated to lose it.

I kept thinking of the nine-plus years I'd spent in reaching this pinnacle: round-the-clock editing sessions in windowless basements; grinding my teeth as technicians, their machinery not working, took two hours to execute one video effect, emerging onto cold, deserted Manhattan streets at 4 A.M., finding no taxis, musing to a colleague, "I wonder what kind of day it was."

Yes, we did these things willingly, even lovingly. And yes, we were well paid. But there was an implicit understanding. This was a meritocracy. We didn't mind 60 hours without sleep in Innsbruck, didn't flinch at driving through a blizzard to meet Cosell in Lake Tahoe, didn't calculate the personal disruption that 25 straight days on the road could cause. It was okay. There was a fabulous prize in store.

Except, what happens if you win the prize and then it's gone in three games? And worse, what if the process seems so savagely, barbarously unfair?

I kept phoning Roone, finally reaching him on Monday evening, Labor Day. He said he'd been busy with other matters, didn't really know the issues, was obligated to rely on the consensus of his vice presidents. He was seductive as always. Emotionally exhausted by then, I didn't press him. This was futile. Another producer had already been assigned and done a full-day meeting with Forte.

I later learned that Arledge had never copied Cosell on the mandate for strong leadership he'd issued me in March. The two were barely speaking at that point.

So it was done. All but the epilogue:

After several more years of grousing about pro football and the *Monday Night* series, Cosell announced to ABC Sports management that he was taking a week off in October 1983. Later that fall, he did it again. At the end of the season, he simply resigned from *Monday Night Football,* saying he'd lost interest.

Meredith lasted only one more season, resigning by mutual agreement with ABC after the '84 season.

In 1985, Cosell published his third book, *I Never Played the Game.* It contained a full boilover of his resentment for the system and everyone within.

"Gifford's voice is thin and monotonic," he wrote, "and he is incapable of using it with rhythm and pace for dramatic effect. In addition, he stumbles over words, and it's not uncommon for him to lose his train of thought."

Of Meredith, he observed "a behavior pattern that I call 'Texas Cruel.' There's a mean streak within him." Of his boss, he wrote, "I never heard from Arledge. I had broken my back for him for thirteen years on *Monday Night Football*, and he never even called or dropped a line to say good-bye."

Spence, then in charge of ABC Sports' day-to-day operations, responded by removing Cosell from the upcoming World Series baseball telecasts. Howard, in turn, resigned from ABC Sports.

Just a few months later, early in 1986, the corporate managers of Capital Cities, Inc.—which had acquired ABC in 1985—split Roone's role as joint head of two divisions, reconfirming him as president of ABC News only. Spence, uninvited to interview for the vacant ABC Sports presidency, resigned from the company.

Forte at first pledged allegiance to his new division president, Dennis Swanson. He even posed for *Sports Illustrated* with a stunning, corporate look—tie and three-piece suit to replace the leather jackets, unbuttoned shirts, and gold chains that had formerly been his fashion. But within months, Chet attacked Capital Cities in print, and Swanson had no choice but to dismiss him.

Slusher's deadlock with Sullivan continued into the regular season of 1980. Two of the four player negotiations, Haynes's and Bishop's, were settled after three games; Owen came to terms after six games. But their return did not come soon enough to help New England into the playoffs that year. Cunningham stayed out the entire 1980 season, finally settling at the end of 1981 preseason. He retired at the finish of 1981, a year that saw the Patriots win two games and lose 14.

Haynes got the $200,000 per season that Slusher had

been asking for 1980–82. He made the Pro Bowl two more times in those three years, missing only in 1980, when he suffered a collapsed lung after rejoining the team. However, in 1983, at impasse once again, New England traded Haynes to the Los Angeles Raiders. He was the last piece of the Raiders' puzzle that year. Playing superb cornerback, he helped his new team to a Super Bowl title.

In 1987, Mike Haynes was still performing at a high level for Los Angeles and earning $775,000—a top wage among NFL cornerbacks and a fortune away from the $85,000 salary that precipitated his first crisis with the Patriots in 1979.

The Sullivans continued to have financial troubles. In 1984, Chuck Sullivan promoted Michael Jackson's rock 'n' roll "Victory" tour and lost $18 to $20 million on the venture. Badly strapped, the family began flirting with a series of potential buyers and/or minority partners for the Patriots. In December 1986, the family relieved a cash flow problem by accepting $21 million from a Philadelphia group in exchange for an option to purchase the club.

In January 1988, the Sullivans allegedly reneged on that option, forcing the Philadelphia investors to file a suit charging extortion, fraud, and breach of contract. This legal action finally forced the family to sell in the fall of '88.

At the time of sale, total debt for Billy and Chuck Sullivan personally, plus their football team and stadium, computed to $126 million.

Howard Slusher, meanwhile, continued to represent athletes in their negotiations with professional clubs and served as chief legal counsel for the billion-dollar Nike shoe company of Beaverton, Oregon.

3

1981: The Watershed

MY DISMISSAL from *Monday Night Football* was quickly followed by reassignment to *NCAA College Football*, agreeable duty with Al Michaels and either Ara Parseghian or Frank Broyles each week.

In the middle of that 1980 season, Kevin O'Malley, a good man and vice president at CBS Sports, asked me to have dinner with Van Gordon Sauter, the new president of his division. I wasn't yet free to discuss employment at CBS, but the notion was as tangible on our table as the salt and pepper shakers.

I felt I'd lost my effectiveness at ABC. Nobody mentioned it to me, but I could feel the questions hanging like rainclouds. A producer needs to inspire the opposite vibrations—confidence, respect of his peers, unquestioned loyalty under fire. Roone, Chuck Howard, Don Ohlmeyer —my role models at ABC—oozed this kind of charisma. I'd been a prospect of sorts, but suddenly nobody was calling me "Arledge Junior," as technical manager Joe De Bonis had during the Lake Placid Olympics.

The only problem with jumping to CBS Sports was . . . CBS Sports. "Execrable" and "abominable" were the adjectives chosen by Bill Carter of *The* (Baltimore) *Sun. Television Age*, a trade publication, once wrote, "CBS Sports seemed to exist only so that NBC wouldn't be last in everything."

To that point, my closest contact with CBS Sports had come on the first weekend of June 1979. CBS was broadcasting the Belmont Stakes that weekend, and what a story line the television gods had arranged.

The colt Spectacular Bid was undefeated and poised to become a Triple Crown winner, having romped in the Kentucky Derby and the Preakness Stakes. There was open hostility between Bid's jockey, Ronnie Franklin, and another rider, Angel Cordero, Jr. Would there be jostling, rough riding? No matter, said the experts. Spectacular Bid was in a class with the other Triple Crown winners of the decade—Secretariat ('73), Seattle Slew ('77), and Affirmed ('78).

But Bid ran poorly in the Belmont, finishing third on a muddy track. Then, incredibly, after all the hype CBS Sports had devoted to this "superhorse," its best producer-director team left the air without interviewing the colt's trainer, Bud Delp.

The next morning, I was waiting on Delp's front lawn in Laurel, Maryland, when he returned from New York. The trainer dropped stunning news: Spectacular Bid had stepped on a safety pin in his stall the night before the race. He was feverish and swollen in the frog of that front left hoof. The colt had done well to run third.

My crew rushed the interview over to ABC News' Washington bureau and fed it to New York. Lengthy excerpts aired that afternoon, and the wire services credited us with a big newsbreak. This was the ultimate embarrassment in sports television—ABC had a scoop on a CBS event.

How indicative was this incident? Listen to Chuck Milton, a senior producer who thrived in CBS Sports' old-boy network.

"In the '60s and early '70s, we used to just shut down all summer," he once told me. "After the Belmont Stakes, nobody did anything until the first football game in September. We kept getting paid, of course. But all we did was play cards."

"Who?" I asked.

"The president of the division, a couple of his vice presidents—really, anybody who was around."

By the mid-1970s, they were working a little harder, but not much better. Johnny Unitas, the Baltimore Colts' Hall of Fame quarterback, once described the low comedy of his five years at CBS Sports:

"I went into it totally unprepared. No training. No coaching, nothing. My first game was a disaster. I finally had something to say and I'm rolling along when suddenly the director is talking into my earphone, 'Commercial coming up . . . ten, nine, eight, ...' I just stopped talking, right in the middle of a thought.

"But for three years, I thought I was doing a good job. Everybody around me told me I was doing great. Then at the end of my third season, I'm working a game in St. Louis. At halftime, I get a call from Barry Frank [then president of CBS Sports]. He says, 'Be in my office at ten o'clock Monday morning.'

"I'm sitting, waiting in his office Monday morning. He's a half hour late. He walks in and says, 'What are you doing here?' I said, 'You called and said to be here.' He said, 'You mean you made a special trip?'

"It took him a while, but he finally said what was on his mind: 'You know, you're butchering the King's English. Maybe you should go back to school and learn how to talk.' I said, 'You mean take some college courses?' He said, 'No, high school.'

"Now I'm so mad I feel like throwing him out the window, but I just sit there and say, 'Yes, sir.'

"I'd been on the job three years and all of a sudden I'm being told I ain't worth a shit. What we decided on was I would work with a special tutor, a guy in Philadelphia. So for nine straight weekends, I drove from Baltimore to

Philadelphia. We went over film clips, worked on my diction, stuff like that. CBS paid for everything.

"But now that I finally had some training, what happens? I'm cut back on the number of games I work and my per-game pay is cut. Two years later, my contract expires and it's not renewed. A friend of mine asked me, 'How's it feel to be fired by CBS?' I said, 'I'm not the first and I won't be the last.' "

Barry Frank soon followed Unitas out the door. Between February 1975 and March 1977, he brought Jimmy Connors against four challengers in a creation called "The Heavyweight Championship of Tennis." It did big ratings, viewers lured in part by CBS's promotion of the matches as "winner take all." Except they weren't. All players were guaranteed healthy appearance fees. Barry Frank took the fall.

His replacement as division president was Bob Wussler, doing a second tour of duty in the space of three years. Then came Frank Smith, a former sales executive singularly unsuited for the job, but a man whose infamy still lives at CBS Sports.

Apparently drunk and marauding through a network Super Bowl party one evening, he fondled an attractive woman, a total stranger, and, ah, paid her a compliment. Somehow, the woman wasn't amused. And, bad luck, she was the wife of an ad agency executive who handled the Eastern Airlines account. Her husband punched out Smith, and a blow-by-blow made newspapers in New York and Los Angeles.

Once again, CBS Sports was in search of a new president, its fifth in six years. This time, the choice was Van Gordon Sauter, the most unusual man ever to lead a network sports division.

Van had been CBS's head censor and chief of CBS News' Paris bureau. More recently, he'd revamped the network-owned station in Los Angeles while living on a houseboat and courting Kathleen Brown, sister of California governor Jerry Brown. Sauter got his sports division appointment virtually on the eve of their marriage.

He was a great bear of a man, perhaps 260 pounds, handsomely layered in sweaters and tweeds, even on the warmest days. His face, too, was covered, by large glasses and a perfectly trimmed salt-and-pepper beard. He cut the figure of an academic, favoring bow ties and a pipe.

This was an incongruous sight at posh, preppy Saratoga Race Course in August 1980 when, one month on the job, Van was obliged to visit a CBS remote, the Travers Stakes. As *Sports Illustrated* later reported, "He recently spent his first day at Saratoga sitting under a tree reading books, one of which was a biography of Henry VIII, a man to whom he bears more than a passing resemblance."

He may have been better read than his predecessors, perhaps a bit esoteric for the world of jock TV, but he was not naive about the task at hand. In that same *Sports Illustrated* piece, he admitted that CBS Sports had "bottomed out." Taking one look around, Sauter realized he'd inherited the worst, most permissive, most unprofessional shop in the history of sports television.

This bombsite called for a sense of humor. Of CBS's freakish trashsport, "The World's Strongest Men," Van said, "We are no longer going to have misshapen men hauling refrigerators up steps to a Playboy Club somewhere in New Jersey." Of the motorcycle jumps by his network's Evel Knievel imitators, he deadpanned, "We are no longer going to have motorcyclists moving walls with their faces."

These embarrassing moments in television history were brought to you by the *CBS Sports Spectacular*. "It is neither sport, nor is it spectacular," Van averred.

Drawing on a lengthy news background, his idea was to make a franchise of sports journalism. He envisioned a studio newsroom that would provide scoring updates, breaking news, and extended features. This on-air signature would wrap around and through all the division's weekend programming. Van wanted to give the name *CBS Sports Saturday* and *CBS Sports Sunday* to both the studio wraparound and the new anthology that would replace *Sports Spectacular*.

It certainly sounded good, but was it real? CBS Sports had been such a revolving door of new faces and unfulfilled plans. When rumor of my meetings with Sauter reached ABC, John Martin chided me, "You *believe* that? How many times have we heard their latest brainstorm? And by the way, who's the president over there these days?"

When my ABC contract expired on the final day in 1980, I was at last able to entertain a CBS offer. Sauter was aggressive, proposing a generous three-year contract and the role of executive producer, cutting edge of his machete at CBS Sports.

ABC's offer was comparable money but not much expansion in my duties as a field producer. Even if I had felt comfortable at ABC—and I didn't—the opportunity to hire and teach a staff, the chance to make over CBS Sports was too tempting.

I was 95 percent ready to switch networks on the second Saturday of January 1981 when I sat down in my living room to watch *CBS Sports Spectacular*. Such anticipation I felt. My colleagues-to-be were covering the longest, most grueling downhill in men's ski racing, the Lauberhorn from Wengen, Switzerland.

I'd been there, seen Franz Klammer win in 1976, just before his Olympic triumph. On the advice of American racers Andy Mill and Karl Anderson, I'd skied the famous course—or part of it. Lulled into false confidence by the gentle terrain on top, I zipped through a blind S turn and . . . OWWW! Suddenly, free fall!

This was the vaunted *Hundskopf* (dog's head), two large boulders flanking a sheer cliff. Somehow I landed on my skis after sailing 20 meters airborne. But then came a sweeping right-hand turn. Carrying far too much speed, I crashed heavily, cartwheeling down toward safety nets that guard the funicular railway.

In my living room, I rubbed both legs and winced once again, awaiting *Sports Spectacular* so eagerly. Would the CBS guys dig into Wengen's lore? The place was loaded with history, standing in the shadow of the Eiger Mountain. On the trip in '76, Jim McKay told me of five climbers who died trying to scale its notorious north face. As rescuers reached the last of them, an Italian suffering from exposure and dangling by his tether, they heard him utter two final words: "*Fame, freddo* (Hungry, cold).*"

Then *Sports Spectacular* came on. I, too, was left hungry and cold. The greatest test in Alpine skiing was reduced to *11 minutes* in order to make room for 35 minutes of the "NFL Cheerleaders' Competition," a made-for-television contrivance of giggles, wiggles, and jiggles. I immediately called my attorney-agent, Art Kaminsky.

"I can't do it," I said. "I can't work there."

"But don't you see?" he argued. "You can change that. That's the whole point of going over there—the opportunity."

Kaminsky had a point. I remembered an insight from Beano Cook, then a publicist at CBS but formerly a colleague of ours at ABC in the '70s.

One summer evening at 6:45, Roone Arledge emerged from his office to see ABC Sports' twenty-eighth floor still half full. It was a Friday in late July. Roone smiled as he surveyed his juggernaut.

"You think the guys across the street are still working?" he asked Beano smugly.

"I doubt it. But let me ask you—do you ever worry about NBC and CBS?"

"I'm not so worried about NBC," said Roone. "But CBS, with their affiliate lineup and all that strength in news and entertainment. If they ever wake up in sports, we're in trouble."

Still, before making the jump, I wanted to test Sauter

once more. Meeting with him and his vice president, Neal Pilson, in Sauter's apartment early one morning, I told them I couldn't come to CBS unless they promised hell-bent pursuit of the NCAA Basketball Championships.

This blossoming tournament, an NBC property for 16 years, was suddenly available. NBC's embattled president, Fred Silverman, had committed all available resources to fixing his disastrous prime-time schedule. He'd ordered his sports executives to reject the NCAA's reasonable asking price.

Sauter and Pilson were briefly surprised at my dogmatism. Their faces said, "To us, college basketball is an important property. But you're telling us it's life or death?"

Exactly. To me, it was the starting point of radical surgery for CBS Sports. Pilson raised questions about regular-season profitability. But Van, recovering a composed expression and reading the moment better, said he understood my arguments. He vowed to give the NCAA negotiation his best shot.

In my final scene at ABC, I met alternately with Arledge and his vice president of finance, Irwin Weiner. For more than two hours, we reworked assignments and compensation, trying to approximate CBS's offer. My mind fatigued during this process, leaving instinct to take control. At last, I looked up and said, "Irwin, you've been very understanding. But I don't want to stay at any price. I want to go to CBS." He and Arledge wished me well.

On January 27, 1981, I parked my car in the same Seventh Avenue garage and walked one block east, just as I'd done for several years. But instead of entering the skyscraper on the north side of Fifty-third Street and Sixth Avenue, I diverted to the south corner. Geographically, it was one block; in terms of professional capability, the difference was several hundred light-years.

What urgency, verging on panic, greeted me that first morning. Sauter had been in office for seven long months without effecting any alteration in CBS Sports' look. Van's strengths were concepts and salesmanship. He'd spent much of his tenure giving persuasive newspaper interviews, promising change in his division. But he dared not implement these ideas without a trusted production chief.

Rival network executives, especially Don Ohlmeyer, who'd left ABC for NBC Sports, began sniping at him. "So where is it?" they demanded. "Where's the revolution?"

Certain voices inside CBS were tempted to join the chorus. Sauter, despite his iconoclastic appearance, was known as an ambitious fast-tracker, widely thought to be angling for the presidency of CBS News. His chances, according to rumor, depended on a quick turnaround of CBS Sports. But after seven months, everyone agreed, the scoreboard showed a fat zero next to his name.

Van's impatience was palpable that first day as he came to my office for a private chat. Frustrated with internal factions and intransigence, he said, "Big guy, we have to get the issues joined here."

He'd called a meeting of his seven vice presidents and me for later that afternoon. He wanted me to be as blunt in this forum as I'd been in our earlier talks. He was desperate to shake CBS Sports into motion.

Sauter's meeting was a series of direct questions for me. He began with on-air promotion.

"Ineffective," I said. The previous weekend, CBS had presented the most unique boxing promo ever. Instead of selling personality or story line or simply two warriors banging, the spot was graphics over an *empty* boxing ring. Unprecedented. Newspaper advertising (which once displayed John McEnroe playing tennis *right*-handed) was just as bad.

When Sauter asked what else was wrong with CBS Sports, I hardly knew where to begin. Their production people had not been introduced to the fundamental techniques of attracting and holding audience. They hadn't developed personalities among CBS's star athletes, didn't heighten interest by reporting legitimate news, didn't preview their coming events with live cut-ins during a broadcast day. Once when the Daytona 500 ended early, CBS Sports' producer did 30 minutes of fill without throwing to the NBA basketball game that would follow.

Van asked about "talent," television talk for commentators. Whom did I regard as the best young talent on the air, regardless of availability?

"Al Michaels of ABC and Bob Costas of NBC."

"Can we get them?" he asked.

"Get them?" I said. "Van, we once *had* them. Both of them."

It was another CBS Sports tragedy. In 1975, Michaels worked regional NFL games for CBS and desperately wanted a regular spot on the network's roster. Bob Wussler, then sports division president, invited all his commentators to that season's Super Bowl in Miami. What might have been a perk or a thank-you became a transparent assessment of their work. Wussler doled out Super Bowl assignments according to his personal ranking ladder. When Michaels found himself consigned to a dingy, forlorn cocktail bar for a meaningless pregame piece, he took the hint and signed with ABC.

At CBS, Al had been slotted behind an ordinary talent named Gary Bender. A few years later, Bender was the issue again. This time, it was 1979 and Costas was the hot commodity, looking for a positive signal from management. He'd done two full years of superior work on basketball and football. But apparently nobody noticed. Frank Smith and his associates preferred Bender. That was okay with Don Ohlmeyer. He wooed Costas and won him for NBC.

By the way Van puffed his pipe, I could tell he'd never heard these stories. Several vice presidents in the room had advised Wussler and Smith on these critical decisions. Their misjudgments had left CBS Sports barren of quality manpower behind its microphones and assured years of good commentary for the opposition. These same men now doodled on their papers as we took up event acquisition.

This was the biggest problem. CBS Sports had subsisted for years on three top-grade properties—NFL football, The Masters golf tournament, and the Kentucky Derby. In 1973–74, CBS lost the Derby and added NBA basketball. This was an unfortunate exchange in the short run. Pro basketball was headed for steep decline. Several star players would be caught using and dealing hard drugs. Later, all professional sports would have this problem but basketball was first. In 1981, many viewers and advertisers shunned the NBA as a "junkies' league."

By contrast, college basketball was beginning to boom. Played in bright, new arenas by fresh-faced college kids, this was the comer in sports television. College administrators had seen its economic viability, compared its 12-man roster to the expense of a 90-man football squad, and sent their recruiters foraging for agile 7-footers. No longer a game of regional limits, college basketball was sinking roots all over the country.

Addressing the entire group now, I delivered the same passionate argument that I'd previewed in Van's apartment a week earlier. Major properties, I suggested, were historically immobile, victims of inertia at all three networks. What rare good fortune to have one come available that was perfectly suited to our needs. In the most heavily watched months of the calendar—January, February, March—we could go from the worst programming in sports television to the best.

Our NBA-PGA golf tandem was failing on Sunday afternoons; it had no audience flow from one to the other. With one bold stroke, we could swipe NBC's biggest gun and strike a mortal blow to ABC, whose *Superstars* and *American Sportsman* were finally showing their age.

My new colleagues just looked at me. Sauter adjourned us.

Within days, that meeting was echoing all through the business. The *New York Post* reported we were dumping the NBA for college basketball, NBC called Costas's agent to negotiate a long-term extension, Al Michaels heard my praise almost verbatim, and CBS Sports' director of on-air promotion told friends I was after his scalp.

This was my introduction to the oppressive, never-ending politics of CBS. It surprised me. I'd figured a last-place outfit might be looking for new direction, a unified purpose. I reread Brent Musburger's words from that *Sports Illustrated* piece on Van: "Since I came to CBS in 1975, we've had five different presidents, and everybody left friends behind. So there are a lot of different factions." And a lot of insecurity.

Privately, Sauter said to me, "You dropped some chins in that meeting. But don't worry. I told the others, 'He's tough, but he's exactly what we need right now.' You just keep going."

So we did. In a whirlwind few weeks, we designed a totally new look for CBS Sports—animated show openings, graphics formats, typefaces, music themes, bumpers, bridges, tags, plus the two most prominent cosmetics—a studio set and CBS Sports logo that are still in use today.

More important, we revamped the production staff. Five new faces arrived from ABC, and a sixth, David Michaels, came at the recommendation of his brother, Al. To my great relief, I found that many of the incumbent producers and directors needed only a blend of retraining and reinvigorating.

To insure the future, we installed Arledge's "farm system," hiring young production assistants to work 60-plus hours a week and learn the business. CBS had never had production assistants, never fostered the loyalty and consistency of growing its own people. From our first two classes came a half dozen young men who will lead CBS Sports' production staff in the next decade.

I fired a handful, too—four or five who weren't good

enough or didn't care enough. And to the many free-lancers who'd gotten work from CBS, I said, "We're going staff-only." How else could you expect mutual trust with your people?

Then I collected both survivors and new blood at my home in Greenwich, Connecticut, for a daylong seminar, followed by an evening of dinner, healing, and reassurance. We'd done it with blurring speed and had probably bruised some feelings in order to meet Sauter's timetable, but we had a team.

In late February, our college basketball battle was far from won. Pilson, the most respected man on Sauter's managerial staff, remained unconvinced that regular-season games would be profitable. He wanted to limit them to eight per season. Carl Lindemann and Kevin O'Malley, also vice presidents, agreed with me that CBS could downsize the market.

We pointed to the exploding competition nationwide. Eager for exposure and recruiting advantage, universities could be whipsawed as low as $40,000 per team, per game, we thought. Besides, the NCAA was saying that unless we doubled our commitment to the regular season, the coveted tournament was staying with NBC.

Our break came on Thursday, February 26, at 11 A.M. —the moment of truth when Nielsen ratings of the prior weekend's sports programs are made available. The sweet aroma of Van's cherry-blend tobacco grew stronger and the rumble of his big, agitated body grew louder as he charged into my office. He waved the ratings sheets theatrically:

"Big guy, what do you think our Los Angeles Lakers and New York Knickerbockers broadcast rated last Sunday?"

I paused, realizing the country's top two markets were involved in a 96–93 game that was contested right to the final buzzer. On the other hand, the scene was Madison

Square Garden, a tomb of quiet disinterest in the home-standing Knicks.

"I don't know, Van. A mid-six?"

"Four point three."

(A rating point represents one percent of all the television homes in America—77.8 million in 1981. Thus a 4.3 rating meant that slightly more than 4 percent of households with television were tuned to the game, just 3.35 million homes.)

"Now what about the shit on ABC?" asked Sauter.

"Twice the number."

"Twice and then some: 9.1 for the videotaped fucking *Superstars*, 12.3 for the *Wide World of* fucking *Sports*. That settles it! I want those fucking college kids, those fucking cheerleaders! I want some fucking lung power!"

The timing of this explosion could not have been more critical. Exactly five days later, Tuesday, March 3, we were due in Chicago to give the NCAA our final monetary bid for the tournament and a commitment on regular-season games.

Leaving me, Sauter steamed through the offices of corporate CBS, securing $48 million for three years of the tournament, 1982–84. He overruled Pilson's arguments about regular-season profitability (which later proved erroneous) and met the NCAA's demand of 14, 17, and 17 exposures in the three years.

On March 4, the television community was stunned to learn that lowly CBS Sports had acquired the NCAA College Basketball Championships.

Exciting as that pickup was, it did not rank on Sauter's immediate agenda with *CBS Sports Saturday/Sunday*. We wouldn't see an NCAA basketball game until the next season, at which time Van was hoping to be in residence at CBS News. But sports journalism and funeral arrangements for *Sports Spec* or (*Sports Dreck*, as some called it) —Sauter had been promising these since his first days in office, nine months earlier.

CBS Sports Saturday/Sunday took the air on April 11, 1981. Immediately, our young zealots showed that sports news could be compelling television. In the first few months, we got the only network interview with Billie Jean King on the weekend she revealed her lesbian affair with a former secretary; broke the story that Indiana University sophomore Isiah Thomas was "going hardship" to the NBA; edited a complete obituary of Joe Louis in 16 minutes when news of his death broke while we were on the air; produced a 27-minute whiparound, mostly live, from ten major league cities on the settlement of baseball's player strike, leaving ABC and NBC—the baseball networks—in our vapor trail; and told the sad tale of Bert Yancey, coming back to professional golf at 42 after a siege of manic-depressive illness.

I thought of Jim Spence when we dug into the Denver Broncos' cocaine investigation and widened the Boston College point-shaving scandal with enterprise reporting. Sauter was guardian of a 25-year CBS relationship with the NFL and knew that the ink was still wet on our prized NCAA basketball deal, but he never flinched in either case.

Instead, he let us send John Tesh to Lexington, Kentucky, for a confrontational interview with Kentucky basketball coach Joe B. Hall. The question: Why wouldn't the Wildcats schedule cross-state rival Louisville? The charge by Louisville coach Denny Crum: Arrogance by the mighty state university. The innuendo: Alleged racism by predominantly white Kentucky against Louisville, the inner-city school that started five blacks.

Tesh framed this question three different ways in search of an answer. On the third pass, Hall removed his microphone and got up to leave the room.

"Cut! Dissolve! Turn that thing off!" he ranted.

It would have been good television for *60 Minutes*. For a weekend sportscast, it was unheard of. *Sports Saturday/ Sunday* was making a reputation.

Bill Taaffe, in the *Washington Star*, called it "the class of the spring in sports TV. . . . [It] has set an unusual standard for excellence since it made its debut." *Newsday*'s Stan Isaacs said CBS Sports "has come a long way from its days as the sports network that heard no evil, saw no evil and spoke no evil."

That kind of thing was exciting for our staff, but I knew it couldn't sustain us over the long haul. The "live video sports page," as we called our reporting, was unpredictable. News flow was necessarily irregular. What we needed to secure *Sports Saturday/Sunday*'s future was a strong event lineup. Events meant a steady, reliable audience each weekend. They were your *TV Guide* listing, your on-air promotion. They were the guts of your series.

But what a daunting assignment, assembling a schedule to compete with *Wide World*. Their program was an American institution, a monolith. They'd virtually transformed its title into a generic term, the way cola drinks became "cokes" and copiers became "xerox machines." On airplanes to Europe, our people would say they were covering figure skating or gymnastics for American television and stewardesses would reply, "Oh, you're with *Wide World of Sports*."

With revenue projections based on *Sports Spectacular*'s meager past, we had only half ABC's budget. But we knew what we wanted. First, the events had to be live or same-day in order to sit compatibly beside our news and information programming. This would distinguish us from *Wide World*, which still operated on two- to six-month gaps between recording and airing some of its material.

Second, I wanted events that we could take all the way to logical conclusion. There was no sense investing in a national championship when the winner would only progress to ABC's world championship. Every dollar of rights money, every moment of airtime, should lead us toward a CBS payoff.

Third, we wanted to take chances, as underdogs should,

knowing that a longtime industry leader naturally grows conservative over the years.

Then there was a fourth element—we got lucky as hell. Decisions we made in the spring of 1981 were blessed with the kind of good fortune that makes TV programmers light church candles. These decisions would make *Sports Saturday/Sunday* competitive with *Wide World of Sports* in less than a year.

In ski racing, for instance, we made a big commitment to the World Cup tour. The U.S. Ski Team story was like ours—underfinanced, neglected, four months on the road, 90 percent of their races on foreign snow.

With these handicaps, who could have guessed that Phil Mahre would win three World Cups in the early '80s and that Tamara McKinney would win a women's Cup? Who knew that Bill Johnson would pick our Wengen race in 1984 as site of the first World Cup downhill victory ever for an American? Or that he'd follow by winning our "America's Downhill" in Aspen, Colorado, the next month?

In cycling, the only event to have was the Tour de France. *Sports Spectacular* had botched it in 1980, then turned it over to NBC for two years. But we decided in 1981 to reclaim the race and communicate its mammoth spectacle.

David Michaels and John Tesh would make the Tour a personal creative statement. Michaels, a filmmaker at heart, learned the sense of discipline and structure required in television. Tesh was a Juilliard-trained musician who traveled synthesizers and emulators along the 2,500-mile route, recording an original score for each broadcast, as well as narrating the weekly programs.

Our good fortune in this event would be named Greg Lemond. No American had ever cracked the Tour's top ten until Lemond turned up in 1984, our second year of coverage. What theater he made—the lone Yank fighting his own French teammates, fearing attack by a Gallic jingoist along the unguarded roadside. All Lemond did was finish third in '84, second in '85, and blessed first in '86. There were some long faces on the Champs-Elysées that day. Astoundingly, an American had won the Tour de France.

We made other pickups in 1981—the Oxford-Cambridge Boat Race, the World Triathlon Championship, and the Iditarod (Sauter's favorite), an 1,100-mile dogsled race from Anchorage to Nome, Alaska.

Some of our luck was inherited from the prior regime. In the late '70s, ABC mishandled its relationship with the World Figure Skating Championships, the single most attractive anthology event. This opened the door for Eddie Einhorn, programmer of *Sports Spectacular*. By the time I arrived, Eddie had departed CBS for coownership of the Chicago White Sox. But we were grateful for his enduring legacy: Katarina Witt of East Germany, Brian Boitano of the United States, the fabulous Torvill and Dean of Great Britain, and other stars of the World Figure Skating Championships.

Sports Saturday/Sunday's luck ran hot in boxing as well. In April 1981, Gil Clancy, our boxing analyst, came into my office and said, "Terry, there's an exciting young kid from Youngstown, Ohio, that I think we should have on."

"Oh, yeah? What's his name?"

"Ray Mancini. 'Boom Boom' Mancini."

Thus began the "lightweight strategy" that made CBS boxing the best on network television in the early '80s. Home Box Office (HBO) had just begun to monopolize both the heavyweight division and marquee fighters from other divisions—Sugar Ray Leonard, Marvelous Marvin Hagler, and others. Even ABC was no match for HBO's budget, though my former colleagues were slow to concede this. While they false-started with a hodgepodge schedule in various weight classes, we seized the affordable lightweight division and made it our own.

In the confusion of multiple champions and alphabet-soup jurisdictions (WBA, WBC, IBF), here was a little corner of understandability for our audience. It was the deepest weight class in professional boxing—more than a dozen guys who could fight like hell. They were reasonable size—135 pounds. We had 'em in black, white, Mexican, Puerto Rican, Hawaiian—Andy Ganigan, Sean O'Grady, Melvin Paul, "Gato" Gonzales, Tony Baltazar, Robin Blake. The viewer could pick a favorite and know they'd all be fighting each other in a kind of unofficial tournament. Every lightweight bout was an investment in our next lightweight bout.

The stars of this programming were three young men who not only could fight but also had great personal stories—Mancini, Alexis Arguello, and Hector "Macho" Camacho.

Mancini was the son of Lenny "Boom Boom" Mancini, whose promised title shot was preempted by service in World War II. Wounded in combat, Lenny never returned to boxing. But Ray vowed to win the belt denied his father, a touching, genuine story that we must have told 15 different times.

Arguello was the best fighter of the group, a glorious boxing name that gave us real credibility. ABC could easily have outbid us and established a relationship with him. But when his career leveled off for a year, Alex Wallau and Jim Spence cooled on him. Wallau later confessed to me, "We made a mistake. We thought he was shot."

Indeed, Alexis, a veteran of more than 80 ring wars, turned 29 a week after *Sports Saturday/Sunday*'s premiere. But the ABC guys didn't calculate his personal motivation. He'd lost everything—house, cars, bank accounts—when the Sandinista government took control of his native Nicaragua. He then moved to Miami and started over.

Arguello was willing—yes, eager—to fight every three months for a purse of $250,000 to $300,000 that was largely funded by CBS. There was never the traditional argument about quality of opponent. His promoter, Bob Arum, told me, "It's the easiest kind of situation. He'll fight King Kong if you want."

It was also the most unusual situation I ever encountered in the backstabbing world of boxing. Once Arguello reestablished his star on CBS, he was free to fight on ABC for bigger money. We had no contract with him. Each fight was a one-shot. But Alexis remained loyal, never forgetting that we took a chance on him in '81. If only he knew. We were the upstarts. We had no choice.

Hector Camacho was the showman of this group, a Puerto Rican from East Harlem who wore sequined trunks and flashed the quickest hands in boxing. I used to see him on street corners while driving shortcuts from Connecticut to midtown Manhattan. I'd come into the office and tell my secretary, "Well, I've been out surveying our major properties. I can report that the 'Macho Man' looks healthy and ready to fight next weekend."

Among them, Mancini, Arguello, and Camacho appeared on CBS 24 times, a staple of our early years. When they grew beyond our budget to HBO and closed-circuit fights (the great irony of this star-making cycle), we adapted.

We took emerging fighters and inflated them to big attractions with the help of their fanatic hometowns. In network TV boxing, there was never anything quite so electric as Billy Costello in little Kingston, New York, Barry McGuigan in Belfast, Northern Ireland, or Donald Curry in Fort Worth, Texas. We asked promoters to recreate the boxing club atmosphere of the 1950s in small arenas and auditoriums. It made us wonder why we'd ever broadcast from sterile hotel-casinos.

From the moment it premiered, *Sports Saturday/Sunday's* mix of live events, hard-edged features, and timely sports news made *Wide World* look like what it was—Arledge's original format from 1961. ABC's reaction, at first, was expressed by Dennis Lewin, coordinating producer of *Wide World*. He was quoted, "CBS's hiring of Terry is very nice, but we are not really in a position to be concerned about it. Why should we be reacting to changes over there when we are *Wide World of Sports*?"

But by the summer of '81, it was trench warfare. When we promoted heavyweight champion Larry Holmes as halftime guest of a prime-time football game, ABC reacted. They were paying Holmes millions for every title defense. One of their associate producers called Larry and reminded him of that. Holmes then called me.

"I can't do it," he apologized. "One of the ABC guys called and told me not to. He said Jim Spence won't buy any more of my fights if I go on with you."

The incident became a volleyball between the two network publicity departments. Our man, Jay Rosenstein, sold his conclusion to Fred Rothenberg of Associated Press, who wrote: "For the first time, ABC appeared to be looking over its shoulder. . . . Calls to reporters and heavyweight fighters seem to say what ABC doesn't want to say aloud—the longtime leader in sports television is hearing footsteps."

Jim Spence took the offensive, charging that *Sports Saturday/Sunday* was nothing but a boxing series. He refused to admit the story-line distinction between our bouts and theirs.

I read a few of his interviews, declined several offers to rebut. But finally, I told my friend Skip Myslenski of the *Chicago Tribune*: "You know, when I got into this business, I missed the part where it says guys from ABC decide what kind and how many fights the other networks are allowed."

We didn't seem to hear another word from Spence.

With the launch of his sports journalism wraparound, Sauter had satisfied his most immediate need. Now to the future and his number one long-range priority. Three weeks after the premiere of *Sports Saturday/Sunday*, I smelled the familiar cherry blend at my doorway once again.

"Big guy," he began, "what do you think of our professional football coverage?"

I knew I could speak the truth. We were alone and Van had no connection to CBS's history of NFL misadventures. Still, I muted my caustic opinion:

"Pretty bad."

Sauter had already decided to break up CBS's lead commentary team, Pat Summerall and Tom Brookshier. Anxious to confirm a new analyst, he asked what I thought of John Madden.

"I don't know," I replied. "I've only ever seen him for thirty seconds at a time."

Madden had been on staff for two seasons but worked barely a dozen games in that time. Confined to regional exposure by prior management, he was invisible in the New York area except for his Miller Lite campaign.

"Ah, those beer commercials," Sauter glowed. "We should never underestimate those beer commercials."

Sauter came from a local-station background and thus understood the value of on-air talent. When the news, weather, and sports are basically the same on all three stations, talent often makes the difference.

In the language of Hollywood film studios, this was the "star system." Roone Arledge had understood it, developing Frank-Howard-and-Dandy, the three-headed institution of *Monday Night Football*. In a somewhat smaller model, NBC Sports was doing the same with Dick Enberg, Billy Packer, and, especially, Al McGuire on its well-received college basketball telecasts.

CBS Sports, in 1981, was without a single genuine star. Sauter knew it and was troubled by it. He sent me to the videotape library, I later realized, not in search of a number one football analyst but in search of a star.

Madden showed promise. At that point, he was not the

funny, outrageous Madden whom America now reveres. He was not doing the "boom, bam, whap" routine yet. But he had something that was honest, real. The quality was hard to define, which made it all the more appealing.

Al Davis, John's boss with the Oakland Raiders, once struggled to capture this essence. Describing the day in 1966 when he first met Madden, then an assistant coach at San Diego State University, Davis said:

"There was a guy standing on that football field, wearing high-cleat shoes, almost up above his ankles. Baggy football pants. A jacket that—I don't know where he got it—it must have come from a rummage sale. A hat, a baseball cap, and he was pretty fancy 'cause he had a whistle on. (Pause.) But goddamnit, when I talked to him, I felt an emotional love of football and something about him that was a little different from those you normally come across."

That's what those videotapes revealed: "an emotional love of football and something about him that was a little different." It was no more explicable than that. But Sauter and I would take it. Madden was on board.

For play-by-play, Van wanted Vin Scully, legendary radio voice of the Los Angeles Dodgers and a network television veteran of football, golf, *Battle of the Sexes*, you name it. I had great respect for Scully, admired his work as CBS's eighteenth-hole golf anchor, had even joined his worshipers for the "transistor stereo rites" one evening in Dodger Stadium. But to partner Madden, I felt he was 180 degrees the wrong choice.

On the occasion of his enshrinement into the Baseball Hall of Fame, Vin had said, in self-portrait, "I like to talk and I relish words. I feel very much fulfilled by doing baseball, especially on radio, where you can paint a mood and put word pictures on the air."

Learned at the hand of sportscasting pioneer Red Barber, this style had served Scully superbly on baseball and golf. But with football's faster pace, there was no time for word pictures, and with recent advances in coverage, there was less need. Now add Madden, who had plenty to say and frequently used the full 30 seconds between plays to say it. The combination would be too much. The viewer, I told Sauter, would be wrung out by halftime.

Van wasn't persuaded. He thought Summerall wasn't in Scully's class. He sent me back to the videotape library with a challenge to find either insight or élan on Pat's tapes.

"Scully is an elegant broadcaster," he was fond of saying.

"But it's not a question of elegance," I argued. "It's a question of styles. After six weeks, we'll all be saying they talk too much, and then we'll have to fight with both of them to cut back."

I tried an analogy from my favorite pastime, the American Ballet Theater: "Mikhail Baryshnikov is the most celebrated dancer in the world. But there are very few ballerinas who can partner him because he's 5-feet-2 or -3. Hell, Cynthia Gregory could probably lift him easier than he could lift her. So he dances with little Gelsey Kirkland. She may not be the best dancer in the company, but she's right for him."

The last statement was arguable. Partnering Baryshnikov, Kirkland had matured perceptibly and by 1981 was well recognized in her own right. But this was another aspect of the case for Summerall—a supposition that he would work harder and raise his level to meet Madden's.

Sauter compromised with me. He let me assign Scully-Madden to four games in September and Summerall-Madden to four games in October. The day after the eighth game, Monday, October 26, we pledged to make a decision. It seemed fair and perfectly in keeping with the combative world of sports—an audition of our two best play-by-play men. The prize: marriage with Madden and assignment to all the top games, including that season's

Super Bowl XVI, which belonged to CBS in the NFL's biennial rotation.

Our next step was overhauling production. In the colorful phrasing of the *Rocky Mountain News*, "CBS has lived in the era of George Gipp, rather than Joe Montana. The network's basic football coverage is mundane, predictable and about as exciting as a fifth rerun of the pro bowler's tour in Dayton."

Sauter issued me a mandate "to get CBS's production values out of the stone age," as the *Los Angeles Herald Examiner* termed it.

But *Television Age*, from the inside view of the trade, had a truer grasp of the problem. CBS football was, it said, "produced in a stodgy, schizophrenic manner almost, it sometimes seemed, half-heartedly."

That slovenly attitude was the topic in mid-May when Madden and I sat down to lunch for the first time. John was unhappy.

"To begin with," he said, "our people think this is a 'show.' They're always saying, 'The show this, and the show that.' Hell, this isn't a show. *Kukla, Fran and Ollie* is a show! *Laverne and Shirley* is a show! This is a *game!*"

"I think we can change that," I laughed. "What else?"

"Well, they don't *know* anything about the game. Don't know and don't care."

"What do you mean?" I asked.

"You know. Football. They don't know whether you blow it up or stuff it."

I asked him to be more specific.

"Take defense," he said. "Simple things, like showing what a zone coverage is. Or showing a pass rusher coming onto the field on third down."

"Yeah. So?"

"So the producer and director tell me they can't show it. Say they don't know it's going to happen till it's over."

"Well, don't they pick these things up when they watch game film?" I asked.

"*Game film?*" Madden exploded, flapping his arms the way you've seen in a dozen television commercials. "*Game film?!* Hell, some of these guys don't even show up until the morning of the game."

I looked at him skeptically, sure he was exaggerating. Next morning, I hunted up one of our vice presidents, a longtime CBS veteran.

"Yeah, it's true," he said.

The director of the prior season's Cowboys-Falcons *playoff* telecast had actually landed in Atlanta on the morning of the game. Never meeting his crew, he simply jumped on headset an hour before air and said, "Okay, who've we got on camera one? Mike. Okay. Camera two? Joe . . . Okay, fellas, we'll do the same shit we've been doing all year." Just like that.

"He actually did one of the better games we had on the air last year," said the vice president.

"Oh," I nodded and wandered away. Madden was right; this was going to be tougher than I'd thought.

I arranged lunch with Sandy Grossman, one of CBS Sports' top directors, to learn more and maybe enlist a respected incumbent to my cause. Grossman had come to CBS in 1957 as an usher after graduation from the University of Alabama. He spent seven years in various network jobs before joining CBS Sports. It was another 12 years before he rose through the ranks to direct his first Super Bowl. By the time I met Sandy, he was 44.

On the day of our first lunch, he was also grim and defensive. He'd heard the news—a 31-year-old kid from ABC was going to overhaul his football coverage. He was ready for me. I never got past the first item on my agenda, placement of the press box–level cameras that cover each play live.

In 1970, with the advent of *Monday Night Football*, ABC had fanned these out to the left 25 yardline, 50 yardline, and right 25. Whichever camera was nearest the ball covered the play. In 1977, when Don Ohlmeyer went to NBC, he took along the same configuration. It was indisputably state of the art. But CBS, in 1980, the year before my arrival, was still without cameras at the 25s. They covered every snap from the 50 yardline.

CBS's NFL telecasts were headed that year by Chuck Milton, the summertime card shark from the early '70s. He played a pat hand, telling reporters, "We think it's the best seat in the house, and we're staying on it. We wouldn't suggest making a lot of changes this year, because we've had a successful product."

Successful product? Chet Forte responded in print, calling Milton's production philosophy "asinine."

Wilfrid Sheed pondered this best-seat-in-the-house argument for *TV Guide* and spotted "the fatal fallacy: it is the best seat *if* you have only one seat. TV has the run of the joint."

Nonetheless, here was Sandy Grossman, firmly shaking his head no as we sat on a cushioned banquette in Mike Manuche's Fifty-second Street restaurant. With packets of sugar on the white linen tablecloth, I had laid out a camera plot, coverage positions at the two 25s and midfield. Sandy kept jabbing the 50-yardline sugar packet with his butter knife.

I thought, "This shouldn't even be a goddamn issue. I'll win this. I'll win all these goddamn things by brute force if I have to. But if these people won't join the rest of the world on the 25 yardlines, how are we ever going to progress to the subtleties?"

I thought of CBS's most recent Super Bowl, a 31–19 victory by Pittsburgh over the Los Angeles Rams in 1980. Surprisingly, the favored Steelers had trailed 19–17 entering the fourth quarter. But Terry Bradshaw connected with John Stallworth on a play called "60 prevent slot hook and go" for a 73-yard touchdown that turned the game dramatically in Pittsburgh's favor.

Grossman's first replay, astonishingly, picked up Stallworth two strides *after* the catch. Analyst Tom Brookshier was left momentarily speechless by this absurd picture. Recovering, he said, "This is the final sprint for the tape, but we want to look at that one again."

Brookshier and Summerall then implicated Ram cornerback Rod Perry, just because he was nearest the catch. In truth, Perry was only responsible for the short zone. Deep help should have come from nickel back Eddie Brown. But when Stallworth, on this third-and-8, ran his hook move right to the first-down marker, both anxious defenders converged. That left him open on the "go."

It was obvious that Grossman and colleagues had not the slightest idea about any of this. Incredibly, they had no isolate of Stallworth, even though Lynn Swann and Theo Bell, the Steelers' only other deep threats, had been sidelined for the evening with injuries. Naturally, there was no wide view of the secondary. In fact, Eddie Brown never appeared in any of CBS's three tight-on-the-ball replays.

Madden was right again. They didn't know and didn't care. And how were we ever going to reach any depth of sophistication when they had their heels dug in at the 50 yardline?

My only option was to ignore the naysayers and construct a detailed plan for presentation to the entire group. The venue: Essex House Hotel in Manhattan. Dates: July 27–28. Attending: All commentators, production staff, and management personnel involved with CBS/NFL coverage, about 90 people.

Carl Lindemann, an import from NBC, had witnessed this meeting the prior two years and wondered, "It costs a fortune to fly these people in from all over the country. Somebody gets up in front of the room for an hour and talks about ratings or whatever. Nothing really. Then we eat lunch and dinner. Next morning, everybody flies home. I don't know why the hell we do it."

In 1981, however, there was a lot to talk about. I started

by handing the commentators Yves Saint Laurent navy blue blazers with a newly designed CBS Sports pocket patch, an on-camera look they still wear today. These replaced tawdry burgundy and gray coats with 1930s-width lapels and a jacket patch that the distinguished Jack Whitaker used to wear upside down. It was so garish, so hideous—the insignia of a berserk naval admiral—that Whitaker figured nobody would notice. He was right; nobody did.

We moved on to production, retooling every tiny detail of a three-hour football telecast. Punt coverage: We would no longer cover punts from the endzone as I'd seen on tape from the 1980 season. We would now use cameras with a profile view of the field. Somebody asked why. I said, "So we can see how far the ball travels."

Individual player statistics: This had been a rare battleground between self-absorbed directors, who didn't want their pretty pictures cluttered with lines of type, and CBS's impotent producers. To show their disdain, directors were matting (superimposing), say, quarterback stats over crowd shots, two-huddle shots, the opposing coach, anything.

"We're gonna make this simple," I said. "We'll matte the quarterback stats over the quarterback. Receiver stats over the receiver. Coach's record over the coach."

Positioning an insert of the game clock: I selected the lower right corner of the screen. Somebody asked why. I shrugged, "Just personal preference."

CBS had always placed its game clock in the upper center of frame. In the 1975 NFC playoffs, Dallas's Roger Staubach beat Minnesota with a last-second "Hail Mary" pass to Drew Pearson. Famous play. But the CBS audience never saw it because Pearson reached up to make his catch *behind* the clock insert. I daren't tell this story. Two guys in the room had produced and directed the game.

Standardization: CBS Sports was the last outpost of

rampant individualism. Each telecast was an independent production. One director went to replays with a circle wipe (video effect), another with a box wipe. One producer used "Minnesota vs. Atlanta" on his graphics, another used "Vikings vs. Falcons." This would stop, I said. Nobody needed to ask why.

Sandy Grossman was on pretty good behavior until I revealed the new typeface and format for superimposing graphic information. As I was finishing, he called out, "Just like ABC Sports."

"Not exactly," I replied. "This is better."

He also fought me on a new division of labor between producer and director. Heretofore at CBS, directors did everything—selected cameras, matted graphics, chose replays, rolled tapes, opened microphones, cued talent. No wonder their production was shoddy. They were doing the work of two men.

I determined to use the ABC and NBC system, wherein the producer made replay decisions after each play while the director was free to cut reaction shots. In the CBS system, producers sat around like spectators. Directors, after each play, searched their tape machines for a revealing angle while the infamous 50-yardline cover camera, still on the air, meandered back to a two-huddle shot. This process yielded a dearth of on-field reactions, as noted by *Sports Illustrated* in reviewing that January 1980 Super Bowl:

> The CBS crew, headed by producer Bob Stenner and director Sandy Grossman, missed on a more basic aspect of big-game coverage: reaction shots. . . . When Los Angeles's Frank Corral missed an extra-point attempt, he surely must have reacted in an animated fashion. We did not, however, get a quick glimpse of him after the miss. . . . On none of Terry Bradshaw's three interceptions did we see an isolated replay of one of the NFL's most animated quarterbacks reacting to his misplay.

The CBS old-timers were impervious to such criticism, dismissing it as the ignorant or jealous view of print reporters carping about television. Nor were they ready to accept my solution, the new producer-director relationship. Grossman filed, but eventually folded, a grievance with the Directors' Guild of America.

Another director, Tony Verna, gave me his vision of the ideal producer: "You know what I like in a producer? A guy who, when you get to the production meeting, has the ginger ale, the beer, the peanuts, and the pretzels all lined up. That's a good producer."

With that novel idea, I took to the road, assigning myself to produce one preseason game each with Grossman and Verna. I wanted a firsthand feel of their skills and their openness to the new system. Later, I would have to choose between them for a Super Bowl director, much like the Summerall-Scully decision.

On Friday, August 28, room-service breakfast arrived in my Dallas hotel room just before 9 A.M. In a few minutes, Summerall, Madden, Grossman, and I would be leaving for the Cowboys' practice facility. The next night's Houston-Dallas preseason game would be the debut of the Summerall-Madden team. If my instincts were correct, this would be the start of something big.

Sprinkling that happy notion on my bran flakes, I opened the *Dallas Morning News*. A headline jumped off the first sports page: "Summerall: 'The Heat's on Madden.' "

> For Pat Summerall, the party's over.
>
> When he joins John Madden Saturday night for the first time to do the Cowboys-Oilers game, it will mark the first time in 6½ years he hasn't worked with color analyst and running buddy Tom Brookshier.
>
> And Summerall doesn't mind admitting that he doesn't look forward to the prospect.
>
> "It puts me in a tough position. Deep down, it's really

true that I'd rather be with Brookshier," Summerall said from his Florida home. . . .

Summerall said he doesn't know what to expect, but it will not be like the good old days of a year ago with Brookshier.

"It was not like going to work when Brookie and I did the games. It was like I couldn't wait to get there. As he is fond of saying, when we arrived we were laughing, and when we left on Sunday night we were still laughing.

"If it were Brookshier and me, we would have had the production meeting, then we would have been out drinking margaritas," Summerall said. "Now I'm not sure what's going to happen. That's why I'm coming in early. I want to get the lay of the land."

In addition to working with a new partner, Summerall will have to learn to deal with a new producer and new camera placements. Terry O'Neil, who left ABC last year for CBS, will be producing his first CBS football game Saturday night. . . .

Summerall said he had received more public and media response from the breakup with Brookshier than any other incident in his 20-year broadcasting career.

"I went into a restaurant in Flint, Mich., last week. The owner was so irate he almost threw me out of the place. He said, 'Why did you do that?' I told him I didn't do it. . . .

"I regret the breakup. I did not agree with the breakup. I think the network made a big mistake," he said. Later, he added, "I'm not sure it's going to be as good as what we had."

On first reading, I flinched, almost knocking over the milk pitcher. I staggered over to the bed and spread the newspaper out wide. Now, on second pass, I began to catch the irony. Summerall would have punched you for saying so, but he had summarized the situation almost exactly as Sauter had back in May. The only difference was that Sauter wasn't laughing about this margarita-festival atmosphere.

Alcohol was the lifeblood of the old CBS Sports. Summerall and Brookshier regularly drank their way through the 4 P.M. football telecasts. After all, it was cocktail hour.

In Sauter's view, Brookshier was the very embodiment of the problem. Tom was a spontaneous wit, a man who entered the booth each Sunday aspiring to a half-dozen clever and original lines. Often he succeeded in that ambition. But lately, the half-dozen were arriving in the nation's living rooms amid the worst jumble of clichés known to contemporary sportscasting.

Yeah, it was a "barn burner" when Van met up with Tommy. There was "a lot of fur flyin'." Van saw Tommy as "some kind of" anachronism in the early '80s and decided to "lay some wood on him." He was "like a bull elephant in heat."

All this gibberish, of course, was filler for an analyst who had done no homework whatever. Reviewing his work in that 1980 Super Bowl, *Sports Illustrated* wrote:

> As for Brookshier, he rambled on in his ever-chuckling, star-adoring way. Brookshier's almost unwavering pattern was this: stalwart makes good play; Brookshier says how good play was; Brookshier says what a great man stalwart is. When Pittsburgh's Jack Lambert made an ordinary tackle, Brookshier said, "He's quite an athlete." Upon Bradshaw's second long pass completion to John Stallworth, Brookshier reported that Bradshaw is a born-again Christian and that "I love him; I've always loved him."
> For many viewers, love is not enough.

Soon after this game—perhaps the biggest of his broadcast career—Brookshier admitted to a reporter, "I let all the parties get in the way of my concentration. A few hours before the game, I suddenly realized that I didn't have a single intelligent thing to say about either team."

It was like Tommy to be in that predicament. And, bless his naiveté, it was like him to confess to a reporter.

You could make an argument that he wasn't solely to blame. After all, CBS had been in town a full week before the game. What kind of schedule was he on? Where was his leadership?

Well, his leadership was hiding, like a Central American government in exile, once Sauter floated the idea of demoting him.

"He thinks he's a cowboy, a western gunslinger," confided Milton, who claimed close friendship with Brookshier. "He wants to fight every guy in every bar, every Saturday night."

Bob Stenner, longtime producer of the Summerall-Brookshier team, told me, "I'm glad they're being broken up. Somebody was going to get hurt. I mean it. All the drinking, the late nights before the games. Some Sunday, you were going to turn on the television and one of them wasn't going to be there."

So they deserted him. His buddies. Guys with the titles and, supposedly, the authority to take him in hand—for his personal welfare and for the good of their telecasts. They had never shown any strength. And now they abandoned him. All except Summerall.

Closing my *Dallas Morning News,* I realized it was fully in character for Pat to make this stand. From what little I'd observed, his best friends were his oldest friends—Ken Venturi, his golf analyst, and Tony Trabert, his partner on tennis coverage. But Brookshier was dearer than any of them. Besides their seven seasons on CBS, Pat and Tommy had worked an additional ten years on a highlight show for NFL Films. Their wives had gotten very close. They'd watched each other's children grow up. The first time I mentioned Tommy, Pat told me, "We're like brothers."

They had a certain exchange almost weekly on the air. I savored it now, leaving my room-service breakfast uneaten and heading for the elevator. Some day, when this turmoil was ended, I wanted to tell them how they'd *made* my Sunday afternoons:

"What'd you do last night?" Tommy would giggle, temptingly.

Summerall in smug reply: "I don't remember. What'd *you* do?"

Emerging into the lobby, I was confronted with Madden's huge presence. He was slouched low in a leather easy chair, wearing the Miller Lite windbreaker and untied tennis shoes that would become his familiar uniform on the day before a telecast. I could not see his face immediately. It was hidden by the *Dallas Morning News*.

I stepped around to John's profile and said good morning. He had folded the paper carefully so that the only type facing him was Summerall's article. I had the clear impression that he'd read it several times. He was seething.

The next moment, Summerall arrived, looking freshly scrubbed, clad in golf shirt, slacks, and black cowboy boots. His "Good morning, John" was neutral, without inference, as if nothing should be wrong. Madden, without making eye contact, mumbled in response, sighed, and rose from his chair ever so slowly. Summerall, by this time, had left him, walking briskly toward the hotel's front door.

One week later, the regular season opened, Scully at Madden's side while Summerall worked the U.S. Open tennis championships. However, commentator pairings were forgotten when A. C. Nielsen delivered its first report of the season. The office hummed with good feeling. Our ratings were 15 percent better than week one of 1980 and far ahead of NBC's numbers.

CBS had always enjoyed an advantage, its National Conference teams situated in larger, more established markets than the American Conference teams that NBC televised. CBS paid the NFL for this edge, an increment 20 to 25 percent greater than NBC's rights fees. The presumption was that CBS would get back its investment with higher ratings and thus steeper advertising rates. But lately, CBS football had been underperforming. Despite the disparity in markets, NBC had made the last two years very close.

In 1980, NBC actually held a full rating point margin after five weeks, maintaining its lead all the way into December. The two networks entered their final Sunday with identical averages. Then CBS, blessed with three big regionals that determined the NFC playoff picture, won the season by three-tenths of a point.

But by the second week of '81, this was ancient history. CBS's ratings again showed huge improvement over the previous year. The third week, our advantage grew even wider.

Beano Cook burst into my office. He was the hefty, impish publicist with whom I'd shared an office during my Olympic researcher stint at ABC. Reunited expatriates from another network and fellow Pittsburghers, we could speak freely. Beano closed the door.

"O'Neil, do you have any idea how many millions of dollars these guys have wasted over the years?"

"What?"

"The NFL ratings, O'Neil. Do you have any idea how much advertising money they've let get away? No, forget that. Do you think the CBS stockholders have any idea? Do you think they know about the fucking idiots who've been doing their NFL maps?"

The "maps," or regionalization of CBS's five-to-eight Sunday games, had major impact on Nielsen ratings. These had been drawn for years by two vice presidents of programming. Beano had once wrangled an invitation to their Monday meeting but lasted only a few weeks.

Seems he tried to explain the rancor between Bear fans and Packer fans along the Illinois-Wisconsin border. It was his theory that if you didn't have Lombardi's venerable Packers to give these people, you gave them a Bears game. Not Vikings or Lions, regardless of division standings. Bears. The rivalry was that deep.

Apparently, Beano was teaching a geography lesson on the senior vice president's desk, outlining the shore of Lake Michigan with his fingertip, when the man told him to mind his own business and get the hell out.

In the brave new world of 1981, Beano was my right-hand man in these networking decisions. He was taking uncommon pleasure in our success.

The fourth week, it happened again—another Thursday morning bouquet from Nielsen. After one-quarter of the season, we were 2.8 rating points ahead of NBC. Our numbers were 14 percent better than 1980. Theirs were 13 percent worse.

Willie Schatz of the New York *Daily News* called me to ask why. What could I say? That America had hated sitting with Milton and Grossman on the 50 yardline? That we had two dummies in vice presidential offices who would've done better maps with darts? Of course not. So I lied.

"I wish I knew the reason," I was quoted in the *News*. "Short of doing an extensive market survey, there's no way to tell. . . . I don't know if we're doing it that much differently from last year."

Beano laughed at me, "Fucking O'Neil. You think you'll get away with that. The writers won't believe you forever."

Truth was we'd done something so elementary that you'd be ashamed to tell anyone it was new to CBS. We simply broke the country into 23 regions or networks. Some of these were strongholds, places where we had National Conference teams. Others were no-win situations, like western Pennsylvania and eastern Ohio, where NBC had three AFC teams—Pittsburgh, Cleveland, and Cincinnati. The last group were areas that had no NFL franchise—Alabama, Tennessee, Arizona. It was important to do something smart in these swing regions.

Each week, we plotted the map with one eye on our schedule and one on NBC's. For instance, if they were showing the Dolphins in Miami at 1 o'clock, we booked a 4 o'clock game there, even if it was a lesser attraction. No matter what the strength of your NFC game at 1 o'clock, going head to head with the beloved Dolphins in Miami was suicide.

Once we eliminated no-win situations, it was simply a matter of *thinking* like a fan in each of the remaining regions. We called sportswriters and television anchors to sample the local mood. Mostly, it was a case of fresh outlook, unencumbered by past practice.

In week five, our lead on NBC stretched to 3.1 rating points, a whopping turnaround of 4.1 Nielsens from one year earlier. But something else happened that was much more significant to the long-term future of CBS/NFL broadcasts.

It was Sunday, October 4. San Francisco was scheduled in Washington. At two wins, two losses, the 49ers didn't really know about themselves. They'd been 2–14 in 1979, 6–10 in '80. If they were still mediocre, this was the kind of game they'd lose, three time zones from home in a noisy snake pit called RFK Stadium. But if they could overcome all that, the players might finally feel they'd turned a corner.

Washington, on the other hand, was 0–4 entering that game. The Redskins had a rookie coach, Joe Gibbs, who came with the reputation of a passing-game wizard. But who knew about his capacity to handle a whole team? Especially after he'd gone oh-for-September.

Gibbs was at odds with the quarterback he'd inherited, headstrong Joe Theismann. The coach wanted Theismann to sit in the pocket and execute his newly installed offense. The quarterback was more inclined to bolt upfield at the first sign of defensive pressure. There was a rumor that Gibbs wanted to trade him for a more compliant field leader.

San Francisco won the game, 30–17. It was just the dose of confidence these 49ers needed to make 1981 their year, too. Beginning with that Sunday in Washington, they won 14 of their 15 remaining games, including Super Bowl XVI. They captured another Super Bowl trophy three seasons later, ultimately ranking as one of the NFL's two finest teams of the 1980s.

The other, of course, was Washington. Theismann threw two interceptions in that '81 loss to San Francisco. Gibbs benched him in the second half as the Redskins' record fell to 0–5. But that night, close to tears, Theismann called Gibbs and asked if he could come to the coach's home. They settled their differences, and Washington won eight of its last 11 games.

The next two seasons, '82 and '83, then again in '87, the Redskins were a Super Bowl entry, winning two of three. Between them, they and the 49ers made seven NFC Championship appearances in the seven seasons, 1981–1987.

There's no estimating how important this was to CBS. NFL football in the '70s had been dominated by three of NBC's AFC teams—Oakland, Miami, and Pittsburgh. From '72 through '80, they won eight of the nine Super Bowls. CBS's NFC had been reduced to the Dallas Cowboys and, stretching a point, the Philadelphia Eagles as watchable "national" teams starting our '81 season.

Washington and San Francisco were perfect breakthrough clubs in every way. Geographically, they were positioned on the two coasts—one to play at 1 P.M., the other at 4. Historically, they had long-term appeal—Sammy Baugh and Frankie Albert, Sonny Jurgensen and Y. A. Tittle. Sartorially, they both had a great look—burgundy and gold in D.C., scarlet and 49er gold by the Bay.

Both played in distinctive, older ballparks with sodded fields—not the circular kind on a riverbank with plastic grass that gives the players concussions.

Regionally, they had broad reach. Before franchise expansion, the Redskins were CBS's southern attraction from the Potomac down through Florida and west across the Gulf states to Louisiana. The Atlanta Falcons and New Orleans Saints should take no offense. Many southern fans were simply waiting for the Redskins to field a quality team again.

Likewise, San Francisco's constituency began in the hills north of Los Angeles and stretched all the way to the Canadian border. Ask no questions about those latecomers, the Seattle Seahawks.

It would be a year or so before the 'Skins and 49ers started paying dividends to CBS, a normal lag in this situation. But in the miracle year of 1981, we didn't need their help. We had divine intervention.

On October 18, week seven of the NFL season, our 4 P.M. doubleheader broadcast was scheduled against game five of NBC's National League baseball playoffs. This was the annual meat grinder. One of our NFL Sundays inevitably faced either the World Series or League Championship Series. In either case, we knew to expect a single-digit rating, rather than the 12 or 13 that was normal for a doubleheader football game in October.

As I sat beside Sauter in a screening room of the CBS Broadcast Center that Sunday, I was prepared to take my whipping like a man. But looking up just before 4 o'clock, I saw an NBC feed that showed Los Angeles Dodgers and Montreal Expos players bundled up with towels inside their heaviest jackets. Olympic Stadium in Montreal was nearly empty. It was snowing! Not raining. *Snowing* in October! The baseball game was postponed.

NBC, of course, had played all its football games at 1 o'clock. Millions of fans who'd cleared their afternoons for this decisive final game of the Expos-Dodgers series would now be looking for an alternative. We were the only game in town.

"Do you know what this means?" I gasped, laying a hand on Sauter's shoulder.

"Big guy," he said, puffing happily, "we deserve it."

Our football doubleheader that day attracted a staggering total of 30.5 rating points, about 10 more than we had a right to expect. The Canadian cold front not only guaranteed a fat, full-season victory over NBC, it also put us on pace for the highest-rated season ever at CBS or NBC.

But the very next week, there was dread where our euphoria had been. It was time to make the Scully-Summerall decision.

Their games had gone off as expected. Vin came armed with heavy statistics, his trademark, and other good information. But Madden's saddlebags were full, too. It was a race to see who would fill the last breathless seconds before commercial.

For his part, Summerall reacted like the athlete-competitor he has been for a lifetime. For the first time in years, CBS veterans said, you could actually hear a heartbeat in his play-by-play. Wisely, though, he turned up the intensity without increasing the quantity. There was still enough space in Summerall-Madden despite John's growing verbosity. In fact, compared to Scully-Madden, it was easy listening.

Off the air, the situation grew tense and nasty. This face-off, such a seemingly good compromise in May, had a big drawback. Fixated on producing a winner, Sauter and I had failed to realize there would be a loser. How would he feel? How would he enjoy answering questions about being a runner-up? Should men of Pat's and Vin's stature be asked to submit to this?

Maybe that's what Summerall meant when, in the heat of August, he looked ahead to the cool of late October and told the *Dallas Morning News,* "It puts me in a tough position and it puts Madden in a tough position." He might have added Scully.

Vin remained the consummate gentleman, never objecting to the audition. He seemed confident. Summerall, on the other hand, had accosted me on October 6 at the funeral of a former CBS Sports vice president.

"I'm going to NBC," he said. "I thought you should know."

He was not threatening. He was *informing* me.

This was the strategy of Pat's newly acquired agents. After 20 years of negotiating his own terms at CBS—a remarkable statement of trust between a man and a broadcast bureaucracy—he had taken on representation "because I'm all alone. I don't have anybody fighting for me."

Sauter and Scully used the same attorney-agent, Ed Hookstratten of Los Angeles. Speculation around the office had it that the deal was already cut, that Scully was a lock. I positively could not believe such an accusation about Sauter, but I dared not ask him. I didn't want the wrong answer.

Summerall enlarged this office rumor—at the instruction of his agents, I felt sure—and injected it with venom: Sauter and I had already assured the spot to Scully; our eight-week trial was designed to let him down easy. When I protested, Pat revised his theory: Sauter had made the promise and I was a stooge for carrying out his charade. I made no reply, except to ask that he continue working hard and wait for October 26.

As we drew closer, however, I couldn't feel Sauter budging on his support of Scully. Monday morning was sure to bring him into my office, quoting Vin's three most graceful constructions of the previous afternoon.

With my concern edging toward desperation, I decided to seek reinforcements. I asked Sauter if we might widen the circle to include his other top lieutenants—five vice presidents and the senior producer of NFL football. This was hardly a decent way to treat my rabbi, outflanking him, but I was tightly in the grip of self-righteousness.

Sauter consented. Actually, this was *his* management style—"collegial decision-making," as he loved calling it

—allowing everyone a voice. Nothing about this business seemed to warm him so much as a gathering like the eight who convened at high noon, October 26, in an executive dining room on the thirty-fourth floor.

It was a rare New York day, brilliantly clear, offering panoramic views across Manhattan to the Hudson River and New Jersey. Served by well-starched waiters, we ate chicken and asparagus off elegant CBS china and wiped our lips with fine CBS linen. Then it was time for business.

Sauter opened by reconfirming his belief in our procedure. Yes, it had been unusual, he said, but the dilemma we faced was unusual, too. Now he wanted our appraisals, plainly stated. The good of the division was at stake, he reminded us.

I knew each opinion in advance. Like a politician at a nominating convention, I had polled the delegation. Of the seven who would respond to Van, four had deep roots at CBS Sports and thus were loyal to Summerall. While acknowledging that Scully had integrated himself nicely in six years at CBS, they still viewed him as an outsider. Considering the staff's widespread paranoia throughout this year of upheaval, these four viewed the potential demotion of Brookshier *and* Summerall as too radical.

The other three responses would be offered by men of varying backgrounds—Lindemann, former programming chief of NBC Sports who was now Van's special assistant; George Schweitzer, who'd followed Sauter through the corporate maze and become a trusted protégé; and me. Presumably, we would bring a more detached objectivity to the question.

"This is what Tip O'Neill must feel like when they're calling roll in Congress," I thought.

One by one, around the oval-shaped mahogany table, each man spoke. I was seated at Sauter's immediate left, and by the time I got the floor, the tally was unanimous. Summerall had all six votes. By the third or fourth endorsement, however, my elation had turned to a sudden sheepishness, an understanding that we were facing down the president of our division—and a good man at that. When it came my turn, I began tentatively.

"Well," I stammered, "I, uh, I guess I'm here to echo some of the thoughts . . ."

"ALL RIGHT!" roared Sauter, slamming a fist onto the table, rattling coffee cups. "I've heard enough. If you people want him, you can have him. But mark my words, you'll have to manage him. I hope you know what you're letting yourselves in for. I'm not going to be responsible for his alcoholic binges."

Whoa. "Alcoholic binges." Apparently, there had been more on Van's mind than blending commentary styles.

We returned to the twenty-eighth floor, Sauter summoning two vice presidents and me to his office.

"Who's going to tell Vinny?" he asked.

There was an uneasy silence, like the moment your waitress puts a heavy check in the middle of the restaurant table and nobody goes for it. Van crossed one arm over his chest, drew heavily on his pipe, and panned our faces slowly. The two vice presidents looked at their shoes. It was okay. This job was rightfully mine.

"I'll do it," I said. "I started this thing."

They looked at each other. Their relationships with Scully were far deeper. I'd only known him for three months. But what the hell, this was a live grenade. Nobody was diving on it.

Crossing back to my office, I gave the Scully phone call not enough thought. It was midpoint of the season. We were shuffling the entire staff as promised, giving every man a chance to show the new executive producer what he could do.

I was thinking about the realignment. Roger Staubach would leave Frank Glieber after half a season and join Brookshier, now doing play-by-play. I'd have to call their producer for a long talk. George Allen . . . Lindsay Nelson . . . Hank Stram . . .

136

My secretary interrupted. She'd found Vin Scully. He was on the line. I hesitated, unprepared for this. But there were still so many phone calls to make. Oh, God. I picked up the receiver. . . .

"Vin, I have good news. You're going to be working two postseason games—a divisional playoff and the NFC Championship. Your partner for the second half of the season is going to be Hank Stram."

Even as I was hearing myself say these words, I knew how wrong they were. Scully was spitting mad. He was in a New York hotel room, between games of the World Series for CBS Radio. I offered to come across town to speak to him. He declined emphatically.

Some months later, he would depart for NBC, turning down a reported ten-year, $7 million offer from CBS. On his way out the door, Scully told CBS corporate management that the Super Bowl disappointment was the largest factor, but another reason was the "good news" phone call from Terry O'Neil.

He was right. It was a hard lesson for me in being direct, *especially* when the news is bad. Faced with parallel situations in the future, I never picked up the phone without thinking of Vin Scully.

If the events of October 26 fractured one relationship, however, they probably sealed another. Years later, when my hometown *Pittsburgh Press* called to ask about me, Summerall said, "He and I have a great rapport, an upfront, 100 percent honest relationship."

Unknown to Sauter, Pat and I had settled the drinking issue on that Dallas weekend in August. An hour before our first telecast together, I met Summerall outside the control truck.

"Pat," I said, "I've told the stage manager there won't be any alcohol in the booth tonight. And I also told him it'd be *his* ass if I find out otherwise. We're going to have one rule around here for commentators, production people, technicians, everybody: No drinking on the day of a game until we're off the air."

He looked at me coldly for an extra second or two, then replied, "Whatever you say." He marched off and we never had a problem. I remain convinced that the only reason he'd previously indulged on the air was that nobody told him he couldn't. He, like Brookshier, was simply a victim of CBS Sports' rampant permissiveness.

Pat's relationship with Madden also improved dramatically once he felt the security of retaining his position. By November, he was saying, "John, I wish I could have played for you. I'm learning a lot." On the air.

Far from his August diatribe, he was now telling newspaper reporters, "I have to work harder. I spend more time looking at film. Part of it is keeping up with Madden, to understand the kinds of things he talks about. . . . It's been an education, a pleasure. . . . It's given me a fresh approach. I probably tightened my belt a little bit and took a closer look at what we were doing."

Our commentary team set, I was free to make the big push toward Super Bowl XVI. The directors' competition between Verna and Grossman was tight. While neither could bring himself to rave about our new methods, I ultimately believed Grossman's good nature would overcome his temporary show of hubris.

The New York *Daily News* once described Sandy as "short, chunky, bearded." They might have added "smiling." He had long laugh lines that creased from the corners of his eyes all the way down to his narrow strip of beard. Once I came to know him, I was deeply grateful for his pleasant manner.

But in 1981, we were a long way from mutual admiration. In one of our November games, I asked him for a shot of an injured running back. He put up the back of the player's head, an "asshole" shot.

"What the fuck is that?!" I screamed.

"It's what you asked for!" he screamed back.

"I want to see his face! He's hurt!"

"That's the best we can get!"

"Oh, yeah? Well, that's not gonna be good enough."

This, finally, was what we needed—the pressure cooker of live television to forge a relationship. The production trucks, the stadiums, game situations—our natural habitat. Not sugar packets on a tablecloth. I had to be patient; for the CBS veterans to embrace my system meant a huge admission about their past. Sandy, meanwhile, had to realize he'd never sat beside a guy who *wanted* it so badly.

Struggling with that contention, we moved into the postseason and an innovation called the CBS Chalkboard. During our May lunch, Madden had asked, "Why can't we show the game the way coaches watch it on film—with all twenty-two men?"

"John," I explained, "they watch it on a projection screen that covers an entire wall. If you took that wide framing and shrunk it down to a seventeen-inch television screen, the players would be tiny ants. The viewer's eye wouldn't know where to focus."

All the while, I was thinking, "But if the viewer had a pointer, a directional marker, maybe even a road map of the play. Then what?"

One autumn morning in the inspired year of 1981, a little package landed on my desk. I swear it was from heaven, but the return address said Chicago, a company called Interand. They'd developed an electronic stylus, connected to a special monitor, that allowed commentators to draw freehand over television pictures. They wanted to know if I was interested.

Was I interested? I stabbed the telephone and dialed Madden. From that moment, without ever seeing the hardware, we both believed what the *Philadelphia Inquirer* later wrote of the Chalkboard: "the most significant improvement in football coverage since ABC's development of the instant replay."

Spreading our fervor through the ranks of CBS management took a few weeks. Interfacing this new technology with CBS mobile units took another few weeks. But we finally had the system ready to debut at a New York Giants–San Francisco 49ers divisional playoff game on January 3, 1982.

The day before, Madden and I had taken a mutual vow of caution. We planned to use our new toy just two or three times, and only after sufficient rehearsal. I swore to him, "John, I'll never call for it unless I give you a commercial to look at the play a few times and practice your drawing."

But then the game started. That's when instinct overtakes the sincerest of promises. We did eight diagrams that day, only two with the benefit of rehearsal. For the record, the first CBS Chalkboard was a 72-yard touchdown pass from New York's Scott Brunner to Earnest Gray in the opening quarter. But Madden and I were just warming up.

Near the end of that period, Joe Montana hit Dwight Clark for a 39-yard gain. This play was typical of a 49er passing attack that had dumbfounded the NFL. Clark was literally 10 yards clear of his nearest defender when he made the catch. Yet on television, the viewer could never understand why.

Live coverage panned with Joe Montana's passes, not revealing the receiver until a split second before he caught the ball. A conventional isolated reply was no good in this case because it only showed Clark, not the full scope of New York's zone defense.

I ordered up a wide-angle view of all 22 men, cued John for the Chalkboard, and edged forward on my chair. I was as curious as our 40 million viewers.

Madden explained that the two Giant safeties were playing deep zones, each responsible for half the field. The safety on Clark's side, Larry Flowers, had been influenced by another 49er receiver who ran a deep route, straight at him. By the time Flowers saw Clark, also working his half of the field, it was too late.

Eureka! After years of hearing the inexplicable term *double zone,* America was now *seeing* it. There were the two Giant safeties—Flowers and Bill Currier. You could see Clark run his pattern through a short zone, where cornerback Mark Haynes played him for 10 yards, then "turned him over" to Flowers. Except Flowers wasn't there. He was locked onto Ricky Patton, the other deep threat. Coach Bill Walsh's design was brilliant, and finally it was *evident.* This was history-making video.

Later in that game, we learned how the Chalkboard could lift decisive plays—the ones viewers would be discussing in barber shops and restaurants the next morning —to an unprecedented level of understanding. We also saw how this cold, analytical tool would fit with the hot, emotional explosion of a game-turning moment.

In the fourth quarter, Brunner's desperate pass was intercepted by 49er rookie Ronnie Lott, who ran it back for the clinching touchdown. Summerall and Madden laid out, letting the hometown roar swell. Sandy cut frenzied crowd, Brunner on his knees, Walsh jubilant, Giant coach Ray Perkins slumped. Our hand-held cameraman *ran* up the sideline with Lott, holding him in glorious profile.

At the time, I saw none of this. I was previewing the videotape that Madden would diagram. Into the commentators' headsets, I said, "They're playing five underneath, two deep. Lott's at the very top of your picture."

After the extra point, our wide framing showed television's first understandable view of "prevent defense"—five pass defenders strung across the field like a picket fence, two deep safeties behind them. Madden circled Lott, showing how he'd read Brunner's eyes and the intended receiver, John Mistler.

It was a two-minute package that captured fans, players, victory, defeat, coaches, and their strategy. If all TV football coverage can be distilled to "emotion" and "analysis," we had them in equal parts.

Unlike his Pittsburgh–Los Angeles Super Bowl, Grossman had time to find reaction shots, the *humanity* of this moment. Independently, Madden and I were preparing a visual explanation that pushed industry frontiers a bit.

It was fire-testing and full certification of our new production system, with all hell breaking loose on the game's pivotal play.

Grossman, however, could not yet admit this. The big overhaul of '81 was still a topic of excruciating sensitivity among network old-timers. It was also a story irresistible to television critics as we approached Super Bowl XVI in Pontiac, Michigan.

Many writers mentioned our overdue move to the 25-yardline positions. Ever-flexible Milton knew enough to remove himself from the "best seat in the house." *Television Age* wrote: "Now, exults senior producer Chuck Milton, 'we've got profile pictures of the ball all over the field.'"

Grossman, however, remained a proud holdout. He told the *Washington Post*'s Bill Taaffe, "Now we're spreading the cameras out . . . but I don't think people at home can tell the difference. It's a media thing."

The men who really committed to our new methods were the technicians. Treated like fools and robots for decades, they loved it when I told them, "Men, in this system, you have to do exactly what Joe Montana does. When the players come to the line of scrimmage, you have to read the formation and react. And you have about as much time as Montana has—two or three seconds."

Before 1981, the watchword of CBS's NFL coverage was, "Keep it simple." But as I explained to our technicians, it *isn't* simple. If it were simple, my little sister could be an NFL head coach. Pro football is terribly complex. The goal of television should not be to trivialize or reduce it to false simplicity, but to make this wonderfully complicated endeavor *understandable* to the viewer.

To that end, we attacked the Super Bowl with 16 cameras and 11 videotape machines. We devised a written preassignment scheme for every cameraman and videotape operator on every down, every conceivable situation. But there were some variables in it.

For instance, we wanted an isolate of San Francisco's pass rushing specialist, Fred Dean, every time he was on the field. He played only on obvious passing downs, but even then, it was hard to find him. The 49ers lined him up all around their defensive front, just to keep the opponent off balance.

Three cameras were instructed to search for Dean on every play: camera 6, located at midfield, above the press box, and cameras 9 and 10, positioned behind either endzone, at field level. If Dean was lined up on the near (press box) side, 9 or 10 would take him, depending on which camera he was facing. If he was lined up on the far side or tucked into the interior line, 6 would take him from the high angle. Absent Dean, each camera would move to its next preassigned priority according to down and distance.

Similarly on offense, we had priorities. Of the five eligible pass receivers for each team, we had facilities to isolate only three. In Cincinnati's case, these were Isaac Curtis, Cris Collinsworth, and Dan Ross.

But Bengal Coach Forrest Gregg told us he had a formation that also used Charles Alexander as a split receiver. Alexander was really a running back. Cincinnati was never going to throw to him. Coach Gregg simply wanted to occupy one of San Francisco's excellent cornerbacks, leaving Curtis or Collinsworth to work on a weaker cover man, nickel back Lynn Thomas.

San Francisco had seen this ploy on film. Its coaches were determined not to waste Lott (who was All-Pro as a rookie that year) or Eric Wright (also a rookie, later to become All-Pro) on a mere decoy. That, I told our cameramen, would be precisely our strategy. We weren't going to waste a camera and tape machine on a receiver who'd never see a pass.

This meant a simultaneous silent "read," without any discussion, among several cameramen. Cameras 1, 2, and 3 were the hotly debated left 25, 50, right 25. On each snap, one would be covering the live play. The other two would isolate the "far side" receiver and "middle" receiver. Camera 9 or 10, whichever was facing the offense, would isolate the "near side" receiver. But their interdependent calculations about "far, middle, near" weren't possible until everybody had checked for Charles Alexander and eliminated him if he were flanked wide.

Got all that? Now add these variables: formation shifts, receivers in motion before the snap, short motion, half motion, reverse motion, slot formations, double slot, double wing, triple formation ("trips"). For our receiver isolates *alone,* it was clear we needed rehearsal.

This was the ideal job for Chuck Milton. I asked him to find me a football team, dress them up in the uniform numbers of the Bengals and 49ers, and run them through some plays we'd seen on film. Our cameramen, meanwhile, could rehearse their various assignments.

Chuck reached the Wayne State University athletic office in Detroit—and not a moment too soon. The school was giving up football as of that season. But they agreed to play one last game, just for us.

It was a big help and a big media occasion. No television crew had ever done anything like this. (Of course, nobody ever needed the preparation as we did.) NFL Films recorded the afternoon, and viewing it now, I have greater sympathy for Sandy Grossman. It was only Friday, still 48 hours to air, but my game face was screwed on tightly.

Spotting a missed assignment, I snapped, "Is Ricky Blane not with us?"

"He should be," Sandy said. "Camera 3? The motion man is yours, Ricky. Remember what we talked about."

I was planning to be nervous on Saturday, the eve of the game. But a group of cameramen both surprised and calmed me as I arrived at the trucks about noon. On their own, they'd come to the stadium early, told a security guard their cameras needed maintenance, then watched the closed practices of both teams through their viewfinders.

Steve Gorsuch, camera 2, said, "You're right about Charles Alexander. They never throw to him. And don't worry about Freddie Solomon's [injured] foot. He looks fine."

So did our Super Sunday. For me, it began at 5 A.M. I lurched awake in a cold sweat. My painfully vivid nightmare: San Francisco kicks a field goal to win at the final gun. We isolate both head coaches, kicker Ray Wersching, everybody but Eddie De Bartolo, Jr., team owner. On my monitor bank, I notice that De Bartolo's reaction is the most expressive, but we don't have it fed to videotape. Groping around my room at 5 A.M., I amended our replay pattern to cover this possibility.

At noon, *CBS Sports Sunday* took the air, featuring same-day coverage of the lung-burning Lauberhorn downhill from Wengen, Switzerland. Just one year after the 11-minute travesty that nearly aborted my move to CBS, we lined the mountain (more than two miles) with 18 cameras. It was the first ever top-to-bottom coverage of a World Cup downhill.

Watching in my Michigan hotel room, I tingled. Everyone in my world was focused exclusively on the Super Bowl. But in many ways, Wengen was more satisfying.

Our people on site were a microcosm of the new CBS Sports. Some, like John Tesh and producer John Faratzis, hadn't even been on staff a year earlier. Others, like skiing analyst Billy Kidd and director Andy Kindle, had merely been waiting for a chance like this. The melding of their efforts was Revolution '81 at its best.

Several hours later, a similar coalition took its place for Super Bowl XVI. I was still three days short of my first anniversary at CBS. My production assistant, Mike Arnold, had been an ABC free-lancer one year earlier. Sandy Grossman, meanwhile, was directing his third Super Bowl for CBS. Associate director Joan Vitrano was working her fourth.

In the moments before air, I took the director's conference from Sandy so that I could speak to everyone—technicians, production personnel, and commentators—simultaneously:

"Men—and Joanie—this is a big moment for us. If you're like me, you're a little nervous right now. But I want you to remember one thing: I'm the only guy who got here on a pass. I'm the only one who assigned himself. The rest of you had to survive the most ruthless competitive process in the history of our business just to be here. Every one of you earned his way with great performance during the season. So if you *are* a little nervous right now, be consoled to know that you're the best. Now's the time to relax and let your talent take over."

Joan Vitrano counted us to air. Grossman was dazzling in the moments before kickoff. He opened a field microphone during Solomon's pregame introduction to hear a teammate exclaim, "They can't beat us today, Freddie." Then he ordered the tightest shot of Montana's eyes you've ever seen. Our video scopes pulsated with excessive blue.

Once the game began, our cameramen found Fred Dean every time. He lived in the Bengal backfield, outquicking Anthony Munoz. They also ignored Charles Alexander every time, zooming past him to their assignments.

Our CBS Chalkboard broke the code on another mysterious football expression: "freeze the linebackers." When Montana faked to his running back and threw to Clark, I punched Madden's headset key and gushed, "Chalkboard 'F.' Watch what this run fake does to the linebackers."

For the first time in TV football, it was all there in one picture. At Montana's fake, both Cincinnati inside linebackers took two giant steps forward to meet the running back. Curling behind them was Clark. Before the "frozen" linebackers could retreat, Montana had a 10-yard space to throw his pass. On our wide-angle shot, those 10 yards were a yawning, dramatic expanse of green.

At halftime, Grossman and I bent an NFL rule—strictly to serve the viewer, you understand.

We were allowed cameras inside the locker rooms, but only for the postgame show. The cameras sat unmanned throughout the game—fired, lenses uncapped, and, Sandy took care, framed and focused on the middle of the room.

Trailing 20–0 at halftime, Cincinnati Coach Gregg spent extra minutes in a fire-and-brimstone exhortation of his athletes. Grossman took the shot. Madden caught the mood. Then, matching his words to the coach's sweeping gestures, John delivered a speech that was probably better than anything the Bengals were hearing:

"I know what he's saying. He's tellin' 'em, 'Look, this is the biggest day in our lives! This is a world championship! We lost the first half, but we have to come out of here now and win this second half! AND WIN IT BIG!' "

Took your breath away.

In the third quarter, Cincinnati scored immediately, reducing its deficit to 20–7. Later in that period, the Bengals had first-and-goal at the San Francisco 3 yardline, a chance to make it 20–14. This was the game's hottest moment, prime time for Summerall to vindicate his selection as Madden's partner.

On first down, Cincinnati fullback Pete Johnson carried to the 1 yardline. Over a replay, Madden used 20 seconds in a pedestrian description of the key block by Bengal center Blair Bush.

Summerall interjected, "Bush got the knock, the block, and the takedown on Archie Reese."

On second-and-goal, Johnson was stopped for no gain in a fearsome collision with San Francisco linebacker Jack Reynolds. We rolled a tight isolate of Reynolds, eyes bulging, clashing helmets with Johnson. Madden went wild, but Pat was more incisive in five words:

"Reynolds led with his head."

Failing again on third down, the Bengals disdained a field goal and put their whole season on the line with a fourth-and-goal gamble. Pat's description:

"They give it to Johnson. And I don't know."

That's all. Without saying another word, he let the players unpile and the officials signal that San Francisco had held. This was the key play in the 49ers' 26–21 victory.

Stan Isaacs of *Newsday* called the CBS telecast "an excellent sight-and-sound show." Jack Craig of the *Boston Globe* wrote, "CBS's coverage of the game came close to perfection." Willie Schatz of the New York *Daily News* offered, "The heroes of Super Sunday included Bill Walsh, Joe Montana, Jack Reynolds, John Madden, Terry O'Neil and Sandy Grossman."

Then came the rating: 49.1 and a 73 share, meaning that 49.1 percent of the nation's television homes watched the game and 73 percent of people using their sets were tuned to us. To this day, it remains the highest-rated Super Bowl of all time.

There was more good news. A. C. Nielsen computed our 1981 regular-season average as 17.5—the highest rating ever achieved by any network with Sunday afternoon pro football. Before or since.

CBS accountants totaled the season in their way. Clearly, advertisers had caught the fever of our improved coverage and record ratings. Regular-season NFL profits were $30.2 million, up from $19.7 million in 1980. Altogether, NFL football delivered a $48.7 million profit to

CBS for the 1981 season, as opposed to $28.4 million a year earlier.

Then came the Emmy Awards. We won not for the Super Bowl or for any single game but as a team for the whole year: "Best Live Series—*CBS Sports Presents the National Football League.*" All producers and directors got statuettes.

One year later, we won a second Emmy for the 1982 season. In fact, our group might have retired that trophy if CBS hadn't withdrawn from the awards after '82 in a dispute over judging procedures. Still, this was a helluva thrill. The same guys whose work had been called "stone age" and "Neanderthal" now had Emmy bookends.

My one regret was that the Television Academy gave statuettes only to production personnel, not to commentators. Wanting to recognize the entire group, I had a jeweler cut my '82 Emmy into little pieces. He mounted each piece on a wooden base with an individual gold plaque for distribution to our 16 commentators.

Roger Staubach, among others, sent me a thank-you note: "When I won the Heisman Trophy, I always said I should break it into little pieces and give one to each of my teammates. Of course, I never did. Now you're making me look bad. But thanks anyhow."

4

Haunted by "Combolations"

AFTER THAT first lunch with Madden in May 1981, after
confirming all his horror stories, I made him a promise:
"We'll educate our producers and directors about football.
They'll become students of the game."

John shot back a look that was somewhere between
"Bullshit" and "Prove it."

In those days, the networks' way of preparing for an
NFL telecast was to invite each club p.r. man to join their
production meeting for five minutes. The exchange often
went like this:

PRODUCER: Hey, thanks for coming. Will you have a
drink with us?

P.R. MAN: Sure. What can I do for you guys?

PRODUCER: Anybody hurt?

P.R. MAN: Nope. I think they all practiced today.

PLAY-BY-PLAY MAN: I had one question. How do you
pronounce Modzelewski?

P.R. MAN: Most people say "mah-juh-LESS-kee." But I
think he likes the way his Polish neighbors say it back in
Pennsylvania, with an *f*: "mah-juh-LEFF-skee." What
else?

ANALYST: Where do you suggest we go for dinner tonight?

Hard to believe, but as late as 1980, this was the extent of "firsthand research" by all three networks. ABC, NBC, and CBS were equally delinquent. Consequently, the game they broadcast was wholly different from the game being played on the field.

Madden once told me, "You know, when I was coaching, I could always tell what the television commentators had said by the complaints I got afterward from fans or even my friends. They'd say, 'I don't know why you left your cornerback man-to-man all day on Isaac Curtis. He's a world-class sprinter.'

"I'd say, 'Well, the cornerback was *never* man-to-man on Isaac Curtis the whole game.' And my friends would look at me like they didn't *believe* me! They'd heard it on TV! Boy, that used to upset me. The television guys were saying things that weren't *true*, things that never *happened*!"

In 1981, we gambled that enough NFL coaches agreed with Madden to permit an improvement in the process. I called the league's broadcast coordinator, Val Pinchbeck, and told him we wanted to become "intimate with the game." I asked that producers, directors, and commentators of every CBS broadcast be allowed to screen film, attend practice, and meet with coaches and players on the day before their games.

Pinchbeck's first reaction was, in rough paraphrase, you wanna do what? But within minutes, he took the position, "What's good for CBS is good for the NFL."

Accordingly, we devised a weekend schedule for all our broadcast teams that was unprecedented in the spotty history of televised football. A sample:

FRIDAY

8:00 P.M. Producer, director, commentators have dinner together to plan the weekend. (Optional: Order room service to the producer's room and screen a portion of the previous Sunday's telecast.)

Saturday

8:00 A.M.	Leave hotel for home team practice facility.
8:30	Screen coaches' film of both teams.
10:15	Watch home team practice.
11:30	Conversations with home team players and coaches.
1:00 P.M.	Lunch.
2:00	Producer and director devise isolation and replay scheme.
3:30	Producer and director present photocopied assignment pattern and diagram several plays in meeting with cameramen and videotape operators.
6:00	Conversations with visiting team players and coaches at their hotel.
8:30	CBS production meeting.

Some of the CBS old-timers blinked at the thought of a 14-hour workday on Saturday. But it was easy to ignore them. I had Madden's support.

The situation reminded me of a story Sparky Anderson used to tell about his early years with the Cincinnati Reds. One day he was visited by Pete Rose, Joe Morgan, and Tony Perez, who told him, "Skip, you can make any rule you want on this club because we're the leaders—white, black, and Latin—and we'll support you. We want to win."

That's the way it was with Madden. The best broadcaster on our staff was also the hardest-working. It was therefore possible to ask virtually anything of the others.

The groundbreaking feature of our new weekend schedule was access to players and coaches. This was the source of hard information for commentary and camera isolations. But in a fascinating way, it also became a human study.

The sessions were informal, free of the stiffness that an on-camera interview generates. In that atmosphere, we were exposed to fear, doubt, hope—all the emotions that are so ripe on a football squad the day before a game.

Coaches, far more than players, wore that enervated 24-hours-to-kickoff look. Their jobs were man-eaters, all-consuming. Worst afflicted were the offensive coordinators, who bore the mental strain of calling every scrimmage play. Frank Broyles had told me about this coaching type when we worked together at ABC.

"The play-caller is a different breed," he'd said. We were on our way to visit Wally English, Broyles's former assistant at Arkansas but, on this night, offensive coordinator at the University of Pittsburgh.

"They're always imagining situations. Third-and-goal. At the 1. Quickly! Need a short yardage play against a gap defense. He's training the mind to react. Instantly. Because there's no time. You have to get that play in to your quarterback right now. And then, sometimes, when it's on the way, you wish you could take it back."

At Pitt's hotel, the desk clerk told us, "I'm sorry, Mr. English is not in his room. I believe he said he was going out for a walk."

Broyles grimaced and turned back to me. It was 11 P.M.

"You see what I mean," he said. "Those play-callers. They can't sleep the night before a game. They're *tormented.*"

It may have been torment, but some head coaches realized that play-calling was too important to be entrusted to an assistant. These men served as their own offensive coordinators.

In 1981, our National Football Conference included five of them—Walsh of San Francisco, Gibbs of Washington, Perkins of New York, Dick Vermeil of Philadelphia, and Tom Landry of Dallas—men who wore both hats as head coach and offensive play-caller. Was it coincidence or not that four of the five qualified for postseason play in '81 and the fifth, Gibbs, was just one season away from winning a Super Bowl?

Perkins we knew for only two seasons. Though he ended an 18-year Giant drought with that '81 playoff appearance, he was never at ease in the organization. The next year, he returned to his alma mater, the University of Alabama.

In a world of general discomfort, Saturdays on the road seemed Perkins's most painful time. Upon arrival at the hotel, club management would throw open its doors for the traditional Giants cocktail party. Said to be the lengthiest and most lavish in the league, this was an open bar and "stand-up dinner" for the team's legendary collection of fans, priests, cronies, and assorted hangers-on.

Previous Giant coaches had joined the fun, Saturday being a day of light to no practice and limited meetings. Perkins, however, disdained the party as having "nothing to do with winning football games."

Instead, he sat in an adjacent room and waited for Summerall, Madden, Grossman, and me. Not especially close with any of his coaches, not interested in watching a college game on television, he simply awaited our meeting.

We entered the room. He greeted us with not a whisper of a smile and . . . The Stare. Perkins was infamous for this. Charlton Heston, playing Moses in *The Ten Commandments,* had nothing on Ray Perkins's piercing blues.

The conversation began. Certain questions would provoke a reprise of The Stare.

Late in '81, as Perkins vacillated between oft-injured Phil Simms and inconsistent Scott Brunner at starting quarterback, I asked him, "In practice, why do you give all the snaps to your starter and none to your backup?"

The Stare.

Perkins said there simply wasn't time to prepare more than one quarterback during the week.

Mini-stare.

Where Perkins's eyes were icy, Dick Vermeil's were often bleary. His Eagles were defending NFC champions that '81 season, but a devastating rookie linebacker had crashed their Eastern Division—Lawrence Taylor of the Giants.

"You sit here for 45 minutes screening a reel of their defense," he told us, "and when it's over, you realize you've spent the whole time watching just one player."

Working at that pace made for long nights. By the time we saw Vermeil on Saturdays, he was often exhausted and overwrought. He'd shake his head at the feeble options for dealing with Taylor's blitzes. He could use Stan Walters—an aging, decrepit tackle—or maybe his tenacious running backs, but they were badly undersized.

Next day, the Eagles would try both. We isolated Taylor on every snap. He took Vermeil's whole scheme and plowed it back into the quarterback time after time. Philadelphia was beaten.

Another time, we found Vermeil frazzled on the day before his home game with archrival Dallas. Typical of his diligence, he always tape-recorded his meetings with the three Eagle quarterbacks, then gave each an audio cassette to play in his car as a refresher.

On this afternoon, Ron Jaworski's cassette couldn't be found. Vermeil had sent him home to search for it while Eagle secretaries turned the team offices upside down. Understand, this was a home Saturday, the only afternoon off for much of the staff during the season.

"I know the Cowboys have gotten hold of it," Dick steamed. "I just know they have it."

The cassette was never found. Dallas won the game, 17–14.

Later, as the teams prepared for their rematch, Vermeil was still aching from a controversial loss to Miami. Unable to hear signals in the deafening Orange Bowl, Philadelphia's offense had been forced five times to retreat from the line of scrimmage. Eventually, the Eagles collapsed in a 13–10 defeat.

That was on a Monday night. A full 12 days later, as we met him on a Saturday in Dallas, Vermeil was still upset. Red-eyed with grief and fatigue, he spent most of our meeting complaining about the officials and crowd in Miami

When we left him, Madden said, "He still hasn't forgotten two weeks ago. There's no way his team will be ready tomorrow."

They weren't. Vermeil's Eagles lost again to the Cowboys, 21–10.

Ultimately, there were too many of these traumas. Football took control of Vermeil's life the way liquor does an alcoholic. The "Little General" was sleeping three nights a week in his office. Indeed, during the season, he never left Veterans Stadium from 6 A.M. Monday until 8 P.M. Thursday, when he went across town to tape his television show.

Madden noted this lifestyle, recognized its symptoms from his own 20 years of coaching. On the last weekend of the 1982 season, without any inside information, he told viewers of an Eagle game: "I wouldn't be surprised if this weren't his [Vermeil's] last coaching game in the NFL. And by his own choice. I just have a feeling—I have no reason—I just have a feeling Dick Vermeil may not be coaching next year, and I don't think he's going anyplace else."

Just days later, Dick retired, tearfully telling a press conference he was "burned out." But in that admission, there was something tremendously appealing. He'd made himself vulnerable in a way that the dogmatists, autocrats, and near-militarists of coaching never do.

View it this way: Woody Hayes of Ohio State felt all the same emotions, but he repressed and repressed until, one night in the Gator Bowl, he slugged a Clemson linebacker who'd intercepted his quarterback. Vermeil, on the other hand, walked into regular team meetings during his last season and, for no apparent reason, began to cry. Which guy would you rather play for?

Another coach who stayed three nights a week in his office was Gibbs of Washington. In fact, he slept on the very same roll-out sofa where we'd sit for our Saturday conversations.

Gibbs once told us what mornings were like with his hyperkinetic quarterback, Joe Theismann.

"I'll just be rollin' out of bed, about seven o'clock," he said, "and I'll hear these little feet. Bip, bip, bip, bip—all over the hallway. It's Theismann."

He groaned and rolled his eyes. Now he pantomimed light tapping at the door.

" 'Coach? Coach, you up yet?'

" 'Y-y-yeah. Yeah, Joe, I'm up.'

" 'You want some coffee, coach? I'm makin' some.' "

Hearing the story, Madden shook his head. "I couldn't put up with him," John said. "He'd drive me crazy."

Madden was thinking of the endless hours that quarterbacks and their coaches must spend together. In his vision, there had to be a certain affinity, if not friendship, such as he'd enjoyed with Ken Stabler in Oakland. But with Theismann?

Arriving in Washington in 1974, Joe immediately pronounced himself a better quarterback than Redskin legends Sonny Jurgensen and Billy Kilmer. Then he opened a restaurant, authored a book, and landed his own radio show—all while playing *third string*.

Washington Post columnist Dave Kindred once wrote of him, "He's the Will Rogers of football. He never met a microphone he didn't like, or a notebook he couldn't fill."

The press may have been amused. But his teammates, charging shameless self-promotion and a touch of "little man complex" in the world of NFL behemoths, disapproved almost universally.

Kilmer, Jurgensen, and other Redskin veterans of that era insisted on calling him "THEES-man"—the accepted family pronunciation in South River, New Jersey—not "THIGHS-man," the affectation Joe had adopted at Notre Dame to rhyme with Heisman (Trophy). Center Len Hauss, a Kilmer/Jurgensen loyalist, welcomed any inquiry on this subject as an opportunity to repeat his sardonic rationale: "His dad's name is pronounced THEESman, right? His mom's name is pronounced THEES-man, right? So what's his name?"

Gibbs felt no more personal warmth toward Theismann than did his players. Indeed, after that 0–5 start in '81, he had the perfect opportunity to dump him. Theismann was in the last year of his contract while promising rookie Tom Flick waited in the wings.

But Gibbs put subjectivity aside, as good corporate managers must, and judged him solely on performance. With those eight victories in Washington's last 11 games, Theismann proved he could play.

Later, in a major concession, Gibbs granted Theismann a few audibles in his tightly framed offense. Rather than fight the quarterback's ambitious personality, Gibbs harnessed it. In 1984, he confessed to us that he installed a few new plays near the end of each week "just to keep Joe's interest." This was indicative of Gibbs's finesse in handling men and situations.

In 1983, his star fullback, John Riggins, proudly converted a toolshed on the grounds of Redskins Park into "The Five O'Clock Club." This was a ramshackle wooden cube, its floor 15 feet square. Riggins crammed it with two large refrigerators, a few beer kegs, ice tubs, and a handful of chairs. The walls he hung with clocks, most of which bore brewery logos, all set permanently to 5 o'clock.

Admission was by invitation only. Theismann, for instance, was never included. No, this exclusive club was for "The Hogs": Russ Grimm, Joe Jacoby, Donnie Warren, Mark May—down-in-the-dirt linemen. Importantly, it was also for Riggins's pals—a local fireman, an off-duty policeman, a team equipment man named "Stretch," a former Redskin center named Ron Saul. What an honor it was for Summerall, Madden, Grossman, and me to be invited when in town.

The Five O'Clock Club existed for only one reason. After practice, rather than be harassed by fans at a nearby bar, Riggins and troupe simply ambled 50 yards from their locker room to the shed. They would drink beer for hours, sometimes until nightfall.

Occasionally, club members would look out through the cracks of their weather-beaten door to see Gibbs running his laps around Redskins Park. The coach was aware, of course, but ignored them—as long as they were winning. During the '85 season, however, when Washington found itself 5–5 after ten weeks, Gibbs suddenly "discovered" the club and banned it. Riggins and mates got the message.

As much for his human skills as for his football acumen, Gibbs is probably the most complete coach of the '80s. There was something very centered about him, something that helped him deal with the torment that Frank Broyles had described.

Madden, who coached with Gibbs at San Diego State, said he'd been a real hell-raiser as a young buck. But between then and now, he'd endured family hardship. His wife, Patricia, had suffered a facial tumor and a mild stroke. Somewhere during that period, Gibbs found religion, too.

He never used language harsher than "doggone." But that made communication during crisis all the easier. When he overturned a blackboard one year at halftime in Dallas and told the 'Skins, "We're getting our butts kicked," they understood. Washington came from behind in the second half.

Besides their midweek sleeping habits, Gibbs and Vermeil had something else in common. Tom Landry sometimes couldn't remember either man's name. Gibbs he called "Gibson." Vermeil he called "Vermillion," a nickname we exploited mercilessly once Dick joined us at CBS in 1983.

Tom Landry, stoic under the hat and headset, was an enigma to our foursome. Visiting him, at first, was a waste of time. Yes, he'd heard those directives from the league office: "The CBS guys want to talk to you. Any information you give them will be held in strictest confidence until they come on the air."

But Landry was slow to buy in. We'd make the courtesy call for every Cowboy game and Tom would dutifully give us 15 minutes of nothing. Then we'd go get some real information from his players and staff.

Madden and I moaned to each other about this futility. But Summerall told us to lighten up. He'd known this man for 30 years, back to their days with the Giants when Pat was a placekicker and Tom an assistant coach.

Landry was gonna be Landry. We should simply take the session for what it was and amuse ourselves by doing something original. Like count the number of *his own* players' names that Tom couldn't·pronounce.

Gary Hogeboom, for instance, was "Hogenbloom." Don Smerek was "Smirk." Once, when discussing quarterback Danny White, Landry called him "Roger." This was three or four seasons after Staubach had retired. Similarly, he called Doug Donley "Golden," for Golden Richards, a look-alike receiver with long blond hair who played for Dallas in the '70s.

On the sideline during big games, the coach could be suprisingly vacant. He'd send plays into the huddle that didn't exist, leaving his quarterback to extrapolate or guess what he wanted. In tight spots, he'd turn and call for a player who hadn't been with the Cowboys for several seasons.

Landry's malaprops extended to medical terms as well. When we once asked him what was wrong with Doug Cosbie's knee, he responded, "I don't know. I think he's got some combolations up in there."

Combolations?

If you listen closely, you can still hear Madden use this creation on the air as a catch-all for general malfeasance.

For instance, "That was a broken play right from the start. They had a lot of 'combolations' in the backfield."

The best of this genre, however, was engineered by Summerall one morning in a stroke of devious brilliance. On the ride to see Landry, he surveyed the Cowboys' depth chart and decided it might be possible to extract two manglings in one breath. Bang-bang. A double-dip.

His targets: Smerek and Jim Jeffcoat. Summerall engaged Landry thus:

"How's your defensive line?"

"Playin' pretty well."

"Are the starters holding up?"

"We hope so," Landry smiled.

"How 'bout behind them?"

"Well, we got some young guys, but they're comin'."

"Who's your first substitute?"

"Well, it depends where we get an injury."

"Say it's at tackle."

"I guess we'd probably go with 'Smirk.' "

Summerall was containing himself nicely.

"And if one of your ends went down?"

"I don't know," mused Landry, looking just slightly puzzled by this deep line of specific questioning. "I guess we'd go with 'Jethcoat.' "

Jethcoat! we screamed later in the car. To this day, the four of us have rarely referred to Jim Jeffcoat any other way.

Jokes aside, it was interesting to observe the decline of the Cowboys during my term at CBS. From the dominant NFC team of the '70s (making five Super Bowl appearances in nine years), they slipped out of the playoffs in '84, below .500 in '86, '87, and '88.

From my perspective, the primary reason seemed to be lack of internal communication. You'd go by Tony Dorsett's locker after a Saturday practice and hear him bitching that he'd gone seven weeks without gaining 100 yards.

But when you asked if he'd spoken to anybody about it, he'd say, "Who you gonna speak to around here?"

You'd ask the cornerback, Everson Walls, how he was doing and he'd say, "Man, I'm on an island. They got me in single coverage every play."

But could he ask one of the coaches for more zones, more combination coverages?

"No, man. Hell, no."

In the '70s and early '80s, the Cowboys still had a few commanding young men as assistant coaches, notably Mike Ditka and John Mackovic. They were ideal to hear out the players and act as intermediaries with the aloof Landry.

But by '83, Ditka and Mackovic were gone to head jobs of their own. By '86, Landry himself was 62 years old, and his top assistants were Jim Myers, 65; Ernie Stautner, 59; Jerry Tubbs, 51; and Dick Nolan, 54. The younger men on staff—Paul Hackett, Al Lavan, and Alan Lowery, all in their thirties—had not yet acquired enough confidence of either generation to bridge the gap.

Landry never seemed to understand this. He grew more remote, knowing fewer and fewer players by name. They, in turn, played more and more listlessly into the '80s. When I asked Madden about my theory, he said, "Some coaches are like that. Tom thinks that if he draws it up, it should work. But it's still a game of *players.*"

However isolated he may have become from his team, Landry did become more forthcoming with Pat, John, Sandy, and me. You still had to read between comments to ascertain his true feeling, but it was there if you cared to search.

All the while, Dallas's on-field performance made our sessions with him more difficult. As the team played worse and worse, there were more tough questions to broach. These fell to me as we struck a "good cop/bad cop" pose, sparing Pat and John.

What did Landry think of the *Dallas Morning News* poll

that listed Hogeboom as the players' choice at quarterback, ahead of his choice, Danny White? Would he trade one of them? How soon?

These were questions that needed asking if we were to do a proper job the next day. But better I should ask. Landry adopted an unspoken compromise with me. He'd answer truthfully, even completely, but without ever looking me in the eye.

Another sensitive topic was Dallas's defensive front, aging through the '80s and getting decreasingly little heat on the passer. Landry, who'd developed the straight 4-3 defense, was accustomed to seeing the old Doomsday foursome, led by Bob Lilly, get plenty of pressure by themselves. Now he was reduced to a scrambling defense that brought as many as eight rushmen on Dallas's "max blitz."

"This must be killing Tom," said Madden privately, recognizing the purist in Landry. "Just killing him."

The Cowboys had developed a method to deal with their inadequacy: Behind the four ineffectual linemen, play no linebackers and seven defensive backs. Since all seven could either blitz or cover receivers with equal skill, devise such a bewildering number of schemes that the offense would never know who's coming and who's dropping off.

It was inspiration out of necessity. But Landry would never admit to it fully.

"How often are you blitzing?" we'd ask.

"Oh, ten or fifteen percent. About the same as ever," he'd reply.

For something so close to Landry's soul, we learned that we needed a player source. Coming up to Thanksgiving Day 1985, a St. Louis–Dallas game, we asked defensive captain Dennis Thurman how much the Cowboys would blitz.

"Depends on how the game goes," he said. "Not much, I don't think."

Sitting beside him was strong safety Dextor Clinkscale. "What do you think, Dextor?" I asked.

Clinkscale dropped his head. A slight leer began growing at the corners of his mouth.

"We'll be comin' after his ass," he said, still looking at the floor, trying to stifle his expression.

"Half the time?"

Tucked down into his jacket, Dextor's mouth was widening to a smile. He looked up through his eyebrows, without raising his head.

"More."

Something about the way he said it, we chose to believe Clinkscale and, armed with his information, reduced the game to a most understandable proposition for the viewer. We junked the traditional opening and had Madden narrate tape of a Dallas "max blitz" against the Cardinals from 1984.

It's pretty simple, John explained with the CBS Chalkboard: Dallas is going to be rushing eight men a lot of the time. Neil Lomax, the St. Louis quarterback, has only seven blockers. But if he can read the blitz quickly and unload the ball before that eighth man gets him, he's got single coverage on his receivers. And if they can do what Roy Green did last year, it'll be a touchdown.

The game unfolded just as Clinkscale had predicted. We must have done two dozen Chalkboard replays. Madden: "Here are the four down linemen. (He circles.) And here come the others. Bates. Here's Thurman. Clinkscale off the corner. And here's the one the Cardinals can't handle —Downs up the middle. He gets the quarterback."

It was Russian roulette. The Cowboys kept pulling the trigger of their "max blitz." But every fifth or sixth time, Lomax had a round of ammunition in his chamber. He squeezed off some big pass plays, but Dallas ultimately prevailed, 35–17.

The man who finally took the bullets out of Landry's Cowboy six-shooter was Walsh of the 49ers. When Dallas brought its heavy blitz package to San Francisco in the middle of that watershed '81 season, Walsh annihilated it, 45–14. This marked a transfer of authority in the NFC. From that day to this, Bill's record against Landry is 4–0.

It's 5–0 if you count what Walsh did on the morning of the 1985 NFL draft. The Cowboys were desperately in need of a wide receiver on the first round. In the early '80s, they'd featured the best trio in football—Drew Pearson, Tony Hill, and Butch Johnson. But in the spring of '84, they traded Johnson, unhappy as the substitute third receiver. Just weeks later, an auto accident ended Pearson's career. Soon thereafter, Hill developed both an attitude and a weight problem.

But the Cowboys eyed a solution on Draft Day 1985. The receiver they most wanted, Jerry Rice of Mississippi Valley State, was still available as New England prepared to make the sixteenth selection of the first round. Dallas, with the seventeenth pick, was ready to celebrate. The Patriots had needs far greater than wide receiver. They were no threat to take Rice.

But what was taking so long? Then the announcement: San Francisco had "traded up" to New England's position. Its choice: Jerry Rice.

In 1987, Rice would be everybody's Player of the Year with an astounding 22 touchdown catches. This was an NFL record for a full season, yet Rice had set it in only 12 games because of the player strike. The Cowboys, meanwhile, stumbled to a 7–8 record that season. Their most glaring deficiency: lack of a quality wide receiver.

It was like Bill Walsh to trade top draft choices for precisely the attacking force he wanted. Walsh was *the* offensive mind of the '80s.

We knew it right away in the '81 playoffs when he succeeded where his buddy, Dick Vermeil, had failed—in neutralizing Lawrence Taylor. Instead of offering Taylor a top-heavy, imbalanced tackle or a tiny running back,

Walsh slid a guard—squatty, quick-footed—to get a more reasonable match-up of physical skills.

One week later, facing Dallas again, this time for the NFC Championship, Walsh had both an inventive ploy and the courage to use it with his whole season at stake. Trailing 27–21 with five minutes to play and backed up on his own 11 yardline, he knew the Cowboys expected pass. They came with their six- and seven-back defenses.

But instead of throwing, Walsh ran sweeps. Dallas's linebackers, their run-stoppers, had been replaced by smallish corners and safeties who were ill equipped to deal with San Francisco's 260-pound pulling linemen. The only problem was that sweeps took 30 seconds apiece. If San Francisco went 50 or 60 yards this way, then made a mistake, they wouldn't get the ball back. Throwing every down, Walsh could count on two possessions. But this way, it was all or nothing.

The 49ers went 89 yards in 13 flawless plays, culminating in the famous Joe Montana–to–Dwight Clark game-winning touchdown pass. In San Francisco, these are still called "The Drive" and "The Catch."

Authored by "The Professor." He was a wonderfully unique image on NFL sidelines—trim body, handsome Californian face, silver-rimmed glasses, wavy white hair, topped by a double-eared headset. His right hand, holding the "ready list" of plays, crossed over his chest. The left thumb and middle finger rubbed gently beside his temple. His face glazed pensively. In this arena of roaring, violent monsters, here stood the real power, quiet and composed in immaculate white shirt and sweater. He was positively scholarly.

Who else, for example, would have "scripted" his first 25 plays and "rehearsed" them—Walsh's verbs, as if this were drama class—instead of "practicing" as other teams did?

When I asked him why, he said, "When we make a big play, we want to capitalize while the defense is back on its heels. We don't simply want to run off tackle until we think of *another* big play."

Thank God we discovered the CBS Chalkboard in the same season we discovered Walsh. There was no other way to explain his creativity. As we learned in that '81 playoff game against New York, he had a tremendous knack for distracting safeties, clearing the deep areas for long passes. These were made-to-order Chalkboard opportunities.

In the '83 NFC Championship, trailing 21–7 with 10 minutes to play, Walsh conspicuously inserted Renaldo Nehemiah. "Skeets" was a world-record hurdler who played infrequently but looked to the Redskins like the target of a desperate 49er "bomb."

Walsh sent him on a "streak" up the left sideline, where he attracted Washington free safety Mark Murphy. That left Freddie Solomon alone in the deep middle for a 76-yard touchdown reception.

In the Chalkboard replay, you could see Murphy pointing at Nehemiah from the moment he broke San Francisco's huddle. Madden said, "The Redskins are all screaming, 'Nehemiah's on the field, Nehemiah's on the field!'" In reality, Bill Walsh's imagination was on the field.

Perhaps his ultimate moment came in 1987 during the players' strike. On a Monday night, Walsh brought his replacement team east to play the Giants. At the start of the second half, he sent his offense out in the wishbone— yes, the college formation that wins national championships for Oklahoma. ABC's commentators chuckled.

On the first three plays, Walsh's quarterback twice kept and once handed to his fullback on the wishbone dive, barely making a first down. Bill Parcells, the Giants' coach, laughed and waved across the field. Walsh grinned and shrugged, palms upturned as if to say, "What am I gonna do? It's a replacement game."

His 49ers kept at it. On the sixth play, Walsh's quarterback made a full reverse pivot and ran the counter option for 16 yards and another first down. The tiny crowd—smallest in Giants Stadium history for this "scab" game—began to ripple with amusement.

Giant players grew embarrassed, however. They may have been stopgaps, but they were professional stopgaps, wearing NFL uniforms. No college offense was going to humiliate them. Cornerbacks and safeties began creeping forward even before San Francisco snapped the ball. They plugged the next two wishbone runs for no gain and happily pounded each other's pads. The 49ers were forced to punt.

Walsh's next possession began at the New York 40 yardline. On first down, ten Giants crowding the line of scrimmage, they blasted San Francisco fullback Mike Varajon after one yard. The defenders slapped hands, banged helmets. C'mon, bring some more of that college stuff!

Second down and 9. Forty-Niner quarterback Mark Stevens held the ball in Varajon's belly again, "riding" with him two steps. The Giants swarmed. But Stevens pulled the ball back and retreated suddenly to a pocket of linemen that formed from nowhere. New York's left cornerback—lunging forward, peeking into the backfield—was helpless. His man, Carl Monroe, flew past him to catch a 39-yard touchdown throw from Stevens.

Of course. It was pure Walsh. He wasn't simply going to put in a formation or run a few plays for novelty. He had a whole *sequence* in mind. While the others were laughing, he ran nine plays on the ground, just to set up the wishbone pass. It was both stunning and nostalgic, recalling Texas's James Street–to–Cotton Speyer and Oklahoma's Jack Mildren–to–John Carroll.

The more you thought about it, the better you understood: There was something at work here besides lighting up the scoreboard. This was a thing of beauty, a human creation. This was Bill Walsh's art form.

By extension, defense was defacement, a hooligan running through the Louvre with razor blade and spray paint. One Saturday, in self-definition, Bill told us, "The guy who invented the nickel defense should be shot."

Madden privately disapproved, but I loved it. The 49ers were not simply a championship team. They were inventive, innovative. The television viewer was *absorbed* watching them. What would Walsh come up with next?

Before the '85 season, I tried to explain this in *TV Guide*. San Francisco had replaced Dallas as "America's Team," I said. This was not a comparison of star players —Joe Montana versus Danny White, Roger Craig versus Tony Dorsett—but, rather, an acknowledgment of Walsh. He was the *x* factor. It was downright *engaging* to watch him coach.

But what a wrenching exercise for him. He was every bit the tormented insomniac that Frank Broyles had described. The first time we met Walsh, he described his creative process: All alone in the 49ers' sprawling two-story headquarters, his office pitch black except for the projector lamp, only the endless clicking and whining to be heard, forward-reverse-forward-reverse, more than a dozen times on some plays, as the clock turned past midnight.

"I know I shouldn't stay up so late at night," he said. "I'll watch reel after reel of the opponent. And the more tired I get, the more I'm convinced, 'There's just no way to attack this defense. We may not score on them.' And then in my hopelessness, I'll fall asleep, right here in my chair."

It was eerie. He sounded like "The Phantom of the Opera."

Later, we noticed that Walsh had begun to use the word *haunt* with disturbing regularity. After a defeat, for instance, he would tell the press about the 49ers' "haunting" penalties. Not needless penalties, or careless, or damaging, but "haunting."

He cleared the deep middle for Derrick Harmon one Sunday against New Orleans, a wide-open play that would have reversed a loss to the Saints. But his rookie halfback dropped the ball.

The next week, Walsh was still crestfallen when we saw him. Dejectedly, not angrily, he told us, "You work and work to devise these things. You set it up early in the game. Then when the time is right, we protect the quarterback and deliver the ball and . . . " He sighed. "It's a haunting thing."

He used the word enough to make it an inside joke with our foursome. By the final week of the 1985 season, it was absolutely predictable. The 49ers were defending Super Bowl champions that year but needed a season-closing victory over Dallas just to make the playoffs.

Going into our meeting with Walsh, I told the other three, "You know, this season has been so tough on Bill, I'll bet we get a 'haunted' today."

Madden agreed. "You know, [John's wife] Virginia has been watching his television show every week. She says he's almost over the edge."

It took till the end of the meeting, but sure enough, on the subject of turnovers, Walsh volunteered, "They haunt you and haunt you."

I gasped, then coughed to cover a laugh. Pat, John, and Sandy looked away and tried to control themselves. It was time to go.

As we shook hands and left his office, Walsh turned to us and asked, "By the way, what time's the game?"

What time's the game?

He was at home. We were the CBS guys. On the West Coast, CBS Sunday games are only ever played at 1 o'clock.

"*What time's the game?*"

As we drove out of the 49ers' complex, Madden said, "You *get* like that. *You do!* He doesn't know he's at home for a Sunday game. Hell, he doesn't know where he is."

Bill Walsh took his 49ers to the playoffs six of seven years between 1981 and 1987, winning two Super Bowls in that time. More important, he invigorated the game with creative touches. Far more than wins and losses, this is his legacy.

Straight-line thinkers that they can be, not every NFL coach was a fan of Walsh. For instance, in that January 1985 NFC Championship, Chicago Coach Mike Ditka was hardly amused to see Walsh line up guard Guy McIntyre in his "Angus" backfield. Ditka knew the media consensus on Walsh—"offensive genius." On his own staff, he had a defensive coordinator, Buddy Ryan, whom the press called a "defensive genius." The day before the "Angus" game, Ditka sneeringly told our foursome, "I'm gonna hang a sign on the stadium tomorrow: 'Geniuses at Work.'"

Mike Ditka did not believe in "genius." He grew up in Aliquippa, Pennsylvania. His father worked shifts in a steel mill that, back then, was the largest in the world. And with those old blast furnaces, it was probably the hottest, too. Mike became an alley fighter of a tight end at Pitt. He took that style into the NFL and made the Hall of Fame—first tight end ever elected. No, he didn't believe in "genius." He believed in "tough" and "long memory."

Early the next season, when Chicago returned to San Francisco for a regular-season game, Ditka had a reply for Walsh. Running out the clock with a 26–10 lead, he inserted 310-pound William "Refrigerator" Perry into his backfield for two carries. His glare across to the 49er sideline said, "You want Angus? You want beef on the hoof? How 'bout this? And my guy does more than block. He *carries* the damn ball."

Thus was born the legend/sideshow/endorser/laughtrack known as "The Fridge." It was 1985, the year that Chicago danced the "Super Bowl Shuffle."

Ditka later said his Bears played with a chip on their

shoulder that season. Similarly, I often thought he coached that way.

Mike almost didn't get his head coaching job in 1982. The Bears' founder-owner, George Halas, had been told by NFL people that Mike wasn't facile enough with x's and o's, that he was too hotheaded to handle the modern athlete.

Ditka proved them wrong in '85. But it didn't seem enough for him. He wasn't satisfied, for instance, to let Perry die as a clever comeback. Instead, he had The Fridge *catch* a touchdown pass in Green Bay—"in your face" to archrival Packer fans—and try to *throw* a pass before the worldwide Super Bowl audience. (Notice that Ditka didn't spring these creations for a Sunday regional audience against Tampa Bay or Detroit.)

On a *Monday Night* in '87, Mike hoped to showcase several more variations of his goalline offense. But this time, like Dr. Frankenstein, he saw his invention lurch out of control.

Leading 14–7 at Denver and controlling the game completely, Ditka had goal-to-go for a two-touchdown lead. On first down, he had Jim McMahon throw to *another* defensive lineman, Steve McMichael. Incomplete. On second down, he nearly got McMahon killed on a novel quarterback sweep. Two-yard gain to the 1. Now he sent Perry rumbling onto the field with his third-down brainstorm.

McMahon was to fake a handoff to The Fridge, then continue down the line in a college-style option with Walter Payton as the pitch back. Here were both of Walsh's innovations from that NFC Championship game *in one play*. A lineman in the backfield *and* the old split-T option. Now who was the genius, football fans?

There was only one problem. McMahon's head was still ringing from the blast he took on second down. Either he didn't want to take another hammering from the unblocked defensive end—as option quarterbacks must, just before pitching—or he thought he had a better idea. In either case, he tried slipping the ball into a vegetable drawer or freezer compartment of The Fridge. This was news to Perry, who thought his assignment was a simple belly-flop fake.

Through his layers of, um, insulation, who knows if he ever felt the ball in his stomach? Whatever, it went rolling free into the endzone, where Bronco defensive back Mark Haynes recovered. The momentum switch was 180 degrees. Denver came from behind for a 31–29 victory. This was the beginning of Chicago's decline in a disappointing '87 season.

It was also a time when I wanted to quote Madden's old Raider axiom: "Mike, just play. You've got the athletes. Just line 'em up and play. Keep it simple on the goalline. You don't need gadgets and kitchen appliances."

But Ditka didn't see it that way. After the game, he flaunted that chip on his shoulder. Of the goalline fumble, he said, "It's a great play, designed by a great coach. . . . It was supposed to be a fake to Perry, and when you fake to Perry, what happens? Right, a lot of people go after Perry."

Well, maybe. But beyond field tactics, there was another level to consider. The Fridge was a disruption among his teammates. In his rookie year, the kindest thing they called him was "Biscuit." Dan Hampton told us, "He came to camp just a biscuit away from 300 pounds."

But when The Fridge's weight soared beyond 330, another Bear told us, "He's a fat tub of shit."

Most didn't believe he was worthy of playing defensive tackle, let alone goalline offense. Ditka ordered him into the starting lineup midway through '85, replacing popular Mike Hartenstein. That was bad enough. Then veterans who'd suffered many dismal seasons in Chicago had to watch this "rookie phony" collect all their endorsement money and Super Bowl attention. They resented it.

Even worse than Perry, I thought Ditka made a serious misjudgment with the team's feared and unique "46" defense. He seemed not to like it simply because Buddy Ryan had developed it.

Ryan was a pudgy, bespectacled Oklahoman, whom Halas had reconfirmed as defensive coordinator when he hired Ditka in '82. Players told us the two coaches didn't speak. This made for razor-sharp team division. In fact, when their Super Bowl victory was finished, the Bears registered an NFL first—the offense carried *its* coach, Ditka, off the field, and the defense carried off *its* coach, Ryan.

The "46" (named for Doug Plank, a former safety who wore that number) was more complicated, more devastating than anything the NFL had experienced in years. In essence, it put eight men on the line of scrimmage to stuff the run and attack the passer's pocket at will. From this alignment, the Bears marauded through enemy backfields like North Vietnamese regulars overrunning an American G.I. field camp. It was a scene from *Apocalypse Now*.

Recognizing the coaches' cold war, we never asked Ditka much about the "46." Nor was Ryan much of a source. But we had our version of Watergate's "Deep Throat" in Gary Fencik, a rare Ivy Leaguer (Yale) in the NFL.

Fencik was a marked man in Chicago's only loss of that year, a Monday night upset in Miami. Dolphin coach Don Shula tried a new approach against the "46." Instead of working just two receivers and keeping maximum protection against the Bear blitzers, he opened up his formation, adding a third wide receiver, veteran Nat Moore.

Eight men committed to the line of scrimmage, Chicago was forced to cover Moore with Fencik. This was a weakness in the "46." Fencik was excellent at reading and roaming to the ball from his free safety spot, but in man-to-man coverage, he wasn't much. Moore beat him for some big plays in Miami's 38–24 win.

As we arrived in Chicago for our telecast of the Giants-Bears playoff game that postseason, with the Super Bowl still two victories away, common belief was to attack the "46" Miami's way, by making Fencik cover.

When Gary walked into the conference room of the Bears' Lake Forest, Illinois, training complex, the four of us asked him about it. He looked left and right, like an informant in a spy movie. Grabbing a piece of paper and pencil from the center of the table, he smiled, "You guys won't tell anyone, will you?"

He then proceeded to draw up a variation defense that Ryan had conceived that week, the "46 nickel."

"If the Giants come with a third receiver," said Fencik, "we'll bring in [cornerback] Reggie Phillips to cover him. The Fridge goes out. That way, I can stay at free safety. And we have a natural cornerback on each of their receivers.

"Then we'll put our outside linebackers on either side, instead of together on the strong side, the way they normally see it in the '46.'

"On the line, we'll only play three men, instead of four. But we'll still cover [play head-up on] the center and two guards, so it'll *look* like the regular '46' to their interior linemen. If they block this like it's the '46' they've seen on film, we'll be on Simms before he can take his drop."

The Giants did. And the Bears were. On our isolations, we could see center Bart Oates call blocking assignments by forming his hands into the shape of a "diamond," New York's term for the "46." His linemates looked at Oates in confusion. If this was the "diamond," why were Chicago linebackers Otis Wilson and Wilber Marshall coming from opposite sides? And from what little Simms saw of the secondary, why wasn't Fencik covering the third receiver man-to-man?

MADDEN: There's that "zircon" defense again, that phony "diamond," with the three down linemen, linebackers on either side.

SUMMERALL: Those two guys on the outside—watch them. Simms . . . [incomplete pass] just threw it away—in the direction of Carpenter.

MADDEN (*Chalkboard replay*): See, here's the thing I'm talkin' about—the "diamond." Here's the thing they call the "diamond" [interior defensive line]. But usually there's a fourth. Now there's only three. You see, it's a three-man line. Here comes Wilson [blitzing outside linebacker] from this side. Marshall [ditto] comin' from up on the top side. Of course, that is a little confusing look. The Giants haven't seen this because it's the first time the Bears have played it. And they're in it again.

Within weeks of Chicago's Super Bowl victory, Buddy Ryan departed for the head coaching job in Philadelphia. That was the time, I thought, for Ditka to wrap his arms around the "46" and all its variations, both as winning strategy and as a gesture of reconciliation with his defensive players. If he didn't buy that, okay, forget gestures. Few other teams played this defense. Certainly, nobody played it like Chicago. Offenses rarely saw it and weren't well prepared for it.

But Mike is Mike, or as John Updike wrote in *Too Far to Go,* "People are incorrigibly themselves." Ditka phased out the "46." Despite winning Central Division titles again in '86 and '87, Chicago was drummed out of the playoffs in its first game both years. The '87 loss was especially galling. With McMahon looking sharp at quarterback, the Bears took a 14–0 lead. In '85, that would have been a wrap. Playing in the January cold of Soldier Field, 14 points would have been plenty. But Washington came back to beat Chicago, 21–17.

Afterward, the Bear locker room was ornery as ever. Ditka, in his anger and disappointment, spoke of giving some "unhappy" players a chance to go elsewhere. In succeeding weeks, he apparently considered moving six or seven defensive starters, including such names as Richard Dent and Otis Wilson.

There was a steeltown stubbornness about Ditka that I recognized from my own personality. Further, there was a charisma and tough-guy appeal that made him the most telegenic NFL coach of the '80s. But there was also an intractability that I was ready to mark as his fatal flaw—until the 1988 season.

Simmering down from that playoff loss to Washington, Ditka invited all but two of his defensive players back. And one of the departed, Wilber Marshall, brought two number one draft choices in return. Then in training camp, Ditka announced that he was delegating play-calls to his quarterback coach, Greg Landry. Astonishing.

Ditka kept 13 rookies on the 47-man opening day roster, a sizable number for a championship-level team. The Chicago press attacked him in week three after a loss to Minnesota, saying he'd turned over the roster too radically. But Ditka stayed the course, showing patience with his young group. When they rewarded him in week five with a big win over previously unbeaten Buffalo, Ditka flashed the old Aliquippa vocabulary in defense of his players.

"Some of you don't like our people," he roared in the postgame press conference. "*Tough shit!* We like our people!"

One month later, the Bears in customary control of their NFC Central Division at seven wins, two losses, Mike Ditka, age 49, suffered a heart attack. For NFL fans who'd known his strength and bruising on-field style for 28 playing and coaching seasons, this was the ultimate proof of human fallibility.

Lying in a Lake Forest, Illinois, hospital bed, Ditka told his doctors he'd be back on the practice field within 48 hours. They shook their heads, said it would be weeks. The patient sank back onto his pillow and philosophized about the strange turns life can take.

The world may not be ready, but I think we're about to witness the full maturing of Mike Ditka.

Ditka was one of three successful NFC coaches whom we met after the '81 season. The other two were John Robinson of the Los Angeles Rams and Bill Parcells of the New York Giants. All three maintained a veto over play selection, but none was a head coach and offensive coordinator like the five we met in our first year.

Robinson actually came to grief in a playoff game for lack of play-calling judgment on the sideline. At a critical goalline moment of Los Angeles's 1984 wild-card game with New York, Robinson's offensive assistant, Jimmy Raye, called on running back Dwayne Crutchfield instead of giving the ball to All-Pro Eric Dickerson. The Rams' failure to score a touchdown in this situation cost them the game.

Madden, Robinson's boyhood chum from Daly City, California, railed on the air, "Why do that? I mean, I'm sure that Crutchfield is a good player. But you have Eric Dickerson. The guy's All-World! He's broken every record in rushing. All you have to do is flip him the ball and let him go! I mean, I don't understand this. I really don't!"

In one of our meetings, I once asked Robinson about the importance of an offensive coordinator, but he dismissed it with a wave of his hand. "Ah, those guys are all the same," he said. "They all call the same plays."

Still, that Crutchfield-Dickerson fiasco marked Raye's last game with the Rams. Robinson then tried Bruce Snyder for two years. When he finally settled on Ernie Zampese as coordinator in 1987, it meant a lost year of completely retooling his offense.

In truth, Robinson's strength is far more atmospheric than strategic. Taking the Rams job in 1983, his first move was to ease his owner, Georgia Frontiere, fully out of the picture.

When the late Ray Malavasi was coach, Georgia was

always hovering around the practice field or talking player trades to the press—needless distractions. When Robinson arrived, all that stopped. I once complimented him on it as we were having breakfast at an NFL owners' meeting. He only smiled in reply.

His other major revision was to create a mood of physical toughness, such as he'd learned under John McKay at the Universities of Oregon and Southern California.

Madden once analogized, "Bill Walsh, say, plays football like a game of chess. John [Robinson] plays it like a game of people." It was curious of Madden to have pulled his punch. He meant that Robinson's football is a game of bumper cars or demolition derby.

When Dickerson was setting records for him, Robinson spoke of "creating an environment for a great running back . . . getting big, 300-pound guys to just get their hands on the defense and push. . . . Then the running back is like a fighter coming out of the corner, trying to kill the other guy, or the other eleven guys."

That kind of rhetoric belies his personal nature. Robinson is well read, a connoisseur of fine restaurants and good movies. He once phoned me to say that he and his wife were taking a New England vacation. Could I recommend a few country inns along their route? That is an unusual football coach.

While Robinson may have been Madden's lifetime friend, I always felt that John's favorite coach was Parcells of the Giants. They had a lot in common—two beefy guys who hadn't made the NFL as players but instead became career coaches in their early twenties. Neither one was afflicted with a young man's customary distractions—playing golf, chasing women, late nights. No, this was a pair who enjoyed nothing so much as ten hours with the film projector—drinking coffee, smoking cigarettes, maybe chewing on a stale Danish, and *watching football*.

The first year we knew Parcells, however, none of us

was ready to predict his eventual Super Bowl victory—Bill included. It was the end of 1983. Parcells's team was headed for a 3-12-1 record in his first season as successor to Ray Perkins. New York general manager George Young, meanwhile, was pursuing Howard Schnellenberger, a hot coaching prospect who, that season, was winning college football's national championship with the Miami Hurricanes.

As we met Parcells in a northern Virginia hotel room, just before his season-ending loss to Washington, he'd heard the Schnellenberger rumors. Everybody had. His team was dispirited. His assistants were quietly making inquiries around the league, expecting to be fired along with their head man.

But Parcells had an even heavier burden. In October, his backfield coach, Bob Ledbetter, had dropped dead of a stroke. The same month, his father underwent open-heart surgery and wasn't recovering well. In December, his mother was diagnosed as having cancer. She would die within a month. His father would die six weeks later.

Needless to say, we didn't talk much technical football in that meeting. Two lamps burned so dimly, the room seemed a morgue. Parcells barely spoke above a whisper. What little he said about his team involved drugs. He knew he had a problem. How severe, he didn't know. But if he got another chance in '84, he promised us we'd barely recognize his roster.

We left. When I turned back to watch him close the door, he seemed so utterly alone. I was certain we would not see him again soon.

But in the next few weeks, the Giants' courtship of Schnellenberger foundered. Did they cast about for alternatives? Who knows? For Parcells, it didn't matter. He had one more year.

Bill responded like a tiger, cleaning his roster of 22 players, almost half the squad. The survivors he drove into

Roone Arledge, the father of sports television as you see it
every weekend. *(AP/Wide World Photos)*

Eddie Hart crossing the finish line ahead of Valery Borzov in the 4x100-meter relay, Munich 1972.
(UPI/Bettmann Newsphotos)

Coach Stan Wright and sprinter Rey Robinson during the European training tour that preceded the Munich Olympics.
(AP/Wide World Photos)

Wayne Collett and Vince Matthews, looking casual and petulant on the Munich victory rostrum after sweeping the 400 meters. *(UPI/Bettmann Newsphotos)*

Stan Wright in tears after being denied an appeal to reinstate Eddie Hart and Rey Robinson in the Munich 100 meters. *(UPI/Bettmann Newsphotos)*

The major players in "Mother Love's Monday Night Traveling Freak Show" (*left to right:* Don Meredith, Howard Cosell, Frank Gifford). *(AP/Wide World Photos)*

As Cosell once said in self-portrait: "Arrogant, pompous, vain, verbose, a show-off. *(Long pause.)* Of course, I'm all of these." *(UPI/Bettmann Newsphotos)*

Van Gordon Sauter, whom *Sports Illustrated* noted bears more than a passing resemblance to Henry VIII. *(AP/Wide World Photos)*

Jim Lampley, one of the few network sports commentators willing to put his career on the line for journalistic principles. *(Athletes and Artists, Inc.)*

Swapping Pittsburgh memories with Tony Dorsett on the eve of a Cowboys telecast.

The aloof Tom Landry, whose fall from greatness in the 1988 season stirred sympathy even among his harshest critics. *(Dallas Cowboys)*

"Iron Mike" Ditka, the son of a steelworker—and he played like it. His heart attack in 1988 was, for many NFL fans, final proof of human fallibility. *(Chicago Bears)*

Jim McMahon—headbands and headbutts, late nights and sunglasses. *(Chicago Bears)*

Lawrence Taylor, who frequently missed our Saturday meetings because he was out drinking, but a television producer's delight for his isolated replays on Sunday. *(New York Giants)*

Bill Parcells, who survived his 1983 nightmare to win a Super Bowl three seasons later. *(New York Giants)*

"The Stare" of laser-eyed Ray Perkins. *(New York Giants)*

Dick Vermeil, the "Little General" who was devoured by pro football. Luckily, that process made him available to us at CBS. *(Philadelphia Eagles)*

Joe Theismann—talkative, sometimes abrasive, but the best quarterback in pro football for the 1982 and 1983 seasons. *(Washington Redskins)*

Joe Gibbs, my selection as NFL coach of the '80s. *(Washington Redskins)*

Bill Walsh, whose absorbing, engaging offense made the San Francisco 49ers "Television's Team," if not "America's Team," in the '80s. *(San Francisco 49ers)*

Joe Montana of Monongahela, Pennsylvania, a two-time Super Bowl MVP and the NFL quarterback of the '80s. *(San Francisco 49ers)*

John Madden in his "Maddencruiser," ready for another cross-country ride. Does he truly fear flying, or does he simply prefer long stretches of isolation? *(AP/Wide World Photos)*

Al Davis, the Brooklyn-bred street fighter who *is* the Raiders, and the only man whom John Madden truly reveres. *(UPI/Bettmann Newsphotos)*

Deep in discussion with Summerall and Madden on the eve of our first Super Bowl, wearing expressions that only active football coaches should wear.

Pat Summerall's description of his working relationship with Tom Brookshier: "When we arrived we were laughing, and when we left we were still laughing."

With John Madden, Muhammad Ali, and Sugar Ray Robinson at the Hagler-Hearns middleweight championship, April 1985 in Las Vegas.

With Phil Villapiano, the former Oakland Raider, at our annual charity golf tournament in Greenwich, Connecticut.

In the mobile unit at a World Cup ski race we named "America's Downhill" in Aspen, Colorado.

With Brent Musburger on the set of the World University Games at Edmonton, Alberta, Canada, in 1983.

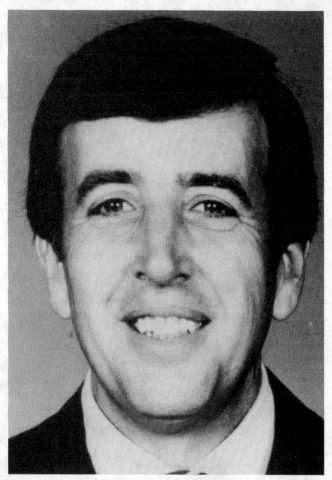
Brent Musburger. *(AP/Wide World Photos)*

his weight room for a prodigious off-season training program.

This was something else he had in common with Madden—an understanding that football victory often belongs to the strongest and meanest. The Giants, dormant in the late '60s and the '70s, had been physically soft.

"They were always a team that looked good in the lobby," said Madden, meaning that their prowess never extended beyond the hotel's sliding-glass door. "They always had their hair combed, wore ties, maybe a little— you know—a little sweater or vest. Just a bunch of blond-haired, blue-eyed guys. Like Brad Van Pelt. Remember him? Skinny, little hips. No ass on him at all."

Madden's Raiders, of course, were just the opposite. Now Parcells molded his bunch in that image—Lawrence Taylor, Carl Banks, Harry Carson, Leonard Marshall, Jim Burt. Bill also took the Raiders' strategic approach with them: Keep it simple, don't beat yourself with a lot of gambling blitzes. Just sit in basic coverages and let your front seven knock hell out of the offense.

Parcells spoke to his friend and Raider guru, Al Davis, every week, sometimes two or three times a week. He came to understand the old Raider philosophy: You've done much of your coaching by keeping them in the weight room all winter and spring. If you can just get 'em into the stadium and lined up by 1 o'clock each Sunday, they'll sometimes do the rest.

From that '83 disaster, Parcells's Giants made the playoffs in '84 and '85, then won it all in '86. The last two years, they blasted San Francisco out of postseason play in an awesome physical overmatch. Bill Walsh may have been playing chess, but his pieces were made of flimsy plastic; Parcells's were heavy alabaster. During the second half of the '86 game, a 49–3 destruction, Walsh actually removed his headset in total capitulation.

"They shattered our blocking," he said later.

If Parcells had captured the best of the old Raider approach, he was also saddled with the worst of it. In 1985, Taylor, the league's best defensive player, began to show signs of alcohol and drug dependency   falling asleep in meetings, withdrawing from his teammates. Parcells was ruthlessly loyal to the player—arranging medical treatment, shielding him from the press—but when he needed someone to share the burden, he turned to Madden.

I never knew whether it was at Parcells's urging or on his own, but Madden began to drop hints about Taylor: "You know, Lawrence Taylor just isn't Lawrence Taylor these days. He used to be such a bright-eyed guy. After practice, he used to stay and play basketball at the hoop the Giants have outside their locker room. He doesn't do that kind of thing anymore."

"Bright-eyed" was Madden's on-air code for "solid citizen, free of drugs." Taylor no longer qualified. His level of play slipped noticeably. Seeing him on film in '85, trying to pirouette around a blocker, Madden exploded to us, "Did you see Taylor? He used to just run over those little halfbacks. Now he's trying to trick-fuck the guy."

Taylor's rehabilitation was not a complete success. But despite occasional drug relapses, he played like himself for most of '86, '87, and '88. If Parcells's use of Madden and CBS played a small part, I didn't mind. My Columbia journalism professors always told me the information blade cuts both ways. Most times, you use the source, so it's more than fair that sometimes the source uses you.

This was the way with Chicago's McMahon. In 1985, he became a national phenomenon/outrage with his headbands and headbutts, late nights and sunglasses. Here was a child of the television age. He knew exactly where our cameras were and what kind of on-field byplay would make air. During the Giants-Bears playoff game that year, while fighting an NFL ban on his Adidas headband, Jim wore another on which he'd lettered "Rozelle." We gave it more exposure than some touchdown plays.

The same afternoon, McMahon caught sight of our

sideline hand-held camera. He wheeled on it and stuck out his tongue. Kind of like Mick Jagger in concert. We played it back in slow motion.

Jim knew he was news, knew we had to cover his antics. In effect, he hijacked CBS's delivery system to build an image in 25 million television homes that day. Later, advertising agencies would lease that image to sell Honda motorcycles, Taco Bell fast food, and Revo sunglasses, in addition to the Adidas sportswear. In 1987, McMahon earned $3 million endorsing such products.

Were we used? Hell, yes. Was it worth it? Absolutely. In a period when McMahon wasn't speaking to any media, he'd wait a full hour while we talked to his nemesis, Ditka, then give our foursome as much time as we wanted.

What's the Bob Seger lyric from "Night Moves"? "I used her, she used me, but neither one cared. We were gettin' our share." That was our relationship with Jim McMahon in 1985.

Joe Theismann was another outstanding player source. Early on, he told us that the "Yellow-30" call he made before every snap was nothing more than a dummy audible. If there was to be a man in motion, "Yellow-30" was his cue to get started. Otherwise, it meant nothing.

"Anything else you hear me say under center probably *does* mean something," Theismann advised.

Once Coach Gibbs began giving him audibles in the Redskins' Saturday night quarterback meeting, I asked Theismann to stop by our CBS truck before going to the locker room on Sunday morning. Once, before a critical game with St. Louis, he warned me:

"If their corners press [play tight against] our receivers, and I read blitz, you'll hear me call, '0–22.' The zero calls off the previous play. The '22' is the audible. It's a quick slant to Calvin Muhammad."

I passed the information to Pat and John before kickoff. Then, because of Summerall's very spare play-by-play, we heard Theismann's audible clearly in the second quarter:

"0–22! 0–22! Set. Hut! Hut!"

Summerall and Madden followed with a clinic on Washington's offense.

Theismann's precious information came at a price, however. A good friend and former '71 classmate at Notre Dame, he loved jabbing me, reducing me to proper size in front of my big-time network colleagues.

In 1983, on the eve of Washington's second meeting with Dallas, I harked back to their first game, when Theismann passed an amazing 21 times on first down. Did this, I asked him in the Saturday session with our foursome, imply that the Redskins preferred throwing against Dallas's base 4–3 defense, rather than the 4–0 substitute defense that often played on second and third downs?

Joe gazed off at the ceiling and began his three-minute reply by sniffing, "Well, to the average layman, it may appear . . . "

Summerall, Madden, and Grossman were convulsing. All weekend long, that's all I heard. Summerall asked me, "What time does the 'average layman' want us at the stadium?"

Madden's first words from the booth during Sunday's rehearsal were, "Hey, layman. Any 'average laymen' down there?"

Where John's tone was jocular in addressing the "average layman," Theismann's voice had revealed the certain testiness that we came to know, and forgive, in players 24 hours before kickoff.

Prior to Super Bowl XVIII, we asked the Raiders' Howie Long about Washington's All-Pro center, Jeff Bostic. Long rose excitedly to the edge of his seat, shook a fist at us and spat: "If Bostic's All-Pro, I don't know what fuckin' league he's playin' in!"

Similarly, we had a tense encounter with Los Angeles Rams lineman Dennis Harrah on the eve of the January 1986 NFC Championship in Chicago. Harrah arrived in our hotel suite as we were quizzing his quarterback, Dieter Brock. I invited him to sample the hors d'oeuvres and drinks that we always provided, while Brock was explaining that the Rams were taking just twenty offensive plays into the game.

"This is madness," I thought. "Twenty plays against the Bear defense? Hell, the 49ers have gone into some games with as many as 120 pass plays alone."

Madden sensed an opening with Brock and began probing for the full list. Twelve runs and eight passes, Dieter said. "Mirrored plays" (same action both left and right) each count in the total. So "46 gap" and "47 gap" were two of the 20.

It went on that way for a few minutes, matter-of-factly and apparently okay for Brock. But when he left and Harrah took a seat, the mood changed explosively.

"What the hell is this?" he demanded. "I thought this was going to be an interview with a camera. I come down here and find you pumping our quarterback for the whole game plan."

The Rams had been criticized all year for their limited offense, and Harrah was probably frustrated at hearing the topic raised again. But he made the mistake of asking Madden what he intended to do with the information, even wondering whether it might find its way back to the Bears.

The mercury rose in Madden's face. He sat forward, matching Harrah's indignation degree for degree until it filled the room.

"Look," he said, "if you think I'm here to carry information back to the Bears, *you got the wrong guy!*"

Harrumph, Harrah. End of conversation.

Madden was right to take it as an insulting, naive suggestion. From the outset, all four of us knew that any breach of confidentiality would spread like a California forest fire. We even went to extremes in phrasing our questions, careful to conceal what we'd just learned from the other team.

In truth, our relationships were just the opposite of what Harrah implied. On the road, especially, we were four familiar faces in the lonely hours before combat.

Bill Walsh once seemed aggrieved when we rose to leave his hotel room after an hour of conversation. "No, no," he protested. "Don't leave. I'll be all alone. I'll just have to rewrite the ready list."

Dismissing the grim, laser-eyed look that Ray Perkins presented us in 1981, Ed Croke, the Giants' publicity man, said, "Believe me, you guys are the highlight of his Saturdays on the road."

For some coaches, our sessions became a confessional. One told us that many of his players had been sleeping with the same woman—17 of them had herpes. Another coach said his club had wire-tapped the hotel room of a player during a road trip. They caught him with $30,000 cash in a briefcase, ready to buy drugs at cheap out-of-town prices.

Still another coach had tears in his eyes. Near the end of a disastrous season, knowing he was about to be fired, his biggest immediate concern was us.

"Don't you know I've been thinking about this meeting for weeks," he said. "I knew we had this national game [telecast] coming up. I knew you fellows would come to see me. I kept wondering what I'd tell you. (Pause.) Well, we're just not very good. Not very good at all—starting with the head coach."

5

Madden

THE WEATHER in Chicago on January 4, 1986, was about what you'd expect: 27 degrees, northwest wind at 18 mph, wind chill near zero. So why were 40 grown men playing touch football in these conditions? Why, indeed.

A year earlier, hoping to foster camaraderie at CBS Sports, I'd organized a touch football tournament for the commentators, technicians, and production personnel of our NFL football broadcasts. It was a season-end frolic and thank-you to the staff.

We played standard six-man touch. Including substitutes, there were ten players to a squad. The four team captains were Pat Summerall, John Madden, Sandy Grossman, and me.

The first tournament had also been booked at this time of year, near the finish of our NFL schedule. That time, however, we'd had the good sense to play in Anaheim, California.

After the games, we quaffed beer and ate catered dinner in a tent beside the field. One of our CBS crews had videotaped the "action," allowing us to roar and groan with the replay.

At the very end of the evening, I presented cheap trophies that we'd found at a local sporting goods store. This was a parody of Super Bowl ceremonies we'd covered. The captains delivered mock-serious acceptance speeches, riddled with excuses and friendly accusations of cheating.

The goodwill generated by this event exceeded my most optimistic dreams. The technicians, especially, rehashed these games endlessly. Spending 150 days a year on the road, as some did, the tournament in Anaheim was always prime conversation.

In the first round of play, Madden's and O'Neil's squads advanced with victories over Team Grossman and Team Summerall, respectively. In the championship, the O'Neils laid a drubbing on the Maddens, three touchdowns to none. The obligation of full disclosure compels me to report that the winning team captain ran for one score, threw for another, and caught the third.

Madden, the third most successful coach in NFL history by winning percentage, had a long memory of this game. For months afterward, he lamented his inept squad with comments like "Son of a bitch, I could kill cameraman X [his wide receiver]. He couldn't catch a thing. And videotape operator Y is *so slow*."

I admit to fueling his gloom just slightly, tweaking him now and then.

As the next season, 1985, progressed, Chicago and San Francisco rose to the top of our National Football Conference. These were the likely sites of our playoff broadcasts and thus the second annual touch tournament. Given that choice, everybody assumed we'd play in San Francisco's moderate climate.

All except Madden. As early as October, he began a campaign: "This year, I want to play where we have some *elements*. Some rain and mud, maybe even some snow. Hell, anybody can play in California. I want to see how Terry does in Chicago. I don't think he has enough body fat to win there."

What the hell did I care? This was a collegial exercise. If Chicago made Madden happy, if it lent the possibility of blizzards, bad footing, and exaggerated retelling for months afterward, well, that was exactly the idea, wasn't it?

So here we shivered on a snow-covered high school field off the shores of Lake Michigan. In other conditions, it might have been picturesque, the Wrigley Building and Sears Tower framing our fluttering passes. But heavy, gray clouds obliterated the city skyline. This was just what Madden had in mind—damp, chilly, the breath frosting before our faces. Another inch of snow would fall later in the day.

By coincidence, the first-round draw and game results were the same in Chicago as they'd been in Anaheim. Team Madden beat Team Grossman, and my squad handled Summerall's group. The championship game would be a rematch.

Madden held a serious huddle with his men. The coach wore Nike running shoes and dark trousers. His huge upper body was draped in the royal blue game jersey, lettered "CBS Sports," that my production assistant had commissioned for this occasion. He wore scuba gloves and a navy blue balaclava—booty from the Chicago Bears' equipment man, whom we'd visited that morning.

Looking at his group and then mine, I suspected that John had tampered with the "blind draft" conducted by our associate director. He had nothing but frisky young kids. My guys this year were a mixed lot, to be kind about it. But what the hell, it was just a game.

Madden won the coin toss and elected to receive. On the first play from scrimmage, he and Chuck "Red-Eye" Milton positioned for pass blocking. They grabbed my pass rusher. Bear-hugged him, in fact. The referee, a college student whom we'd hired for the afternoon, threw his flag and marked off 10 yards against Team Madden. John went crazy.

"We'll hold every play!" he cried. "We're not gonna take penalties!"

As the poor referee stood chewing his whistle, John

marched the ball ten steps back toward our goalline. His paces being longer than the referee's, Madden actually gained a few yards on the exchange. I walked away laughing. What the hell, it was only a game.

On the next play, we intercepted, then started a long march. On first down, I ran for 12 yards. Coming back to the huddle, I thought, "Yeah, it's only a game. But as long as we're out here, we might as well win."

Three plays later, we had a critical fourth down near midfield. Madden, stewing on the sideline, brandished a snowball and told his substitutes, "This is the seventh man on defense."

Then he "hid"—as best John can—behind the referee, throwing the snowball at me as I took the center snap. To no effect. I hit Big Carl, one of our free-lance gofers, for a first down.

Steam appeared from the balaclava that form-fitted Madden's head. Only his nose and a crescent of his red face were visible. He began to pace and flail his arms as he'd done on NFL sidelines in the '70s. He exhorted one of his men, who dropped a sure interception:

"Rich, c'mon, you gotta catch those. . . . What? . . . Baloney, don't worry about gettin' hurt. Just play!"

A few moments later, I slipped out of the backfield on a delay pattern, taking Big Carl's perfect pass. From the corner of my eye, I saw a massive, hooded roadblock angling toward me.

It was Madden. He'd come off the sideline to tag me, much as Alabama's Tommy Lewis had done against Dicky Moegle of Rice in the 1954 Cotton Bowl.

"Dicky Moegle!" I laughed at Madden. Then, jogging past him back to my huddle, I imitated a football announcer: "Somebody came off the bench to get Dicky Moegle!"

I could see a wider gap in the balaclava. To my surprise, there was real tension and frustration in John's tight smile.

"Why, you little . . ." He lunged at me. This was decidedly *not* a game to him.

"How much time, ref?" he demanded. "Hey, ref, you stiff, how much time?"

Our team kept moving. In a fourth-down huddle near Madden's goalline, I asked Big Carl to hit me in the endzone on a post-corner pattern. John, meanwhile, exhorted his defensive players as if they were Matuszak, Hendricks, and Tatum:

"That's it, Mike! C'mon, right here. . . . Hey, Red-Eye, Red-Eye, keep containment!"

Big Carl's pass described a perfect arc through the leaden sky, but I slipped making my cut and the pass fell incomplete. The first half ended scoreless.

I looked around to find that, almost universally, people were again enjoying the afternoon. My production assistant had induced the Bears' cheerleaders, known as the Honey Bears, to join us. Outfitted in orange body suits and navy and orange pompoms, they did their Soldier Field routines as if we ragtags were Jim McMahon and Walter Payton:

"Do it, do it, get right to it, oooh, ah. Do it, do it, get right to it. . . ."

On the adjacent field, I noticed that Summerall had caught the right mood. Playing Grossman's team in the consolation game, he held his beer can aloft and advised, "Time to suck it up, guys."

Madden, on the other hand, was deep into halftime adjustments with Red-Eye Milton, associate producer Mike Arnold, and cameraman George Rothweiler, a weightlifting fanatic known as "Hulk" after Lou Ferrigno's TV character on *The Incredible Hulk*.

MADDEN: Okay, huddle up. Here's what we have to do. Look, look, Terry's the guy in the middle, so if we had someone come and block Terry . . .

"HULK": Oh, can I please?

MADDEN: Yes, you got him.

"HULK": Wait a minute. Let me get this straight. You're ordering me to knock Terry out, right?

MADDEN: I'm— Knock him out, yes.

"HULK": That sounds fair.

MILTON: And Mike'll produce the game.

MADDEN (*scanning his players as if making a statement for the record*): Mike Arnold said for "Hulk" to knock Terry out.

As we lined up for the second-half kickoff, our team to receive, "Hulk" stretched his thick arm, ready to throw the ball. The referee, whose control of the game was in serious doubt, told him to punt or kick the ball off the ground.

"Bullshit!" Madden raged from the sideline.

Wanting to be helpful, I observed that nobody had been throwing kickoffs all afternoon. Madden, several steps onto the field and shorn of his headware, roared:

"But you're in the *championship* now!"

I shook my head at this reenactment. The wild hair, the boiling face, the agitated body, the referee-baiting—this was the coach of the Oakland Raiders, deadlocked with the Pittsburgh Steelers in an AFC Championship game from the '70s.

How little the public had known him then, shadowed as he was by Raider legend Al Davis. How much better the public thought it knew him now, seeing him every week on CBS. But in the face of such an outburst—so excessive, so inappropriate—could any of us truly claim to know this man?

The son of an auto mechanic, John Madden grew up without luxury in Daly City, California, near San Francisco. His youth was heavy with pool halls, caddyshacks, and inventive entries into Kezar Stadium, home of 49ers.

After high school, he drifted through several colleges. A brief stay at the University of Oregon seemed to cast him for life. He once said:

"That was the first time I was ever aware that I didn't have any money. My roommate in the Sigma Chi house had a closet full of clothes, and I didn't have any. . . . It was easy for me to understand people who didn't have any money, but not the ones who did. Hell, I still hate to be presentable."

Plenty of wealthy, prominent people have come from humble be ginnings to attain the "American dream." The difference with Madden was that some part of him was still caddying for the rich men at San Francisco Golf Club.

On the day before a telecast in Washington, D.C., Ethel Kennedy called and invited him to dinner. This was a Kennedy tradition, begun by family patriarch Joe, Sr., in Boston and Hyannis—inviting a well-known stranger to dinner. Dozens of Kennedy children were enriched in this way.

"Can you believe that?" John asked me, looking dazed as he fingered his phone message. "Ethel Kennedy wants *me* to come to dinner!"

"Why don't you go," I suggested. "We can fit our schedule around it."

"Ah, no. I can't go to dinner with the *Kennedys*."

Another college experience seemed to mark him. In 1958, John was a third-string senior tackle for Cal Poly–San Luis Obispo in California. While flying home from a game at New Mexico A&M one evening, he heard the pilot announce that the airplane's hydraulic system wasn't working. The landing gear wouldn't lower into place. They would be circling Santa Margarita Lake, the pilot said, trying to reverse the problem. But if their fuel ran too low, they'd have to make an emergency landing.

Madden huddled his 250-pound frame at the emergency

exit door. Out the window, he could see fire trucks and ambulances gathering on the runway.

Then, suddenly, he felt a rumble below his feet, in the belly of the plane. That was followed by the pleasant, hydraulic whirring which normally accompanies descent. The wheels had unlocked.

Two years later, after John had graduated, the Cal Poly team was not so lucky. Their charter flight crashed near Toledo, Ohio, killing 16 players.

By now, everybody knows that Madden gave up flying soon after he left coaching in 1978. He claims, however, that this is not for fear of 30,000 feet but rather for the claustrophobia an airplane cabin gives him.

Instead, he rides trains or a private bus. Is this a travel alternative, or is it because of the claustrophobic feeling that people sometimes give him?

He'd call me from the train station in Oakland, California, minutes before starting cross-country for a telecast.

"I'm just checkin' in," he'd say, "because I'm going to be nowhere for the next three days."

"But John," I joked, "everybody has to be somewhere."

"Not me. I'll be nowhere. No phones. Nothing."

The train was his isolation, his time capsule. He'd read, think, prepare for his next game, take as much bar-car conversation as he chose. But when he'd had enough, he knew it wasn't rude to get up and leave people sitting with their drinks. Those liberties are granted among total strangers. John would simply say good night and retire to his Pullman berth. He'd sleep till 1 or 2 in the afternoon.

There were other idiosyncrasies. At game sites, our production assistant would have to book him a first- or second-floor hotel room so he could avoid elevators. Those left him feeling enclosed.

"I'm a weird guy," he once told me.

I just smiled. What do you say to that?

"I *am*," he protested. "I'm *crazy*."

He wore loose-fitted clothing: baggy pants, oversized

jackets, untied tennis shoes. He bragged that the only time he wore a necktie all week was for Sunday's opening on-camera. John didn't want to be bound at the neck or feet.

During pregame coverage of Super Bowl XVI, we gave him a shot from inside the Cincinnati Bengals' locker room. I asked him to relate the anxieties that flutter in players' stomachs just before kickoff.

Madden said, "That locker room gets smaller and smaller, the closer you get to game time. It all starts to close in on you. All you want to do is just bust out and get on this field."

Claustrophobia.

It could strike him anywhere, particularly in restaurants. John would never sit on a banquette, against a wall or hemmed in by fellow diners on both sides. No, he needed a freestanding seat at the end of the table nearest the door. Even then, there were sometimes problems.

One Friday night, moments after we'd been seated in a moderately crowded restaurant, I heard him stammer, "Wh . . . wh . . . wh . . ." I looked over to see his big head shaking, eyes popping and darting. He pushed back his chair abruptly, dropped his menu, and blurted, "I'll see you guys later."

Restaurant claustrophobia.

A related form was music claustrophobia. One afternoon in Tampa, days before Super Bowl XVIII, we'd finished viewing coaches' film and fell into relaxed conversation in our hotel suite. The group was John, two productions assistants, and me. Facing the tedium of writing out camera and videotape assignments, I put on some soft rock, Jackson Browne's "Lawyers in Love" album.

From an all-out slouch across the length of a sofa, Madden sprang to his feet.

"I gotta go," he insisted.

"John, is it the music?" I asked. "We can kill the music."

"No, I gotta go work on my spotting board." And he was gone.

But these phobias were mere accents in the Madden folklore. They were not his essence. They did not *define* him. Who is this man?

"If there's one word that describes me best," John told *TV Guide* in 1983, "it's *enthusiastic*."

Well, yes. But honestly, that was nothing more than his *TV Guide* answer. There had to be more. Look at it this way: Before arriving at CBS, Madden spent one season on injured reserve with the Philadelphia Eagles, the next seven seasons coaching college football, then 12 glorious years with one of the most successful franchises in team sports history. One supposes that those 12 years, ages 30 to 42, are revealing of Madden, the man.

His players were renegades, the outlaws of pro football —Ken Stabler, Fred Biletnikoff, Pete Banaszak, John Matuszak, Otis Sistrunk, Ted Hendricks, Phil Villapiano, Alonzo "Skip" Thomas, Jack Tatum.

The team's summer training camp in Santa Rosa, California, 60 miles north of Oakland, produced more colorful tales than any in the postmerger NFL. Unlike most teams that sequestered themselves on rural college campuses, the Raiders headquartered at the El Rancho Tropicana Motel.

It came complete with two football fields, plus a bar and disco just off the lobby. The very next building, a short walk away, was another bar, The Bamboo Room. Hot afternoons, after the second practice, the thirstiest Raiders frequently drank there *in their uniforms*, without even bothering to shower.

At night, they normally had 90 minutes to drink between the evening meeting and 11 o'clock curfew. Bed check involved an assistant coach's knock on the front door. But each motel room had sliding glass at the back, and the players used it for their escape into the night. Married or not, many of them had girlfriends in town.

Several had illegitimate children in Santa Rosa. A few players had more than one.

In March 1987, these infamous Raiders gathered at Lake Tahoe, Nevada, for "The John Madden Roast and 50th Birthday Party." It was to be a testimonial to John and, at his insistence, a reunion of the 1976 team that won Super Bowl XI for him. One of Madden's closest friends had asked me to produce the evening.

I agreed on one condition: I wanted to hear Al Davis introduce John and each of the players. That was the only way to get an accurate taste of these very flavorful characters.

Searching back through a 20-year association with the guest of honor, this was Davis's overriding memory: "Winning a hundred games in ten years is a tough job to do. But John did it. He wanted to win for the organization. He had to take care of this group every day, and it isn't easy to take care of fifty guys every day who have their own diverse ways. (Pause.) Especially the particular crowd we had." (Knowing smiles all around.)

It was Davis's philosophy, but John didn't need to be told, that a coach who's younger than some of his players —Madden was 32 when he got the head job in 1969— didn't go looking for confrontation. So John established just three rules for his squad: (1) Be on time. (2) Pay attention. (3) Play like hell when I say so. Even this triad was deemed too complex and later reduced to one of John's pet phrases: "Just play." Davis's variation was "Just win."

The "be on time" business proved unattainable. Wide receiver Mike Siani, a rare island of sanity in this ocean of madness, once told me, "Let's say our first obligation of the day was a meeting at noon. John would be standing at the front door of our training facility and guys would still be coming in at five, ten, fifteen after twelve. Our meetings rarely started on time."

Madden stood there holding the door, his already florid

face flushing and flushing until it was nearly the color of his hair. The players noticed as they brushed past, nicknaming him, "Pink" or "The Big Pink" or, when he was really stifling a volcanic eruption, "The Big Pink Elephant."

The "pay attention" part was less difficult. Villapiano recalls: "We didn't really have the kind of meetings you imagine when you think of the NFL. We always played the same defense—never blitzed, never did anything different. So our defensive coordinator, Don Shinnick, figured we were better off telling jokes or having magic shows—anything but watching film. One day, everybody had to tell a story about the best fuck he ever had."

The coaches' thinking went like this: Having gathered the best athletes and the nastiest dispositions in the league, let's allow their physical abilities to take over. Let's not inhibit them with our x and o contrivances. It's enough to hope that they practice every day.

That was a goal not always met. Matuszak, the notorious "Tooz," would sometimes disappear for two or three days at a time. His teammates never knew where he was. They never asked when he returned.

Davis's introduction of Hendricks at the roast included this recurring nightmare:

"In the morning, the secretaries would come in and say, 'Mr. Davis, Ted Hendricks is on the line.'

" 'Good. Keep him on the line. At least we know where he is.'

" 'I don't like where he is, Mr. Davis.' "

Some players came by the trainer's room in the morning only long enough to be treated for their hangovers, then returned home. Cornerback "Skip" Thomas was tougher than that. He practiced in sunglasses to hide his bloodshot eyes.

Those defensive backs, especially, were hard to control. Davis introduced the other cornerback, Willie Brown, as "the only guy in our secondary that everybody thought *might* be able to read and write."

But Madden's problems with the other three—Thomas, Tatum, and George Atkinson—ran deeper. Shaking his head, he once told me:

"Every Friday night, they'd take a projector to Atkinson's or Tatum's house and spend all night watching film and drinking beer. Saturday morning, they'd show up for practice and 'Skip' would say, 'Coach, we saw something last night. Every time we see a man go in motion, I'm gonna say "yellow." Then At's gonna go here, Tate's gonna go there. . . .'

"We spend all week puttin' in a defense, and they want to change it Saturday morning!"

Amid such chaos, you ask, how did they win? With such rampant individualism, how did they prevail in the ultimate team game?

Very simply. Madden convinced them that their only common denominator was the one thing that counted in pro football: a passion for "knocking somebody's dick in the dirt."

Columnist Jim Murray phrased it more acceptably for his family newspaper, the *Los Angeles Times.* After Oakland's Super Bowl XI victory, he wrote, "They play football like terrorists crashing through skylights."

Listen to Davis's roast-night introduction of Villapiano: "In 1971, we thought our team lost a little *toughness* and so, in the draft, we said, 'We're goin' for the *toughest* guys. We want guys who are *tough,* who play this game *tough.*' Our second round draft choice was out of Bowling Green. *Tough.*

"I remember sitting in my living room one year and I heard them say [on television] they were going to have a player talk about the Raiders. And this guy gets on and says, 'We play *tough* football. We smash people! That's the Raider way!' That was just great for the commissioner:

'We smash people!' But a great *tough* player, great competitor. We love him. Phil Villapiano."

The crowd of 2,000 shouted for Villapiano, a handsome Italian stallion from New Jersey, who gave the Raiders nine years of fierce linebacker play.

Davis's eyes flashed as he moved to the secondary: "The defensive backs—one of the greatest secondaries ever to play professional football because they were *tough.*"

He began with "Skip" Thomas, slow-walking, sleepy-looking, but a wood-splitter of a cornerback. On the field, he'd worn a small towel at his waist, adorned with skull and crossbones, lettered with his nickname: "Dr. Death."

Davis shone with a vivid recollection: "In the late nineteen seventies, into the National Football League came a great player from the University of Nebraska who played for the San Diego Chargers. His name was Johnny Rodgers and we always felt that, within our division, new players had to be handled very early before they got the idea that they could roam the secondary when they were playing the Raiders.

"As luck would have it, they tried to throw a slant to Rodgers real early, and I'm not sure if it was Tatum who got him or Thomas, but I remember Rodgers laying there and Thomas standing above him, tellin' him to 'get the hell off the field and never come back out here again.' And he called him some names that I didn't think he could call one of his brothers. It started with 'mother-.' (Laughter.) It's a funny thing, but the guy very rarely ever came back."

This was becoming a pep rally. The crowd roared, as if in a stadium instead of a hotel showroom. Davis wore a tuxedo, befitting his position on the dais, but it hung incongruously under his leering grin. The earthiness, the Brooklyn-bred street fighter in Al Davis was coming to the surface like a good sweat. His superb word pictures were bringing the '76 Raiders to life like a highlight film.

The audience sat forward, knowing who came next. Al

resumed: "I told you in 1971 we wanted *toughness*. We took Villapiano number two. The guy we took number one was *tough*. To this day, he's the guy who sets the standard of excellence for *toughness* in the secondary. From Ohio State, Jack Tatum."

Wild applause.

Tightening now, Davis's voice took on the tone of a locker room exhortation: "We were playing Miami in those days and they had a great receiver, Paul Warfield. Somehow or other, we had to handle him. Warfield was from Ohio State. Jack Tatum was from Ohio State. And in a big game, Tatum got Warfield down the field—Warfield had slipped in the mud at the Oakland–Alameda County Coliseum, where John [Madden] used to water the grass. (Laughter.) Tatum stood over Warfield—kicked him, spit at him . . ."

On stage, the player did not shrug or shuffle his feet nervously. He looked at Davis and smiled with all the others. This was the feared Jack Tatum, whose autobiography was titled *They Call Me Assassin*. From now until forever, he will be remembered in pro football as the man who paralyzed Darryl Stingley of the New England Patriots.

It was 1978. Preseason. An exhibition game in Oakland. Stingley came over the middle. The pass was too high, well beyond his reach. Tatum either didn't know or didn't care. From his customary centerfield or free safety spot, he struck a shattering blow, driving the crown of his helmet into Stingley's neck. The receiver collapsed to the turf, his cervical vertebrae ruptured.

Such devastation was Tatum's calling card. Siani once asked me, "Do you remember the 'Immaculate Reception' when Franco Harris caught that ricochet pass, and Pittsburgh beat us in that playoff game? Tatum easily could have knocked that pass down with an arm. He probably could have stepped in front of 'Frenchy' Fuqua and intercepted it. But Jack always wanted the big hit. He always wanted to time the arrival of his helmet with the arrival of the ball. And splatter the receiver."

After splattering Stingley, Tatum showed no remorse. He never phoned, never visited. The Patriots, of course, had to return home. So the job of keeping vigil was open. John Madden took it.

The day after his cataclysm, Stingley lay in a suburban Oakland hospital. In his biography, *Happy to Be Alive,* he remembers:

> When I woke up there was a hulking figure staring down at me. His eyes were red, and there were tears running down his cheeks. His hair was disheveled, the way it always was. . . . He held my hand and touched my face, the way a father would. It was John Madden, the head coach of the Oakland Raiders.
>
> "Darryl, it'll be all right," he said to me, his voice so soft, so tender.
>
> "Coach, what's the matter with me?" I tried to ask him. "Coach . . . Coach . . . Coach . . . why won't they tell me what's wrong with me?" The coach kept shaking his head slowly from one side to the other.

Virtually every day, for two months, Madden drove to Eden Hospital in Castro Valley. Sometimes, when Raider staff meetings went late, he'd arrive at midnight. Once, he came directly from the airport after flying home from a game in Denver.

Stingley needed him. The player was a classic psychological study—first shocked, then depressed, angry, bitter.

Was there any hope to walk again? Were the therapists being truthful? Were these doctors good enough? What were the Patriots doing for him? Where was Tatum? Why hadn't he called? How could he make that kind of hit in a *preseason* game?

Darryl Stingley had gone from professional athlete to paralysis tragedy in the snap of a finger. There were no answers. But at least Madden cared enough to listen to his questions. Darryl later wrote, "I can't tell you the love I have for that man."

John wrestled mightily with the Stingley question. Seeing Darryl's head and neck immobilized in a steel brace, watching the weight and strength slipping from his body each day, you know it must have occurred to him: I coached the technique that allowed this to happen. *Caused* it to happen.

Madden was hardly oblivious to the reputation of his Raiders. Two years earlier, Atkinson had blindsided Pittsburgh's Lynn Swann with his "bone" (forearm), knocking him cold *25 yards away from the developing play.* Steeler Coach Chuck Noll attacked the Oakland bunch as "a criminal element."

Madden is a bright man. He came within a few credit hours of a doctorate in psychology before coaching swept him away. No doubt, he examined all sides of this issue. And when his introspection was finished, he drew for himself a clear distinction between illegal play and the necessary *toughness* of pro football, his passion and his livelihood: Atkinson's shot on Swann was wrong and should not be condoned. But Tatum's blast was legal, part of the game. No penalty flag had been thrown. Darryl Stingley was an unfortunate victim in a risky game.

"Violence is not something that is necessarily dirty," John later said. "Football is violent. When two big, fast guys run into each other, it's violent. I'm not for anything that's illegal. But some of the most violent things that happen on a football field are pretty legal. . . .

"Unless you saw what happened with Darryl Stingley and Jack Tatum, you shouldn't really talk about it. It was a terrible thing. But over the years, as the story gets told by people who didn't even see the incident, it gets turned into a cheap shot. It wasn't a cheap shot."

So this was the accommodation of an educated man who coached the roughest gang of football players ever. Was it also a statement of self, an endorsement of *tough-*

ness? Is it his "physicality" that ultimately defines John Madden? Or was this rationalization of his bedside grief?

Darryl Stingley was paralyzed at the start of the 1978 season. At the end of that season, Madden retired from coaching forever.

What happened next was that he brought the Raiders' attitude, mixed with his own complex essence, to television. When San Francisco's Ronnie Lott poleaxed a Dallas receiver in the secondary and stood snarling over his motionless form, the flashbacks must have been warring in Madden's mind. But on this occasion, instead of recalling Stingley, he said into his CBS microphone:

"Lott's tellin' him, 'Don't come in here again. You understand? Make your plays on the outside, if you can. But don't come over the middle again. Or I'll be waitin' for you.' "

It was only slightly modified from the way Jack Tatum and "Skip" Thomas had said it to Johnny Rodgers and Paul Warfield.

And you know what? America went wild. They loved it. They loved his "physicality."

Consider their alternatives. They'd been listening to NBC's Merlin Olsen, he of the Shakespearean earnestness, and ABC's Don Meredith, whose fires were all but banked. Olsen endorsed flowers by wire and get-well baskets. Meredith sipped, pursed his lips, and confessed to being a tea lover. Now here came a guy who burst through brick walls, flapping his arms, to sell beer. His definition of "real football" was "no domes, no plastic turf, no waves, no mayors making bets." It was no contest.

Siani says, "When I hear him on TV, I have to laugh out loud. This is the same shit we used to hear every day at practice. All that stuff about the look in a linebacker's eyes, the 'booms' and the 'bams.' He was the same with us. He hated gloves on receivers, hated kickers, loved the rain and mud, loved goalline offense."

Siani recalled Madden's weekly exercise of breaking

down goalline film, ostensibly searching for a new point of attack. Every week, John concluded: Let's run left behind Gene Upshaw, Art Shell, Dave Casper, an extra tight end, and a fullback lead by Mark van Eeghen. Trailing that convoy, it didn't matter who carried the ball.

In the '80s, it sometimes dismayed Madden to see San Francisco's Walsh finesse the goalline with bootlegs, waggle throwbacks, and wingback drag patterns. Walsh believed, "It's not a question of whether our man can bludgeon the man across from him." John would lower his head, so Walsh couldn't see the rolling of his eyes.

But it truly thrilled him to see the Washington Redskins, whose goalline formations were called "Heavy" and "Heavy Jumbo" and whose goalline running plays were called "40 chip" and "50 gut."

"Look at this determination!" he'd scream. "This is *goalline!* This brings out everything in a man! They just get in there behind big Grimm and big Jacoby. Boom! Here comes big Riggins. Whap! He just pounds that thing into the endzone. Now that's football! That's a goalline offense!"

Siani laughed, "It took me back ten years to our offensive meeting room. John would say, 'We're gonna run left. We know it, they know it, everybody in the stadium knows it! Let's see if they can stop us.' Then he'd line everybody up on the blackboard and show us each block. 'Wham! Bam!' There'd be chalk flying everywhere.

"That's the part of football John loved most. At training camp, he used to go crazy for the one-on-one drills. He'd put Bubba Smith up against Bob Brown, 'The Boomer.' The whole practice would stop. Guys working on specialties forty yards away would come over and watch. He taught *us* to love it."

Now with a wider audience, Madden was teaching millions to love it. He cleaned up his glossary of Raider phrases and introduced a new vocabulary to football broadcasting. After a big defensive hit, for instance,

Raider coaches watching film would say to each other, "That'll knock the snot out of his locker." In his new line of work, John would say, "That'll clean out his sinuses."

Some athletes were spurred to an All-Pro afternoon by making a big play in the opening minutes. Otis Wilson of the Chicago Bears was such a player. Watching him sack a quarterback viciously in the opening series, the Raiders would have said, "His dick gets hard." In commentary, Madden would now warn opposing offenses, "You don't want Otis Wilson running around your backfield in the first series. His veins stick out."

Madden was also quick to appropriate phrases that we picked up from coaches around the league. New England Coach Ron Meyer once told us, "We're not good enough to win without giving total effort. We have to empty our buckets every Sunday."

"Bucket" and "full bucket" became Madden favorites.

Before Super Bowl XVI, Cincinnati Coach Forrest Gregg described his free safety, Bobby Kemp, as willing but not terribly physical. "Oh, he'll hit you," said Gregg, "but he doesn't bring a very big load." It was the perfect phrase for "Refrigerator" Perry when Mike Ditka moved him into the backfield.

"Some guys are tough runners on the goalline," John exulted, "but Perry—he brings a LOAD! Whoa!"

You could also hear the excitement in his voice when he found a defense with an inspired, roughneck name. San Francisco defensive coordinator George Seifert began calling his five-lineman variation "Fever." Giant Coach Bill Parcells devised "Fire Lion Zero," a five-man front that covered all the offensive blockers, leaving Lawrence Taylor protected to "scrape" or roam behind them as a middle linebacker. Parcells cautioned Taylor to "keep your feet clean," that is, don't get tripped up.

"I like that kind of talk," rasped Madden. " 'Scrape with Taylor. Keep your feet clean. Fire Lion Zero!' "

But John brought more than the language of his physicality to broadcasting. Like a quarterback who can throw long and short, read defenses, call audibles, and scramble for a first down, he had an amazingly diverse game.

First and most important was his ability to see and synthesize the game. Watching film with him was a postgraduate education in the NFL. He wasn't kidding when he matter-of-factly told me he could simultaneously watch all 22 players on every play.

Preparing for a Redskins game one Saturday morning, we were watching a reel of their defense. The opposition happened to be Houston. On an Oilers' running play, John exclaimed, "Oh, Jesus Christ, look at Casper."

We didn't care about Dave Casper. He now played for Houston. He wasn't involved in the next day's game. Plus he was on the opposite side from the action. But Madden had seen him cross his feet making a block and end up trying to chicken-fight his man on one leg.

"Jesus Christ," John fumed, "you'd think we never taught him a thing."

Better than doing it in the film room on Saturday, Madden would deliver these goods live on Sunday afternoons. During a Giants-Bengals game in 1985, he glimpsed a two-second shot of Parcells talking to his holder just as New York's field goal team was taking the field. It was fourth-and-plenty for the Giants.

Madden advised, "You know, you just saw Bill Parcells talk to Jeff Rutledge, the holder. I think we ought to be alert here for a fake. You know, fake a field goal and run some type of play."

Sure enough, Rutledge went down the line with an option play and pitched the ball to kicker Jess Atkinson for a Giants touchdown.

The best former coaches in television are the ones who can *accept* coaching, and Madden was all of that. It took only one conversation to persuade him that he must be critical of certain on-field decisions.

In a 1982 Dallas-Washington game, the Redskins trailed

17–10 with three-and-a-half minutes to play. On fourth-and-five at his own 41, Washington Coach Joe Gibbs faced a big decision: Go for the longshot first down? Or punt and hope to get the ball back?

Madden didn't take a side either way. He simply outlined Gibbs's alternatives. The Redskins punted. Dallas then marched 79 yards to seal the victory.

I phoned Madden the next day and began recounting: "You said . . ."

"I know exactly what I said," he snapped.

"But John," I countered, "the viewer wants more than the options. He wants to know what *you* think."

Madden said it wasn't a matter of friendship with Gibbs, his former coaching colleague at San Diego State. He didn't like showing up any coach after a bad decision.

Okay, I said, how about making your call before the play? Then you're on the line just as firmly as he is. John agreed. Years later, when Atlanta Coach Dan Henning attacked him in print for his "second guesses," Madden retorted, "I don't second-guess. I *first*-guess."

Madden could be plenty indignant when someone questioned his work. He got up and left the table in a San Francisco restaurant one evening when Hank Stram disputed his tablecloth diagram of a Bill Walsh pass route. Underneath that teddy-bear TV personality, the Oakland Raider still clenched a dagger in his teeth.

Madden's competitive spirit was most often unleashed on opposing-network coverage. He used to direct his *Monday Night Football* complaints to me, as if I were somehow responsible:

"Goddamnit, Terry, they've got this thing down to 'skeleton' [an offensive drill involving only the quarterback and eligible receivers]. No linemen play on Monday nights. No defensive players play on Monday nights. Just backs and receivers. And their isolates of the receivers are so tight, I haven't seen a cornerback yet. This is disgraceful!"

Madden was stupefied by NBC's telecast of Super Bowl XX, a 46–10 destruction of New England by mighty Chicago. NBC had added Bob Griese in the commentary booth to cover for Merlin Olsen's deficiencies in analysis. But, together, they fired a double-barreled blank in summarizing the Bears' dominance:

> MERLIN OLSEN: I don't know that we've ever seen a defense with the kind of shut-down power these people have. I don't think I've ever seen one.
>
> BOB GRIESE: I can't figure out what they're doing half the time and I've been watching the whole game.
>
> OLSEN: Ha, ha.
>
> DICK ENBERG: Just glad you're up here, huh?
>
> GRIESE: Exactly.

When I spoke to Madden the next day, he despaired for our business. Chicago had been *the* story of the NFL that season, yet NBC had somehow done a four-hour telecast without one revealing picture or comment on the mesmerizing "46" defense.

Madden's tone was genuinely sad, not boastful or superior, as he sighed, "It was like they'd never *seen* the Bears. I knew the game was over in the first three plays when New England didn't block [Chicago's] Otis Wilson. You could see his dick get hard. But the NBC guys had no idea."

Madden had never had any formal experience as a journalist. But he came to feel that *reverence* for truth, as good reporters do, and disdain for the lazy or incompetent who sullied his profession.

He dug hard and got great information because coaches and players responded to him so positively. Our exclusive pipeline to Jim McMahon, for instance, in the hectic Chicago season of '85 was mostly due to the quarterback's fondness for Madden.

McMahon kept us current on his continuing feud with "the asshole," as he called Mike Ditka. On the night before our telecast of a Chicago–New York Jets game, Jim revealed that he hadn't spoken to Ditka in a month. We broke the story during our broadcast.

In that same meeting, McMahon took a swig of his beer, patted the side of his spike haircut, and confided that oft-injured Jet tackle Joe Klecko wasn't the player he'd been. McMahon said he was trying to compensate for a bad leg by anticipating the snap count. Said he'd made New York's whole line jumpy.

"I'll pull them offside five times tomorrow," McMahon promised. Turned out he was wrong. He only got the Jets four times. But Madden used his prediction as a running story line for the afternoon.

McMahon was an old Raider, unfortunately born too late. John regaled him as "the kind of personality the NFL needs." Another time, he said, "Of all the players in the league, I think I'd have more fun coaching him than anyone else."

This was the ultimate for a pro football player in the '80s. Forget big contracts. Forget Super Bowl rings and All-Pro selections. Forget best-selling autobiographies and million-dollar endorsements. Earning status as Madden's special kind of athlete/man made all other dreams attainable—or irrelevant.

Players openly courted this designation. McMahon once copped a plea on behalf of teammate Kevin Butler, a rookie kicker:

" 'Butthead' wants you to know that he's not like the rest of those kickers you talk about. He hangs out with me and the offensive linemen, drinks a little beer. We make him buy, of course, but he's not a bad guy."

"I know," said Madden. "I saw him last week with his

sleeves rolled up, trying to show a little arm like the line-men."

"Yeah, he lifts weights," McMahon glowed. "He's back there with the rest of us, pumping up right before the game so we look good for the girls."

"Who would've thought?" Madden sighed. "The kicker lifts weights!"

John's objection to kickers, of course, was that they weren't physical. The worst of them had tiny pencil necks, too weak to support their helmets, so they looked like bobble-head dolls. And their bodies! Most had little twig arms poking out from under their oversized shoulder pads, like stick figures. In Madden's phrase, they couldn't "fill out a uniform."

He loved the story Redskins Coach Joe Gibbs told him about kicker Mark Moseley. In 1984, Washington won the NFC East on the very last tick of the regular season. Said Gibbs, "I turned around to hug somebody, anybody, and the first guy I grab [Moseley] smells of *perfume*, after-shave lotion or something. I threw him out of the way and said to myself, 'Gimme a *real* player.'"

Apart from kickers, the only players Madden didn't like were those who showed him ulterior motive. When we finished talking to 28 Redskins and Raiders in preparation for Super Bowl XVIII, Madden asked me, "Of all the guys we spoke to, do you know there was only one I didn't like?"

"George Starke," I said.

That was easy. Starke, an offensive tackle, had been more concerned with his T-shirt and promotion company, Super Hogs, Inc., than the Raiders. The look on John's face during that interview said, "Goddamnit, this is the Super Bowl! After Sunday, you can worry about the fuck-ing T-shirts for the rest of your life!"

Two Jets incurred his wrath. Punter Dave Jennings, bumped by a defender, went into a writhing-and-crying performance for our sideline camera one afternoon. Mad-

211

den knew the blow wasn't that wicked. During a commercial, he charged, "That guy knows more about a camera than I do."

Defensive end Mark Gastineau was a frequent Madden target. One Friday at Jets practice, we saw him catch teammate Pat Ryan's arm, nearly hyperextending it, during a passing drill that was supposed to be noncontact. I asked John what he'd have done as coach in that situation.

"I'd run his ass right off the field," he said.

It always seemed Madden drew his CBS Chalkboards of Gastineau with extra zest. A one-dimensional pass rusher concerned primarily with his sack total, Mark was not Madden's idea of a defensive end:

"You see Gastineau here. He always takes a big, wide pass rush. So you just turn him out. Now you get a hole this way (circles vertically), plus you get a hole this way (circles horizontally), and that equals a big hole (circles three times, furiously). Then you can run your draw right there (initials his masterpiece)."

Players heard these comments and agreed. Their respect for Madden was total. Not only did they want to be designated among his special breed, they also wanted to embrace his coaching philosophy.

In 1984, when the 49ers were on their way to a second Super Bowl title, Madden theorized on the air that Coach Walsh's game plans were front-loaded. Walsh's script of 20 to 25 plays to open each game was his best stuff, John reasoned. Opposing defenses shouldn't be demoralized to yield even 10 points to the script. Thereafter, the job should get easier.

The week after he'd announced this hypothesis, we met with Chicago middle linebacker Mike Singletary on the eve of the NFC Championship. Asked in general terms what the Bear defense had to do, Singletary began, "Well, if we can survive their first 25 plays . . ."

So Madden had all the football insight that 20 years of coaching could instill, and reportorial skills, too. Then he had the gift—humor. He had an ability to see something funny where nobody else could. It might be as simple as a player's drooping socks:

"Look at that guy. He's got bad socks. Left one down around his ankle. Right one halfway. Bad socks."

"Refrigerator" Perry was a never-ending source of comedic material. When Ram punter Dale Hatcher, a Clemson teammate of Perry's, told John that this 310-pounder had been briefly on the varsity *diving* team, Madden turned it into an hilarious image:

"Can you see 'The Fridge,' wearing one of those little bathing suits like Greg Louganis wears, bouncing on the end of the board at Clemson?"

After years of self-deprecating after-dinner speeches, he knew the humor in big bodies. "Bad bodies," he called them. Perry and "Chilly" Billy Bain of the Rams were the inspiration for his mythical organization, BUBBA— Brotherhood of United Bad Bodies Association.

"For information about joining," John advised, "dial 1-800-YO-BUBBA."

He came up with a motto for his new group: "You know how people say, 'Your body is your temple; be careful what you put in it.' We say, 'Your body's a garage; put anything you want in it.' "

So he had the whole package. That was another phrase he'd picked up in the '80s. In John's era, the same 11 men played offense or defense most of the time. Now, with wholesale substitution according to down and distance, he asked, "You notice how everything is 'packages'? They got their 'nickel package,' their 'dime package,' their 'third-down package.' I like that kind of talk."

As a broadcaster, Madden's package still included the frozen image of Darryl Stingley. He hadn't forgotten the agony of Eden Hospital, the distinction he'd made between tough and dirty. He brought these right into the television booth along with his spotting board.

On Thanksgiving Day 1982, in Detroit, Leon Bright of

the Giants stood under a punt, waving his arm for a fair catch. The Lions' Leonard Thompson bore down on him in a 40-yard sprint. With the ball still hanging 15 feet above Bright's head, Thompson drilled him just under the face mask. Bright lay stretched out on the turf as Madden flew into a frenzy:

"I'll tell you, [Giant coach] Ray Perkins is really upset and he should be. That is the cheapest shot in football. The most unprotected man—he's tellin' the official now: 'Give him fifteen, but the guy oughta be thrown out of the game.' See? 'Throw him out,' he's sayin'. (Over replay) Watch it. He's lookin' up. He's unprotected. He can't do anything. The ball isn't even close.

"They gotta do something about that. You wanna protect players? They want safety? Prevent injuries? Okay, start doin' something about that. . . . The fifteen-yard penalty doesn't do Leon Bright any good. That's wrong. I mean, there's good play. There's hard play. It's a very physical game. But then there's uncalled for. To me, this is uncalled for."

You had to know John was thinking of Stingley as one Giant trainer immobilized Bright's head and another called for the stretcher.

He was light-years beyond any analyst in television—any sport, any network. In a business renowned for its cattiness, I came to use him as my yardstick for rival executives. If a competitor was secure enough to recognize Madden publicly, I marked it well.

Michael Weisman, executive producer of NBC Sports: "There is a common-man attractiveness that he has. He's overweight, his hair is unkempt, his shoes are always untied, and his collar is never closed. John Madden is not perfect."

Jim Spence, former senior vice president of ABC Sports: "I happen to think he overtalks. He's colorful, but he says a lot of things that I don't think are necessary."

Don Ohlmeyer, former executive producer of NBC

Sports, who openly laments not hiring Madden for his network in 1979: "If a person says interesting things when he speaks, then he isn't talking too much."

For my part, I was asked dozens of times to characterize Madden. I, too, mentioned his "everyman" quality. But I wish I'd had the eloquence of Helmut Schmidt, former chancellor of West Germany. In his memoir, *People and Powers*, he writes of one "Great Communicator," but he might have been writing of the other:

> Reagan has an astounding ability to talk to his countrymen exactly how they talk among each other. With Reagan, Americans had the instinctive feeling that "he is one of us—we can trust him."

In chilly Chicago, our touch football game stalled. Would the second-half kickoff be punted or thrown? "Hulk" Rothweiler, the weight lifter-cameraman, shrugged at me as if to say, "You know Madden. What am I gonna do?"

"Hulk" strong-armed a pass the length of the field. My kick returner, a production assistant named Steve Williams, ran away from it, presuming the ball would bounce out of the endzone. But it died in the snow, and one of Madden's men recovered for a touchdown.

As Williams made a mild protest to the referee, John stormed onto the field.

"You can't let a kickoff go in the endzone!" he bellowed. "Where'd you ever play football, Williams? That's the worst play I've ever seen!"

On the next series, my pass glanced off a video technician's hands, Mike Arnold intercepting for Team Madden. I dived at him unsuccessfully, landing headfirst and jarring a lens out of my glasses. Arnold was high-fiving in the endzone.

In the final moments, "Hulk" finally nailed me, rattling my teeth with a muscleman's shot that he later apologized for delivering. He said he was under orders. Team O'Neil was bruised and beaten, two touchdowns to none.

A few months later, Madden invited me to visit his new home and play a round of golf in northern California. Near the end of a congenial, relaxing day, he showed me his trophy case.

The two most prominent items, displayed front and center, were a game ball from Super Bowl XI and the touch football trophy he'd won in Chicago.

6

Teaching, Bonding, Mythologizing

THE THREE questions most frequently asked of network television producers are these: (1) How did you get started? (2) Can you arrange a job for my son/daughter/nephew/third cousin? (3) What's the difference between a producer and a director?

The answers are as follows: (1) "Just fell into it." (2) "Gee, I wish I could help . . ." (3) "Glad you asked."

In sports television, production work falls into two categories—events and nonevents. The latter consist of features, profiles, interviews—any programming that isn't recorded at an event.

These are normally handled by a producer-director, one person who conceptualizes the piece, directs its recording, often conducts interviews, selects music, edits videotape, and sometimes even writes narration. On many of these pieces, the commentator whose voice you hear has no involvement other than reading copy after the piece is fully shaped.

Sports producer-directors who do this sort of work are actually more akin to news producers. Often they are young people, in their twenties, just promoted from the rank of production assistant. Nonevent pieces are opportunities for them to show their skill and their willingness to run through brick walls.

Nobody lasts too long in this role, however. At some

point, even these young enthusiasts begin to make a calculation: Four days of travel and recording in Europe, two days of editing, a day of writing and music selection, a half-day of narration and audio mix—all for a two-minute profile of a figure skater?

In addition, they begin to understand that the networks don't value this kind of programming highly enough to pay well for its creation. No, the rewards—big salary, airtime, public attention—come with event production.

The two kinds of events are videotaped and live. The former is an ever-shrinking, underappreciated corner of the business. Assignments like the Tour de France and Iditarod dogsled race require the touch of a documentarian. These ask that a weeks-long event be stuffed into mere minutes of programming. An eye for story line is essential —again, much like a news producer.

Other taped programs are simpler condensations of an event that might have been live, except for its length or the conspiracy of time zones. In this kind of program—gymnastics, track and field, volleyball, skiing—the editing goal is to create something "plausibly live." A producer formats elements, both inclusions and exclusions, so that the viewer believes it's all occurring in real time.

This is the great comfort of *ABC's Wide World of Sports.* Its producers may show only seven skiers out of 60 in a World Cup downhill, but the seven are presented so "plausibly live" that the viewer feels satisfied he's seen the whole event.

Unlike the secret recipe of Kentucky Fried Chicken or the mysterious syrup of Coca-Cola, *Wide World* 's editing formula is available to the public every Saturday. It always amazed us at ABC how the competition could remain so far behind.

On *CBS Sports Spectacular,* for instance, you'd see a downhill racer blast into the finish area, still breathing hard from his run. Then CBS edited to his interview. Whack! Suddenly, he was fully recovered, wearing his warm-up suit. Worse, instead of airing the whole interview, finishing smoothly with "Now let's go back to commentator X," they'd snatch the second answer out of a three-question exchange.

Their product didn't just fail the "plausibly live" test; it was downright jarring. The viewer felt like a spring had gone "boing" in his easy chair. He may not have known *why* he felt unsettled, but he was changing channels nonetheless.

In 1981, it didn't take long for our people at CBS to learn these techniques. As I'd told Sauter, this isn't rocket science. Soon after *Sports Saturday/Sunday*'s premiere, we were forced to air a five-month-old auto race. This was an unavoidable obligation inherited from *Sports Spectacular*. At home that night, I turned on WCBS-New York for the 11 o'clock news. The sportscaster was showing highlights of our race, saying, "In auto racing at Daytona today . . ."

Our production people were rightly smug about their convincing performance, but management never acknowledged this kind of artistry. Outside of ABC Sports, seamless editing was hardly noticed, let alone valued. Fairly or unfairly, the business managers of network sports reserved top status for live-event producers and directors.

Live events are center ring in this circus. They yield 80 to 90 percent of each network's sports revenue. That is the yardstick, not a comparison of skill or creativity, by which the "air traffic controllers" of live events make the largest salaries.

It works like this: Just outside the stadium is parked a 40-foot trailer, a television studio on wheels. Working back to front, the rear of the vehicle houses four or five videotape machines, each with an operator. These are the replay sources.

In the middle of the truck is a large audio console with 24 inputs. It has a channel for every audio source in the production—commentator microphones, "effects" mikes for field and crowd sounds, cartridge and reel-to-reel decks for prerecorded music, two channels coming from each videotape machine.

A single technician operates this audio board from within soundproof glass. He mixes his 24 inputs into a single output for air. His cues to open and close individual "faders" are sometimes taken verbally from the producer and director, but more often, they're prearranged according to the video he sees. Elevated slightly, he looks through his glass at a wall of monitors covering the front end of the truck. This is a "picture window" onto the event for those encapsulated in the truck.

Between the audio man and the monitor wall, sitting lower on swivel chairs, are the three key figures—producer, director, and technical director.

The technical director, or T.D., is supervisor of all engineering personnel who operate the hardware "hands on" —camera, videotape, audio, lighting, maintenance, utility. The T.D. personally operates the most important piece of equipment, the video switcher.

This is the terminus of every video source in the production—cameras, tape machines, electronic graphics devices called Chyrons, machines that store individual "still frames" (as opposed to moving pictures).

Each video source is represented on the switcher by a row of colored buttons sitting in a rectangular console. If production were as simple as "taking" or "hard-cutting" one video source at a time, we'd need only one button apiece. But the process involves "mixing" video sources— dissolves (blending one picture into another) and wipes (replacing one picture with another in a geometric pattern). The rows of buttons make it possible to mix one video source with every other video source.

In recent years, the T.D.'s electronic empire has grown. Boxes mounted near this switcher now allow him to make video fly, swoop, cube-turn, page-turn, 180-turn, enlarge, shrink to infinity, and so on.

The T.D. performs all these gymnastics at one end of this front-row threesome, taking commands from a director, who sits in the middle. The director is responsible for issuing direct commands to technicians that, in aggregate, yield the audio-video product. He's the man who calls cameras ("Stand by 3 . . . take 3"), puts videotape machines on the air ("Ready to roll VT-A . . . Roll 'A,' track it, put 'A' on the line"), superimposes graphics ("Matte Chryon 1 . . . lose it"), and so on.

The director issues those commands through a communication line called the "director's conference." Speaking to and hearing from his technicians, he wears a one-flap headset. (On entering a sports production truck, one can always assess a director's relationship with his producer by observing which side he wears his headset. In my first year at CBS, it took a game or two before Sandy Grossman gave me his "open ear.")

The third man in this "front row" is the producer. The buck stops with him. He is ultimately responsible for every aspect of the broadcast. While the director executes audio and video functions, the announcers do commentary, and the production assistant handles graphics, a producer's overall responsibility allows him to override in any of these areas.

More commonly, however, his job is to keep all the oars of a production stroking in the same direction. Think of it as the rowing race, "four-oared shell without coxswain." Every element of a broadcast can be reduced to four categories—live audio/video, taped video (replays), commentary, and graphics.

The producer is like the racing shell's "stroke." He not only determines cadence and barks orders in the boat, he also mans one of the oars. He's responsible for the "taped video" category. After each play in a football game, for instance, the producer decides whether a replay is in order and, if so, which one(s).

These decisions are the essence of a broadcast. Coverage

during play is formula for all games, all networks. It's the work *between* plays that defines a football production. Each 25 to 30 seconds between plays is a precious opportunity, once exercised, never to be regained.

The producer faces 120 to 150 of these decisions per game: Is this replay worthy of air? Is it only half the story without a companion replay?

Producers know that the price of every replay is "burying" the live moment: Should we see Coach X debate his play call on fourth-and-1? Is this the moment to reset time remaining and timeouts? Should we check the bench and see if injured Quarterback Y looks ready to play the next series?

Having made this decision in an instant, a good producer communicates his plan to the other three "oars" immediately. (This was my biggest problem in the early days at ABC. Joe Aceti—a superb director and my mentor on *Monday Night Baseball*—used to say, "Kid, you've got some great ideas. You just have to let the rest of us hear them.")

The producer also wears a headset, connecting him to a stage manager in the booth, production assistants in the Chyron room, and, importantly, to videotape operators. In addition, he may put his voice into one ear of his commentators' headsets by depressing a lever or "key" in front of him. This system is called "interrupted feedback" (IFB). Commentators hear feedback of their own words in both ears, except when the producer interrupts with an instruction on the IFB.

The front-row threesome stares transfixed for three hours at its monitor wall. This contains a black-and-white monitor (13-inch diagonal for cameras, eight-inch for videotape machines) showing every video source. Camera monitors are aligned in front of the director, each with a number and first name of the operator, such as "Cam 1. Mike." In front of both the producer's and director's position are outputs of videotape machines, each lettered, such as "VT-A. Joe."

In the middle of this monitor wall, prominently near the top, are two color monitors. At the left is "color preview." Here the director may see one of his video sources in color without putting it on the air. To its right is "line." This is what the truck is feeding a New York "control studio." The studio integrates commercials and retransmits this "line" picture to the home audience.

So what do the producer and director actually do to each other, or with each other, or against each other? That question, so commonly asked, fails to recognize the other creative components—commentators and, to a lesser degree, the production assistant.

Good producers run a kind of limited democracy. If there are 140 snaps in a football telecast, 70 times the game situation will dictate an obvious direction between plays. Another 25 times, the producer will see something and steer his colleagues onto a certain course. But following those other 45 plays, he'll say nothing, allowing his director or commentators to take the lead. Occasionally, even the production assistant will "sell" a statistic that shapes the half-minute between plays.

Allowing, indeed encouraging, creative freedom in the booth is important because of the commentators' unobstructed vision. The producer and director can only see what their cameras are showing them. Thus those two large speakers in the truck's monitor wall are just as important as any video screen. Through these are heard the audio mix of commentary and effects (crowd sounds, player collisions, etc.).

In the moments before air, one of the most critical decisions is finding an audio balance, such that (1) the producer hears everything in his headset, (2) the director hears everything in his headset, (3) both hear commentary through the speakers, and (4) the producer, director, and T.D. hear each other in their "open" ears. There is no explaining it, but in the same way that Madden sees what all 22 players do on every play, experienced production people hear every word that is said.

So the producer, director, and commentators are speaking and listening to each other nonstop for three hours. And everybody feels a limited creative freedom. What happens when there's a big play and everybody has a viewpoint that he's dying to express? What keeps the four oars from crashing into each other?

Let's take a play from Thanksgiving Day 1983—St. Louis at Dallas, a 55-yard touchdown run by Tony Dorsett.

Summerall's call of the play: "Two tight ends, one lone setback, two wide receivers. (Snap.) Dorsett—behind Donovan. Dorsett! Gone! GONE!"

When Dorsett was still five to 10 yards from crossing the goalline, I knew what I wanted to do. Summerall, Madden, and I had evolved a pattern such that they'd give me a beat at the end of each play before resuming commentary. If I wanted control, that was the moment to say so. If not, my silence meant that they and Grossman were free to initiate a direction.

But on a big play like this, everybody looked for leadership—like the four-oared shell that wants a higher stroke rate to match an opponent's surge. Creative people don't want suffocation in this circumstance but leadership—a plan that's definitive, yet loose enough that they may insert their own contributions.

Even before Dorsett crossed the goalline, I depressed my key to the commentator headsets. Pat hadn't yet finished calling the play, but hearing the interrupt was a signal to him and John that I had made a decision. Whether a producer's idea is good or bad, commentators like to know he's got something in mind.

When Summerall punctuated "GONE!" the second time, I said, "No commercial." Turning to Sandy, I repeated it. Producers select commercial positions within a broadcast, but too often they miss great moments by placing them in the obvious spots after touchdown plays.

By waving off, I let everybody know we'd have space after the extra point to do our replays. That meant Sandy was immediately free to cut reactions, especially smiles about Dorsett, who disappeared briefly up the stadium tunnel. Pat and John fell silent ("laid out"), signaling the audio man to reach for home-team crowd.

During this interlude, I told the commentators, "Three replays. First, endzone. Then, I'll give you Doug Cosbie isolated. Watch how he 'hooks' Curtis Greer, John. Then I've got a block downfield by Tony Hill."

In familiar body language, Sandy and I moved an inch closer to each other, meaning our heads were about two inches apart. He continued looking straight ahead, still directing action along the Cowboy bench, preparing for the extra point. Quartering just slightly, but not looking at him, I said, "Sanford, it's 'N,' 'A,' 'B.'" ("Sanford," Grossman's given name, was a term of endearment with me.)

Looking back at "T-Bone's Video Arcade," as associate director Joan Vitrano nicknamed my double-column of videotape monitors, I said, "Cue it 'N.' Cue it 'A.' 'B,' stand by to play it for me." This was VT-B operator's warning that he would be previewing his replay for me while "N" and "A" were on the air. I wanted to see whom Tony Hill blocked.

Sandy covered the extra point, matted the score, and turned toward me, asking, "Which is first?"

" 'N,' Nancy."

Madden picked up: "Let's watch the play again. Here it is, just a pitch to the outside. Now watch Pat Donovan's block right there. Boom. He takes E. J. Junior, knocks him to the outside, in fact, darn near knocks him out of bounds. . . . "

Once that was under way, into my headset, I said, "Play

it for me, 'B.' " This was a phrase the CBS technicians had never heard before 1981. It was a preview command that I used to distinguish from Sandy's "roll," which was an air command. For whatever reason, the CBS engineers loved it. They walked around football remotes imitating my urgent tone: "Play it for me, 'B,' *play it for me!*"

"What's next?" Sandy asked.

" 'A,' apple."

Madden: "I tell ya, but the thing that got it started was the tight end. Now watch eighty-four, Doug Cosbie. He's gonna be blockin' here on Greer. See now, he gets him to the inside, invites him in . . ."

When he finished that second replay, I quickly fed Madden the information that "play it for me" had gleaned: "Hill's block on Benny Perrin."

Madden: "I tell you, any big play by a running back, it has to be a block by a wide receiver. That was Tony Hill. He came in and blocked the weak safety, Perrin."

Nothing to it, right? Now let's add the Chalkboard. And rather than take the leisurely period after a touchdown, let's select a play that was part of a continuing drive.

In that January 1985 "Angus" game for the NFC Championship, San Francisco's Joe Montana avoided a safety blitz by Chicago's Dave Duerson and threw a 15-yard pass to Mike Wilson. This is exactly how it sounded among our foursome:

GROSSMAN: Ready 3. Take 3.

SUMMERALL: Montana, chased by Duerson. Gets rid of it to Wilson.

GROSSMAN: Hold it, 7. Take 7 *(crowd shot).*

Out of bounds. It'll be first and goal for the 49ers at the 3.

O'NEIL: "N" Chalkboard. Circle Duerson, John.

GROSSMAN: Ready 9. Take 9 (*Wilson high-five*).

O'NEIL: Cue it forward, 'N.' I want to see Duerson, the safety. Forward, forward . . .

GROSSMAN: Ready machine 'N' with Chalkboard effect.

O'NEIL: . . . that's him, back, freeze. "N" Chalkboard, Sandy.

GROSSMAN: Fly "N." Matte Chyron 2 ("CBS Chalkboard"). Lose it.

GROSSMAN: Roll "N."

GROSSMAN: Freeze. Fly 1.

(*Brief commentary "layout" to accommodate crowd roar.*)

MADDEN: Last week, I said Joe Montana's the best quarterback in football. This is the reason he's so good. We can see that he's going to get Duerson (*circles*) comin' through free here. Most quarterbacks go down. Montana just takes the ball, runs out (*draws*), and then finds somethin' down here.

Watch him. Here comes number 22 (Duerson). He's free! He has a free shot at him! Montana gets away. . . . He gets outside and gives a little jump shot out there to the 3 yardline.

There were other replays I might have chosen after this completion—an isolate of Wilson, ground-level of Montana's sprint out. These possibilities surely occurred to my three colleagues as well. But our pregame preparation, always done as a foursome, had defined an important story line: Could the blitzing Bears sack Montana? With nothing more than the shorthand code, " 'N' Chalkboard. Circle Duerson, John," we got all oars stroking toward that theme.

Describing this process, Neil Amdur of *The New York Times* once wrote:

> The O'Neil–Grossman/Pat Summerall–John Madden team has unquestionably been pro football's finest for a variety of reasons. . . . The thoroughness of CBS coverage in recent weeks underscores the success of O'Neil's system. And because everyone is so finely tuned to the operation, coordinating thoughtful commentary from Summerall and Madden to Grossman's pictures works even easier.

It was a kind of Zen. Four men of widely differing backgrounds had conditioned their minds to react identically to any given stimulus. Even though we were sitting in pairs, connected only by telephone wires, the four of us could actually *feel* each other with a certain sixth sense.

In his 1987 film, *Broadcast News*, director James L. Brooks explains this phenomenon superbly. Tom Grunick, a vacant sportscaster-turned-newsanchor played by William Hurt, is coaxed through a live special by producer Jane Craig (Holly Hunter). Meeting in the newsroom after their mutual triumph, Grunick expresses the mystical quality of good IFB communication:

"You're an amazing woman! What a feeling, having you inside my head!"

"Yeah, it was an unusual place to be," replies Craig.

"It was, like, indescribable," exults Grunick. "You knew just when to feed me the next line. You knew the second before I needed it."

On his knees now, grabbing both armrests of Craig's chair, Grunick pulls her toward him in subtle erotic simulation. She throws her head back with a throaty laugh. He grunts with animal pleasure:

"There was, like, a rhythm we got into! It was like great sex!"

No offense to Pat, John, and Sandy, I can't say our

work ever rose to the heights of lovemaking. But it was certainly better than any men's club I've ever joined.

Ultimately, this was the experience that bonded us. After all the bullshit of 1981—the outsider-versus-incumbents battle—it was the communion of making good television that brought us together.

Several forces were at work: pride in suddenly realizing we were the best at our little craft, exclusivity in knowing we had access to privileged information, joint vulnerability—actually *needing* each other on the air. This last notion bred interdependence, which begat real friendship.

Summerall, a CBS blueblood of 25 years' standing, allowed himself to be quoted in *USA Today*: "We're after the end result. The most important thing is that all of us contribute—producer Terry O'Neil, director Sandy Grossman, John, and myself."

United at long last, the four of us were unburdened. We were finally free to make a contribution to the state of the art.

For instance, Sandy and I took the guesswork out of reaction shots by feeding players' and coaches' faces to videotape as they watched a critical play. This had been done occasionally—notably by NBC's Harry Coyle when Carlton Fisk waved his Fenway Park home run "fair" in the 1975 World Series—but never on a systematic basis.

For crucial plays that were guaranteed to produce an emotional response on both sidelines, we programmed less field coverage and more faces into our isolation pattern. Knowing the director couldn't simultaneously cut all these reactions live, we played back the best from videotape.

In 1983, when 12–2 Dallas met 12–2 Washington, the Cowboys' Danny White tried a risky fourth-and-1 audible against Coach Tom Landry's instructions. Our replay caught Landry in an astonishing fit of pique, screaming, "No, no, Danny, no!"

Other times, we had San Francisco's Walsh gasping, "Oh, fuck," after a blocked field goal try. The Rams' John Robinson tried to calm his team after a turnover in noisy RFK: "Relax, relax." Mike Ditka could be counted on for a triple arm pump when his Bears intercepted in the play-offs. These reactions we often folded into a quick montage that was far more visceral than simply reviewing the play.

In game-ending situations, these montages were an explosive climax, but often they came without warning. That's when our system of written preassignments worked like a safety net. In '84, St. Louis kicker Neil O'Donoghue rushed off the bench for a field goal attempt that would decide whether his team was going to the playoffs or not. It was the last play of the *season*. The Cardinals were out of timeouts. The clock ticked from 0:09 to 0:02 as their field goal unit raced onfield and snapped the ball.

In those seven seconds, all nine of our cameramen and six videotape operators found their assignments. Sandy simply called the code, "Field goal." Knowing which direction O'Donoghue was kicking, everybody reacted according to plan. (By the way, he missed—wide left.)

One sports television reviewer, reaching for a story, asked me if our written preassignments constituted a "breakthrough." He was fascinated that we'd adapted the coach's "ready list" and used similar categories—short yardage, goalline, punts, placements, kickoffs, and the like.

This may have been an improvement on the haphazard guesswork of the past, but "breakthrough" was an overstatement. The only true innovations in televised football were the advent of videotape replay (1963) and the birth of the Chalkboard (1982). Other advances were evolutionary, not revolutionary, and, as I tried telling the TV critic, utterly dependent on good research for their effectiveness.

For instance, the low endzone camera had been a sporadic, unremarkable element of football coverage until we made it a CBS staple in 1981. Positioned behind the endzone, with its lens only 10 feet off the ground, this camera showed a wide receiver running his route directly into your living room, or Lawrence Taylor, head on, overpowering a blocker and cartwheeling a quarterback to the turf.

It made for awesome television. St. Louis's Roy Green once broke off a post-corner pattern so sharply in front of this camera, it put a crick in your neck.

But low endzone positions, like every other production improvement, only showed their real value when we complemented them with hard information.

San Francisco's Dwight Clark had a favorite pass pattern that was made for low endzone replays. It was called "The Shake." He went upfield, faked toward the goalpost, faked to the corner, then made a final cut to the post. Joe Montana told us about it on a Saturday morning.

Seeing "The Shake" on our low endzone monitor was like watching a magic show. With that last move to the post, Clark made his defender, *poof*, disappear. Into Madden's headset I cried, "It's 'The Shake!' John, it's 'The Shake!'"

We first saw Clark work it for a touchdown against Dallas in the 1981 postseason. Four seasons later, he and Montana hit the Cowboys with it for two more touchdowns on the last Sunday of the '85 regular season.

But when Tom Gilmore of the *San Francisco Chronicle* —the most football-knowledgeable reviewer in his business—wrote about our broadcast, he mentioned not our replays, not our camera positions, but our research:

> Madden and the CBS crew don't come by their gameday insights by chance. They develop them by being one of the best-prepared crews on TV. That was never more evident than on the first 49er touchdown.
>
> Just seconds after Dwight Clark had caught a 49-yard

TD pass from Joe Montana, Madden informed us, "That was the Shake Pattern."

The Shake Pattern? "They've worked on that all week," Madden said before the replay came up. "Usually Clark just makes two fakes—to the post and to the corner, but that time he went post-corner-post."

Similarly, in that 1983 Washington-Dallas epic, the Redskins' Art Monk ran a stop-and-go-route into our low endzone camera that made viewers *clutch* in their living rooms. His defender, Ron Fellows, was paralyzed. The play clicked for a 43-yard touchdown.

But the only people who ever mentioned this classic replay—so gorgeous, it looked like it was staged—were a few associates in the business. That's because we followed the touchdown catch with some of our best reporting.

Monk was part of a Redskins sixsome called the "Fun Bunch." When any of them scored a touchdown, all six circled round in the endzone, swung their arms in unison, then jumped for a high-five.

The Cowboys had noted this act with displeasure. On the eve of the game, Dallas's Everson Walls told us quietly, "They ain't gonna do that shit in our stadium."

"What are you gonna do about it?" we asked. "What if one of the Fun Bunch scores?"

"We'll get in the middle of it and stop them. They ain't gonna jump in Texas Stadium."

When the confrontation developed, Sandy was right on it. Instead of cutting his normal pattern after a touchdown reception—quarterback, sideline reactions—he knew to stay with Monk, who led him into the fray. The Fun Bunch celebrated around and over Walls, whom we could see flailing and screaming at the 'Skins.

Once again, the principles of good journalism showed themselves more valuable than any camera position or any hardware in our $8 million mobile unit.

I spent a whole career learning this lesson. Whether the

job was the Munich Olympics, the Moses Malone investigation, or pro football production, there was no substitute for information. Any thinking professional could see its value. Everybody was drawn to it, galvanized by it.

Before the last game I ever produced for CBS, a technician asked me about his isolate in the preassignment category, "Rams' Offense Moving Left to Right."

"Terry," he said, "when Los Angeles goes to double tights . . ."

" 'Double tights'?" I smiled to myself. "These guys have come a helluva long way. They've even got the lingo."

After that game, in our traditional season-ending toast, I told the technicians, "If knowledge is power, you guys are the strongest bunch in the history of televised football. There's never been a group that knew more about the game."

Enjoyable as the "road" and line production may have been, that was about my fourth most important responsibility to CBS/NFL football. This was a billion-dollar enterprise over the five-year 1982–86 contract. It needed supervising.

When I arrived in 1981, Van Sauter put it to me in these terms: "Big guy, do you realize that professional football subsidizes CBS Sports? Everything we do around here, other than the NFL, breaks even, maybe loses a few million dollars. Pro football covers the losses and provides our yearly profit."

With those kinds of stakes, my priorities were (1) meticulous networking to ensure that the right game appeared in every living room every Sunday, (2) critiquing the entire staff so that all eight broadcast teams maintained top quality, and (3) "romanticizing" our conference, making NFC football the only kind to watch.

Networking was a crossword puzzle that came in two varieties. On eight regular-season Sundays, we televised one game to each market while NBC had a doubleheader. On the other eight, we reversed.

On doubleheader days, the custom was to regionalize five or six games at 1 o'clock and have a single national game at 4. But when Chicago got hot in the mid-1980s, I asked the NFL to consider the converse. Why not a national Chicago game at 1 P.M. and six regional games at 4? The league bought it. No point in denying any region the Bears at 1; no point in trying to elevate a weaker game to national exposure at 4 just because that was tradition.

On single-game weeks, we found a way to provide two games (ergo, twice the rating) in the unique Baltimore-Washington market. Since television signals from those two affiliates overlapped, we always tried to schedule their games in opposite time periods. The best scenario was a 'Skins game at 1 o'clock in Washington and a game involving the hated Cowboys networked to Baltimore at 4. Effectively, this was a doubleheader, and a blockbuster, on our single-game weeks. When the Colts left Baltimore, moving to Indianapolis after the '82 season, NBC had no team in this populous dual market. Our strategy became so ratings-productive, it almost felt like cheating.

Equally important in my weekly routine was an honest appraisal of everybody's performance. To producers I wrote regular notes like these: "Payton's cartwheel drew gasps from your commentators, but no replay." "Alzado replay meaningless on the Ferragamo intercept—his pressure not a factor; would rather have seen Chalkboard to know where defenders were placed." "Need more scores of other games." "Why are we seeing and talking about McMichael's face shield when there's a raging controversy about whether Archer fumbled or not?"

I always included enough items like "Great replay— Henry Lawrence holding." But this wasn't a garden club. It was a publicly held company. Employees should understand that. Besides, sometimes the issue was larger than mere aesthetics.

One of the old-guard CBS producers was a weak-kneed guy who inserted his commercials at the first opportunities of every quarter. I always urged that they be spaced for programming advantage, the way you'd spot them in an edited show. But this fellow was afraid he'd "bring one home," that he wouldn't have enough opportunities. It was a ludicrous, baseless fear, left over from the days when a CBS producer's job description was, "Get the commercials in and get off the air as scheduled. Period."

One morning, the vice president of CBS Sports Sales sent me a memo. Cadillac and Pontiac were considering dropping their $17 million account with CBS/NFL. They'd been tracking this producer's performance. He was jamming four of their commercials into as little as 11 minutes of real time, then allowing 30 minutes to pass without commercials before the next quarter began.

Compressed this way, the client's message wasn't merely wasted on the same 11-minute span of audience. No, Pontiac and Cadillac were actually irritating viewers, who blamed the advertiser for absurdly frequent interruptions. The two auto giants were spending $115,000 per commercial to alienate their target!

This was the kind of error we discussed at the annual season-opening seminar. I'd ask everybody to check both ego and personal sensitivities at the door. Then, for sake of the whole group, as a communal learning experience, I screened a reel of the most educational moments from the previous season—good, bad, and ugly.

In a 1984 game, for instance, play-by-play man Jim Kelly forgot the "muff rule": If a return man doesn't take possession of a punted ball, the kicking team can *recover* his "muff" but can't *advance* it like a fumble.

Call me brutal, I rolled Kelly's very excited play-by-play in the seminar: "Nelms mishandles at the forty-seven! And the Eagles get it back! PHILADELPHIA TOUCH-DOWN!! MIKE REICHENBACH! NO FLAGS! THE ROOKIE FROM EAST STROUDSBURG! (Pause, then very sheepishly) However, on a muff, there is no advance."

We had talked about the muff rule for four years, but nothing ever drove it home to the whole group like playing that tape at the July 1985 seminar.

In the backslapping, attaboy, self-deceptive world of CBS Sports, this kind of accountability was a cold shower. Some guys shivered; some lathered up.

The ones with coaching background, like Hank Stram and Dick Vermeil, were most receptive. Vermeil took detailed notes during the seminar; in season, he wanted to be critiqued every week—and hard.

Tom Brookshier, who turned out to be a helluva guy and a serviceable play-by-play man after his split from Summerall, was often the seminar's comic relief. He'd suffer my criticisms, then joke, "What is this? A roast?"

Others, like Dick Stockton, didn't enjoy it one bit.

At halftime of a 1984 L.A. Rams–St. Louis game that Stockton broadcast, the Cardinals led, 13–3. More important, their defense was completely dominating the game. They had held the Rams to only nine yards passing in the first half.

Failing to move on its first possession of the second half, St. Louis lined up in punt formation. Incredibly, Coach Jim Hanifan ordered a fake. But his players botched it, several linemen illegally downfield on a forward pass from the blocking back. It was Rams' ball deep in St. Louis territory.

Sitting in the studio with me that Sunday was Jack Kemp, New York congressman and 1988 presidential candidate. He had been a gritty, effective leader with the San Diego Chargers and Buffalo Bills, AFL Player of the Year in 1965. Kemp's son, Jeff, was the Ram quarterback this day. Since the game was networked only to Missouri and the West Coast, Jack came to the studio to watch.

When we saw this fake punt, the congressman and I

looked at each other in amazement. St. Louis led by 10 points and had total control of the game. They'd shut down poor Jeff Kemp so thoroughly that his father was squirming. Why give the Rams life with this needless trick?

Surely, our commentators had the same reaction. I turned up the volume slightly and suppressed a proud grin. They would now show Jack Kemp why CBS football was the best in captivity.

Or would they? The referee momentarily forgot the rule on illegal receiver downfield, almost giving the ball back to St. Louis. Stockton followed him off the cliff, fabricating some ridiculous rationale for Cardinal possession. He didn't know the rule either.

Eventually, the officials admitted their mistake, but Stockton, ever insecure, tried an embarrassing smoke-screen: "I was surprised. But, y'know, you always know the officials are gonna have the right call. And if you haven't seen something lately—and there are always new things coming up—maybe you're not totally sure. And we weren't totally sure."

What a mess. Worst of all, Stockton's ignorance distracted him and partner Stram from the real issue, Hanifan's coaching blunder. They made no mention until I, mortified in front of Jack Kemp, was forced to phone the truck.

What happened next was season-killing for St. Louis. Just two plays after the disastrous fake punt, Congressman Kemp's son threw 53 yards for a touchdown. Zip—momentum switch. The Rams came back for a 16–13 victory. Los Angeles made the playoffs by one game that year; St. Louis missed by one game. This was the margin for both squads. And we'd blown the turning point.

When we played this sequence at the seminar, Stockton was in such obvious discomfort that I diverged from normal policy. For the first and only time, I turned down his commentary and did my own explanation as the video played.

With our production people, it was much easier to maintain a proper seminar mood. All I had to do was include a few errors from my own games. In 1985, for instance, I showed a terrific isolate of Chicago's Mike Singletary absolutely mugging San Francisco's Russ Francis.

"Feel privileged," I said. "You are the first audience ever to see this clip. I was ready to play it last year, but I got sidetracked by the referee. He announced the penalty on Duerson when he meant Singletary. And like a dummy, I went hunting through my replays for Duerson. Of course, he was nowhere near the play. But by that time, it was too late. So I didn't replay anything. You are now getting to see this 'illegal chuck' for the first time in a special, private screening."

"Why didn't you roll it anyway?" asked one producer. "Summerall could have said, 'Either the referee made a mistake, or here's a penalty they didn't catch.' "

"You're right. I blew it."

By association with me, Sandy Grossman suffered the same fate. In the '82 seminar, I played one of his worst Super Bowl moments—that game-turning, goalline stand by San Francisco against Cincinnati. On fourth down, Bengal coach Forrest Gregg decided to go for a touchdown, disdaining the field goal. Sandy had great coverage of Gregg mouthing the words, "Go for it." But *30 seconds later,* he cut to Cincinnati kicker Jim Breech, warming up into a sideline net.

Summerall tried to cover for him: "Breech is getting ready, just in case."

"But Madden couldn't tell a lie. He gulped and said, "I think Breech is getting ready to kick off."

Mike Arnold, the associate producer who helped prepare clips for each seminar, later told me, "Everybody's always asking me, 'Did I make the tape? Did I make the tape?' Nobody likes to be embarrassed in front of the whole group. But they love it when you show mistakes from yours and Sandy's games."

If networking and teaching were two of my priorities at CBS, the third was just as important—"romanticizing" the NFC. No, make it "mythologizing." If that sounds like a manipulation, trust me, it wasn't. We simply got so intimate with the people, rivalries, and emotions of our conference, we couldn't help but communicate them.

Roger Staubach had a properly ethereal description of this phenomenon. Several years after he'd departed our staff, I saw him at a Super Bowl party.

"I don't know exactly what it is," he said, "but CBS is just more *into* the game than anybody else."

Everybody on staff made a contribution to NFC mythology. Mine was the 60- to 90-second videotape introduction, called a "tease," that aired at the top of each game. This was another form virtually unknown at CBS in 1981, one that ABC Sports had pioneered to personalize and dramatize its broadcasts many years earlier.

To this day, the best teases ever done are Jim McKay's setups to *Wide World of Sports* broadcasts. They began as a matter of necessity. *Wide World*'s events and athletes were so little known that Roone Arledge recognized the need for preamble. His bonus, it turned out, was McKay's ability to write the most lyrical copy in the history of sports television.

Even with a subject so well known as pro football, what better way to get the viewer's blood running than memorable faces and plays?

VIDEO	AUDIO
George Allen (sound on tape) amid Redskins' huddle.	"Just remember this—forty men together can't lose."
Allen on sideline (Summerall voice-over).	It was George Allen who turned the Redskins-Cowboys *series* into a *rivalry* . . .

Larry Brown run.	Allen who sent Larry Brown hurtling into the Doomsday Defense twenty-five and thirty times a game . . .
Redskins' punt coverage.	Allen who gave the name to special teams and set them loose on Dallas. It was Allen who fired this rivalry with real passion.
Allen (sound on tape).	"Go after 'em. Go after 'em."
Redskins bench (sound on tape).	"Shut 'em down now. Take the ball away."
'Skins Bill Malinchak (sound on tape).	"Die you dogs, die. Die, you yellow dogs."

That was the mythology of Dallas versus Washington, the NFL's hottest rivalry in the '70s and early '80s. But if a match-up didn't have such deep roots, we looked for another angle. When St. Louis visited Washington in '84, needing that season-closing victory to make the playoffs, we tried to define the fable of RFK Stadium, the best "scene" in pro football.

VIDEO	AUDIO
Neil Lomax to Roy Green, 83-yard TD (Summerall voice-over).	The first thing to know about the St. Louis Cardinals is that they have some fine players. Neil Lomax and Roy Green, for instance, burned Washington for this eighty-three-yard touchdown earlier in the season.
Anderson run.	And O. J. Anderson continues to be a punishing, effective runner. The
O'Donoghue field goal.	Cardinals beat Washington in October on this Neil O'Donoghue field goal.

240

Cardinal celebration.

But the second thing to know about the Cardinals is this: They don't have nearly the big-game experience of the Redskins. None of the Cardinals has ever played a game with so much at stake. Never have they found

RFK aerial.

themselves in this kind of pressure cooker . . . in this kind of stadium . . .

RFK crowd.

with this kind of crowd . . . singing this kind of song.

Montage: Touchdown plays, crowd, Riggins, Theismann (sung by fans, played by Redskin Band).

"Hail to the Redskins, Hail Victory, Braves on the Warpath, Fight for Old D.C."

The goal of most teases was goosebumps. I played three or four consecutively one year at a seminar, just before the midmorning coffee break. This was the dead of summer, six months after the pieces had aired. But on my way to the men's room, Madden stopped me, his huge shoulders hunched up in a shiver. "Jeez," he said in wonderment, "those teases gave me a chill."

Teases also inspired a new vocabulary among our group. After that St. Louis–Washington game, for instance, I could never mention an upcoming assignment at RFK without Summerall saying, "You mean we'll be in 'this kind of stadium,' listening to 'this kind of song'?"

Sandy would add, "Cut by this kind of director?"

Madden's favorite tease phrase was "Who would've thought?" from the '83 wild-card game. Honestly, it was a mediocre piece, explaining that Ram quarterback Vince Ferragamo had been playing in Canada while John Robinson and Eric Dickerson had been in college football just a few years earlier. "Who would've thought" they'd now be leading Los Angeles into the playoffs?

But for some reason, Madden latched on to the phrase. Even today, he'll caption a game's improbable moments with, "Who woulda thought?"

Madden was a big fan of teases, but he was also perceptive in picking up my hidden agenda. When two Notre Dame quarterbacks met for the 1983 NFC Championship —one from the Pittsburgh area, the other my classmate— John mocked, "Oh, shit. I can see the tease next week. It'll probably start with the Golden Dome [a Notre Dame landmark]. Up in the sky—in the clouds. Probably spinning like a big hubcap or something."

I couldn't disappoint Madden, could I? So I did the expected, finishing with the line, "Montana and Theismann. After today, one of them is going *back* to the Super Bowl. But *only* one."

This became another phrase in our bizarre glossary, though it was crucial to imitate Summerall's basso baritone: "But *ooonly* one."

Worse than a Notre Dame bias, Madden knew I'd find any excuse to take care of Pittsburghers. This was a running battle between us, and one I couldn't help but win, for two reasons. First, his alma mater, Cal Poly–San Luis Obispo, sent virtually nobody to the NFL, so he had no comeback. But more self-incriminating, John loved Pitt guys.

His favorite player among the Redskins was guard Russ Grimm, a Pitt guy. In Dallas, he liked Tony Dorsett, another Pitt guy. Doing a Green Bay game for the first time, we spoke to cornerback Tim Lewis. When he left the room, Madden said, "God, I like him. What a bright-eyed little guy."

"John," I asked, "you know where he's from?"

"Ah, don't tell me."

"Yep. Pitt guy."

Before a Dallas–San Francisco game, I grabbed Matt Cavanaugh, then the 49ers' backup quarterback and an old friend whose games I had produced at ABC. He was part of my favorite quarterbacking quinella: Cavanaugh, of neighboring Youngstown, Ohio, had led Pitt to the '76 national collegiate championship. He understudied Montana of Monongahela, Pennsylvania, who took Notre Dame to the '77 national championship.

Introducing Cavanaugh to Pat, John, and Sandy, I announced, "You know, everybody thinks tomorrow is a big game with all kinds of playoff implications. But to some of us, it's bigger than that. It's a chance to see Cavanaugh and Dorsett on the same field again. Whew."

Madden almost threw us both out of the room. Still, he sensed something of his old Raider squad in Pitt players. He loved, for instance, hearing about the annual reunion of Pitt's 1980 senior linemen at a hunting cabin in the rural hills of northwestern Pennsylvania.

Greg Meisner of New Kensington, Pennsylvania, then a nose tackle with the Rams, told us, "We all get up early to go track deer in the woods. It'll be cold, snowin', but we get our rifles and go. All except Grimm. He just sits in the cabin all day and drinks beer. By himself. When he has to piss, he just goes to the edge of the porch. Then back inside for another beer. We come back in the afternoon and he says, 'Well, d'you guys shoot me any dinner?' "

When we relayed this account to Grimm for rebuttal, he said, "Damn right. It's right after the end of the season. I got a bad ankle, a bad elbow. My back is sore. I got a pinched nerve. And these crazy bastards want me to go slippin' around in the woods when they all have guns? Hey, I *know* these guys too well for that."

Deny it all he might, these were truly Madden's kind of men. He was a Pittsburgher at heart, tragically consigned to emptiness and unfulfillment in California.

Coming up to a Chicago–New York Jets game in '85, I told him, "Well, John, we got the ultimate tease next week."

"What do you mean?"

"Both coaches are from Pitt."

I overran our budget somewhat by sending Joan Vitrano to western Pennsylvania to shoot steel manufacturing and mood exteriors of Aliquippa. Then we gave Madden the whole history:

VIDEO	AUDIO
Map: Western Pennsylvania, animating Beaver River.	Students of American geography and professional football know that the Beaver River Valley of western Pennsylvania has produced some of the NFL's greatest players. The 15-mile stretch between Beaver Falls and Aliquippa is home to Jim Mutscheller of the Baltimore Colts, Vito "Babe" Parilli of the Boston Patriots, Mike Lucci of the Detroit Lions, Joe Namath of the New York Jets, and Tony Dorsett of the Dallas Cowboys.
Locate towns.	
Still: Mutscheller.	
Still: Parilli. Still: Lucci.	
Still: Namath. Still: Dorsett.	
Steel mill/river (Bruce Springsteen track up.) Smokestacks.	"My hometown . . . my hometown . . ." The Beaver Valley looks like this, feels like this. It's a place where the biggest nights of any year are Friday nights of high school football season. A place where you either won a scholarship and wore a football helmet or wore a hardhat and worked the midnight shift. Joe Walton of Beaver Falls won himself that prized forty-seven-mile trip down the
Sagging row houses.	
Hardhats at dusk.	
Still: Walton '56.	

Walton footage.

road to the University of Pittsburgh, where he was a tough, two-way end in an era when everybody played both offense and defense. Four years later, Mike Ditka of Aliquippa followed Walton to Pitt and then into the NFL as number one pick of the Chicago Bears . . .

Still: Ditka, '60.
Ditka footage.

Blast furnace.

Two sons of western Pennsylvania. They've shaped football teams to reflect that upbringing. Two first-place teams poured and cast in the image of their coaches. Forged in the heat of the Beaver Valley. (Music and effects up.)

Grizzled steelworkers. Pouring molten steel. Fiery sparks half-dissolved over vicious defensive hits.

Though the danger of cliché was ever-lurking, I couldn't resist going for heavy, intense themes. Working late-season and postseason games only, it was easy to convince myself that every Sunday was apocalypse. Besides, I was writing for Summerall's voice, surely the most dramatic in "tease history."

Sunday mornings, he'd arrive at the truck and intone in his deepest octave, "I walked through the graveyard on my way from the hotel. I'm ready."

Mixed with a cut called "War" from the *Rocky IV* soundtrack—our musical score in '85—he was the "voice of God" in these minimovies. The reaction he got from viewers and friends was a kind of creative approval he'd never heard. Whereas at first he didn't ask to see his copy until Sunday, suddenly Pat wanted to rehearse against the video in Saturday's production meeting. These opening moments became his baby, too.

After the 1985 NFC Championship, as we were riding

back to the hotel, he told me, "God, you should have seen the Halas family in the press box. They were in tears over the tease."

VIDEO	AUDIO
Bears entering the field.	The first temptation is to say that today's game is for the most obvious, the most visible Bears . . .
Otis Wilson isolate.	For the blitzing Wilson and
Richard Dent isolate.	for pass rusher Dent, who terrorized the Giants last week.
Jim McMahon headbutt.	For McMahon, the quarterback who'd rather be an offensive lineman.
"Fridge" TD catch.	For "Refrigerator" Perry, who made this football season fun for an entire nation.
Soldier Field aerial.	But the truth is these most visible Bears are the *new* Bears, and maybe the *next* one is for them, but today is not. Today is for the Bears who never knew the slimmest chance of a title game in Soldier Field. For Dick
Dick Butkus montage.	Butkus, whose unfortunate timing it was to arrive in Chicago two years *after* the Bears' last NFL championship. For Gale Sayers, easily
Gale Sayers montage.	the greatest running back of his era, but a man whose era was too brief. He limped out of pro football after seven years without ever making a playoff appearance. Among the current players, today is

Gary Fencik montage.

Walter Payton montage.

George Halas montage.

Ditka as Bear rookie.

Ditka/Halas two-shot.

Ditka in pregame huddle
(sound on tape).

Sunset on lake (with star fil-
ter).

for Gary Fencik, who suf-
fered eight dark seasons
when the only fun was trying
to knock someone cold in the
secondary. For Walter Payton, who became the NFL's
all-time rusher even though
he never had a Pro Bowl
lineman in front of him until
this season. But most of all,
today is for George S. Halas,
one of pro football's founders
and a man who gave these
Bears sixty-three years of his
life as a player, coach, and
owner. His final gift to the
team four years ago was
recognizing that his crew-cut
tight end from the early sixties was just the man to
restore the Bears' fierce pride.
"All we gotta do is want it as
much as we know we want it!
And if we want it that bad,
let's go get it!"
Somewhere beyond the hori-
zon of Lake Michigan, you
can believe George Halas
wants it, too.

So Summerall and I had our way of mythologizing the
National Football Conference. And Madden, naturally,
had his.

Again, it was not manipulative. With his relentless enthusiasm, Madden could have been broadcasting high
school games every week and found a reason to make
teenagers watchable. It was simply CBS Sports' good fortune to have him selling our players in his infectious, irresistible way.

For instance, he regaled Dallas defensive back Bill Bates, just because John liked his reckless style on special teams. Understand, Bates was a free agent, not drafted among 336 picks his senior year. He wasn't much bigger than me.

Until Madden got hold of him, Bates had only one claim to celebrity. In 1980, Georgia freshman Herschel Walker served notice on college football in his very first game by flattening a safety from Tennessee. It was a devastating steamroller job. The Tennessee player was in perfect position—crouched, flexed, ready to make the tackle. Walker just took him head up and, *wham*, left him for dead. The victim's name: Bill Bates.

Madden was undeterred. He watched Bates fling his body headfirst into a kickoff wedge and couldn't help but make him a star. He even drew Summerall into Bates-mania.

MADDEN: I saw Bill Bates in the hotel last night and he was tellin' me, he said, "I broke a helmet last week. I broke a helmet on a tackle." He was proud of that. He had to get a new helmet.

SUMMERALL: Someone was telling me that Bates was six years old, back in grammar school, you know, where they write comments on report cards, like "most likely to succeed" and stuff like that. On Bill Bates's report, the teacher's comment was "bully of the schoolyard." At six years old.

MADDEN: That could be his nickname. "Bully Bill Bates."

Another case was Ram offensive tackle Bill Bain. Madden adopted him just because he rode the train to practice and had a "bad body, just like me." Los Angeles coach John Robinson got to a point where he didn't think it was funny.

"You're really fuckin' me up with this guy," he said.

"What do you mean?" asked Madden.

"You talk about him so much, all of a sudden, he thinks he should be trapping and pulling and leading sweeps. All I want him to do is get his big hands on the defensive end and push. But no, he says, 'Madden says I'm a complete player.'"

Once I understood the value of this, I actually began to look for opportunities. In the '83 postseason, for instance, I arranged a conversation for Pat and John with the Rams' new long snapper, Mike McDonald.

The long snapper is a true specialist, able to fire a tight spiral, bulletlike, from between his legs, seven yards to the placement holder or 15 yards to the punter. It's a knack, relying on strong hands and wrists. The long snapper doesn't necessarily need to be a great athlete.

Mike McDonald qualified in spades. He'd actually been out of football for *four years*—unheard of in the NFL— when Robinson called in 1983. McDonald had been a fireman during that period, but from the look of him, the job had no fitness requirement. An ample beer gut overhung the belt of his football pants and made the 63 on his jersey pear-shaped.

Never mind. He was Madden's type. In the first quarter, as the Rams' punt team lined up, I waved off a commercial in order to replay McDonald's snap and hilarious wobble downfield. It was just the space Pat and John needed.

SUMMERALL: There is center Mike McDonald, who's quite a story. . . .

MADDEN: Yeah, the last time he played football was in 1979 for USC. John Robinson needed a long snapper, a center, last week for the punts and stuff, and he said, "Call that Mike McDonald." Somebody said, "Hey, coach, he hasn't played in four years." Robinson said, "I don't care. I know he can do it." So they called him. He was on the golf course. He was on the fifth hole. He got this call. He came off the course, reported to the Rams. Now he's playing in a playoff game.

SUMMERALL: One thing about McDonald. We erred last week when we said he was married. That's a serious mistake. His girlfriend was very upset.

MADDEN: And his friends said, "Hey, jeez, that was some good news. You know, you got to play for the Rams, you're playin' against the Cowboys, you're doin' all this stuff. But if you're gonna get married, you gotta tell us that, too, man."

When John Robinson recognized the link among Bates, Bain, and McDonald, an idea came to him. He told his boyhood buddy that we should collect all these crazies at the end of each season in an "All-Madden Team." You know, All-Pro, All-America, All-Conference—now we'd have All-Madden. The only qualification was that the player had to be John's special kind.

For instance, in 1984, San Francisco had a rookie tight end named John Frank. He was a backup who rarely played. But as the 49ers were running out a playoff victory over the Giants that year, Frank got into a wrestling match with New York's Lawrence Taylor.

You can imagine how much Taylor enjoyed this. An All-Pro, he'd played his ass off in a 21–10 loss. Now in the dying minutes, here came a rookie, fresh off the bench with a clean uniform, blocking him after the whistle. They fell to the ground, locked together, rolling over and over.

MADDEN: That John Frank is a rookie. Bill Walsh was sayin' this guy is always in fights 'cause he always blocks guys and stays with them. He said, "He can just glue to you." And that's exactly what he did with Lawrence Taylor. Look, he just glued to him. (*Imitating the hysteria of a pro wrestling announcer*) Taylor has him! Frank gets a reversal! Taylor's going for the reversal! Frank gets

250

a pin! Referee says that's it! NO MORE! One, two, three! WHAP!

SUMMERALL: I tell you what, that should be broadcast on Saturday morning somewhere.

MADDEN: I love that. Guys jump from the ropes and stuff.

John Frank may have been a backup for San Francisco, but he was the starting tight end on our '84 All-Madden team. (By chance, I saw the 49ers' starting tight end, Russ Francis, while skiiing two years later. Riding the lifts, we got to talking about Frank. "The son of a bitch," said Francis. "He's been living on that All-Madden thing for two years.")

Other guys proved you could be a good player and still make the team. Washington's 310-pound offensive tackle, Joe Jacoby, for example, was a Pro Bowler, but also an All-Madden selection: "Look at Jacoby. Look, his shirt-tail's hangin' out. Stuff hangin' off him—grass 'n mud 'n stuff. Now he looks like a BIG JOE JACOBY!"

Some positions were harder to fill. Madden didn't really like any wide receivers—not physical enough. One year, I said, "John, you know Jim McMahon and John Elway both caught passes from halfbacks this year. Maybe they should be your wide receivers."

"Yeah," he said. "That's a great idea."

This All-Madden nonsense may seem a meaningless goof until you compare it with NBC's treatment of the American Football Conference and ABC's *Monday Night Football*. When have the other networks ever created watchable commodities out of journeyman players like Bill Bates, Bill Bain, and rookie John Frank? (I exclude Mike McDonald; it would be hyperbole to call him a journeyman.)

Think about AFC football in the '80s. Are there five players whom you felt compelled to watch? My list only goes two deep—Elway and Dan Marino (of Pitt and, only incidentally, the Miami Dolphins). In terms of raw statistics, they are probably the quarterbacks of the decade. Yet when you think of that position, do the names Montana and McMahon not spring to mind? Do you guess Madden had anything to do with that?

Consider McMahon for a moment. With his loud, punk arrival in '84, there's every chance he might have been labeled an ass, or worse, if Madden hadn't put the imprimatur on him.

What about John Riggins? He got drunk, told Supreme Court justice Sandra Day O'Connor to "lighten up, Sandy baby," then passed out under his table at a formal Washington dinner. But was he a boor? Hell, no. On the air, Madden had called him "a man's man, a fullback's fullback."

Other players drank just as much, got themselves into the same kind of scrapes. The Minnesota Vikings had nine players arrested on drunken driving charges in just two years, 1986–87. But they were dismissed as a problem club. Madden didn't do many Minnesota games.

In my five-and-a-half years at CBS, I never raised this issue, but I also never knew an executive who understood it. Collectively, CBS paid Pat, John, Sandy, and me more than $2 million in 1985. If you asked our bosses, they'd say the big salaries were simply a response to market conditions. They never had a clue that "mythologizing" their NFC was the most valuable thing we did.

Hell, the guys at the other networks didn't know it, either. As we drubbed NBC Sunday after Sunday, they kept moaning that AFC teams were located in smaller markets. That ruse got them through the regular season. But in postseason, both networks had strictly national telecasts. All markets received the same game. In my five seasons, 1981–85, CBS and NBC competed on 21 playoff exposures (wild cards, divisional playoffs, conference championships). NBC outrated us four games. If you throw out the quirky strike year of 1982, NBC beat us once in 16 tries. In the last three years, 1983–85, they were oh-for-12.

How much of our success grew from mythology, and how much may be traced to NFC teams winning six of seven Super Bowls for the seasons 1981–87? Who can say? But this much is clear: The six "most watchable" teams of the '80s all come from the same conference.

1. *San Francisco*: On-field success, stylishness, charisma, longevity. They've been champions since '81.

2. *Chicago*: Might be number one with McMahon, Payton, "The Fridge" and the "46," except they were late to arrive, not making the playoffs until '84.

3. *Washington*: Most Super Bowl appearances (three) and a home stadium that literally trembles when they score.

4. *Dallas*: Forget their recent play. With Landry and the Cowboy cheerleaders, this remains America's Team below the Mason-Dixon line.

5. *L.A. Rams*: Need a focal point to replace Dickerson, but that horn on the helmet has long-term appeal.

6. *N.Y. Giants*: Watching their defense in '86 was like gaping at a weekly auto wreck—you couldn't keep your eyes off it.

7. *Denver*: Third-best "scene" behind Washington and San Francisco, but a team that badly devalued itself in two Super Bowl losses.

8. *L.A. Raiders*: The skull and crossbones still have meaning. Damn if Madden isn't partly responsible for this, too.

7

The Caracas Caper and Other Misadventures

HAVE YOU EVER considered the overwhelming appeal of television bloopers?

Nobody gets much thrill out of a bank error—unless it's your checking account and there are lots of zeros involved. Nobody cares too much about the mistakes of bakers, florists, postmen, or traffic cops. But the failures of television people are cataloged in countless newspaper columns and outtake videos.

Apparently, there is something so arrogant, so privileged, so insulated-by-vast-resources about television that its errors are cause not just for amusement but for celebration. Bloopers confirm the fallibility, the humanity in all of us.

Therefore, as a public service—and, in some cases, at great personal sacrifice—I present the worst bloopers of my era in sports television. (Or is it the *best* bloopers?)

ABC's Monday Night Baseball, in its early years, was "blooper heaven." The sport had been televised superbly for 29 years by NBC, since the 1947 World Series. But we changed that, beginning in 1976. Oh, yes. We were going to revolutionize baseball coverage.

For instance, we announced a plan to "personalize the athletes," an ABC trademark, by rolling in videotaped interviews during play. You've seen this technique. The player appears in an upper quadrant of the screen, answering a question, while the game continues.

The problem was our technical directors. This new effect was an intricate process on their video switchers, requiring three separate actions. Once achieved, it was just as complicated to escape. If, while the interview was rolling, a batter hit the ball, it wasn't as simple as punching one button to lose the videotape. ABC producers, consequently, would order one of these inserts, then sit there praying, "Don't hit it, please don't hit it."

One Monday night, Philadelphia's "Downtown" Ollie Brown *disappeared* behind a talking head, into the corner of the screen, to make a game-saving catch against the right-field wall. There was no other angle for replay. ABC viewers never saw it.

Such moments produced this kind of exchange in the truck:

"Lose it!" the director would command.

"W-Wait a second," the technical director would plead, fumbling with his switcher.

"I can't wait! Lose the effect! Lose the fucking tape!"

Cameramen overhearing this conversation at ear-splitting volume finally came up with a solution for their harried directors. In the '78 American League East playoff between the Yankees and Red Sox, Carl Yastrzemski was a dramatic figure, having never played on a World Series winner in his legendary career. Perhaps this would be his last chance. Ample reason to insert an interview, yes? One pitch after the videotape rolled, *crack*! Yaz drove the ball deep to rightfield.

The director screeched, "Lose the effect! Get it out!" While his T.D. groped, the cameraman knew immediately. He simply framed the soaring home run in the right half of his viewfinder as Yastrzemski continued talking in the upper left. No question about it, we were revolutionizing baseball coverage.

These great moments were brought to you by our so-called "A" production team. I, meanwhile, produced the secondary or "B" (as in *blooper*) games.

One evening in 1977, ABC Engineering assigned us a technical director who had just converted from a career as senior audio man. He had never switched live video *in his life*, but his bosses seemed confident.

"Besides," they said, "your telecast is the second game of a double header. We'll schedule the entire crew for the first game. You can use it as rehearsal."

Rehearsal? Right. It was more like a final cigarette while the firing squad was ordered to lock and load. This poor T.D. shouldn't have been permitted to use the remote channel-changer in his own home, let alone switch a network telecast.

Times like this, I inched a little closer to Joe Aceti, our director. Aceti was a former All-America catcher at Colgate in the late '50s. Sometime between then and now, he'd taken on the imposing look of a Japanese sumo wrestler—massive, squatty, but still very vigorous in his forties.

This physical presence belied his gentle soul. Joe was so genuine, such a humanist in the political underworld of network television, that people rallied to him instinctively. He had endless patience with the pickup crews and malfunctioning equipment that we seemed to draw every week. A mainstay of ABC Sports all the way back to the '68 Grenoble Olympics, he was the ideal director for blooper, er, "B" baseball.

Between games of this doubleheader, we stood in the parking lot of old Metropolitan Stadium in Bloomington, Minnesota, just outside our truck. Next to Aceti, I was a mere child—26 years old, quaking at the specter of the next three hours. Together, we had survived the loss of all three slo-mos in Houston one night, the death of our main cover camera (high above home plate) in Atlanta, a union slowdown in Pittsburgh. Aceti always made it work. Now I wanted him to promise me another miracle.

"Kid, we don't have a chance," he insisted.

"Wh-what?" I stammered.

"Not a fucking chance. This guy is brain-dead."

"But Joey, we just gave him a whole game to rehearse."

"Kid, we can rehearse from now until February. It wouldn't matter. This guy is going to make a hundred mistakes tonight."

"A hundred?"

"You count 'em."

Sure enough, it was the worst telecast I've ever seen. I didn't count, but 100 mistakes for the technical director would be a conservative estimate. He was red-faced, mumbling apologies in what would be his only attempt at video switching. After this telecast, he returned to audio.

At one point, I threw a felt-tip pen at the monitor wall. It rebounded and stained my white sweater. Later, Aceti threw his headset down on the console.

"Take any fuckin' camera you want!" he screamed at the T.D. "Go ahead! You're gonna take what you want anyway. Why should I waste my time callin' 'em?"

Incredible, but true, the technical director was only half our problem this night. The other half was roosting in the announce booth—Mark "The Bird" Fidrych of the Detroit Tigers.

Fidrych had been a sensation in '76, compiling a 19–9 record and winning the American League's Rookie of the Year award. He attracted sellout crowds wherever he pitched that season. But now in '77, he was dogged by shoulder and knee problems. Idling on the disabled list, he was Jim Spence's idea of a guest analyst.

In advance, we'd known they didn't call this guy "The Bird" for nothing. He knelt down to manicure the pitching mound by hand, then *spoke to the baseball* before delivering to home plate. As a broadcaster, he stayed right in character.

In commercial before the eighth inning, Aceti framed a shot of the announce booth, just as we'd agreed in our production meeting. But "The Bird" had flown.

"Where's Fidrych?" I asked Al Michaels, a godsend as "B" play by play man in those early years.

"I don't know, T-Bone. After the last out, he jumped up and ran out of here without saying a word."

Leaving Michaels's IFB open, I said to Aceti, "You know, this whole night has been such a disaster, let's have some fun here. Can Camera 2 see Fidrych as he comes back?"

"Anything you want, kid," said Aceti.

"Al," I said, "you're on your own."

We came out of commercial to the kind of behind-the-scenes shot that David Letterman's show has made popular. Fidrych—shirttail hanging out, ABC-provided necktie askew (he didn't own one), Harpo Marx curls drooping—slid along a railing, hopped down three steps like a wounded whooping crane, and went *plop,* swoop-diving into his chair beside Michaels.

This was on the air.

Al said, " 'Bird,' we're doing a game here. Where've you been?"

Fidrych, dead-blank of expression, looked Michaels right in the eye and said, "At the commode."

"The commode." Same place he was taking our careers, I later told Michaels and Aceti.

When Fidrych wasn't leaving "Bird" droppings on us, our regular analysts were Bob Gibson and the late Norm Cash. Like the rest of us, they felt the strain of being "B" team for a network that had never broadcast baseball. Sometimes they compensated by trying to be funny. Operative word: *trying.* One night, before Baltimore had refurbished its downtown waterfront area, they treated the audience to this exchange:

CASH: I like it here in Baltimore.

GIBSON: What do you mean by that?

CASH: Well, for excitement last night, I went downtown and watched hubcaps rust.

MICHAELS: Stay tuned for a few minutes, folks, and we'll give you Cash's home address, because Gibson and I don't want to hear from you.

Yeah, we were going to revolutionize TV baseball. One of my brainstorms was to ask the managers if they'd wear wireless microphones during our telecasts. Surprisingly, Major League Baseball had no policy against this. Nobody had ever asked. But rather than tempt fate with a formal request to the league office, I simply asked individual managers once I'd established a relationship. My journalism education was at work once again: Cultivate sources, establish mutual trust, ask for access. Most managers said okay.

It made for great television, a more inside view of the game than previously seen. One night in Houston, we heard Cincinnati Manager Sparky Anderson tell one of his coaches that the game would eventually turn on a match-up between his reliever, Fred Norman, and Astros pinch hitter Leon Roberts. At that moment, neither player was yet in the game. But sure enough, a few innings later, Norman struck out Roberts with two runners on base to preserve a 4–2 Cincinnati victory.

Even NBC was impressed. They copied our technique, doubling the chance for X-rated baseball vernacular to scorch the airwaves. One Saturday on an NBC game, the Dodgers' Joe Ferguson cruised into third base on a teammate's hit. It was an easy play—he didn't even have to slide. Yet third-base coach Tommy Lasorda, wearing an NBC microphone, launched into a fusillade of false chatter: "Attaway, Joe. Attaway, baby. Way to go. Way to hustle. Way to dig."

In a tight close-up, Ferguson looked at Lasorda like he was crazy. Clear as the game commentators, Ferguson was heard:

"WHAT THE FUCK IS WRONG WITH YOU?"

One moment too late, Lasorda jumped away and clapped both hands on his wireless mike. He had that caught-in-the-cookie-jar look.

Undaunted, I approached Texas Rangers manager Frank Lucchesi one June evening in Arlington, Texas. Lucchesi was a lovable little Italian elf. He was especially receptive this night, coming home from a fabulous road trip, riding an eight-game winning streak—longest in club history.

When I asked him to wear a mike, Frank immediately started unbuttoning his uniform shirt. His brown eyes brightened at the thought of network exposure.

We discussed his vocabulary.

"I never use *fuck*," he said.

"Never?"

"Never."

"What about the hyphenated words?"

"You mean *'cock-sucker'* or *'mother-fucker'*?"

"Yeah."

"No. Never."

"How 'bout *'son of a bitch'*?"

"No. I'd say the only thing you might hear from me is *damn* or *hell.* You know, like, 'What the hell is Randle doing so close to the line?' Or 'He hit Nellie's best damn pitch.' Is that okay?"

"Sure, that's okay, Frank."

I then spent 10 minutes going through the clubhouse, telling every player about Lucchesi's mike. Most felt that the best strategy was to stay away from him. Nellie Briles and Jim Sundberg, the battery that night, promised they'd be positive altar boys if their manager came to the mound.

And they were. When Chicago had runners at first and third, the Rangers were like church mice in a conference with Lucchesi to deploy their infield. Later, when a brief rain squall threatened to wash out the White Sox' 4–0 lead in the fourth inning, we heard Frank tell the ground crew,

"Take your time" covering the field. It was nice, harmless stuff.

In the ninth inning, with Chicago leading 6–3, the Rangers' first two batters were retired easily. I instructed Michaels to read the commercial billboards and prepare for a "panic close." This uneventful telecast was soon to be video history.

Suddenly, the next two Rangers reached base. Texas could tie with a home run. But coming up was Bill Fahey, the team's worst hitter. Lucchesi would love to have pinch-hit in this spot, but Fahey was his last available catcher. Earlier, Sundberg had been removed for a pinch runner. And the previous day in Boston, catcher John Ellis, the team's hottest hitter at .419, had suffered a grotesque compound fracture of his leg.

Lucchesi's front office had promised a replacement in time for this game, but there'd been a snag. The new catcher wouldn't arrive until the next afternoon. His hands tied, his eight-game winning streak headed down the drain, Lucchesi sadly watched Fahey leave the on-deck circle. He then looked to the heavens, just as Aceti took an extreme close-up and ordered his microphone opened.

"WHERE'S MY FUCKING CATCHER?"

Within weeks, Major League Baseball banned my little innovation on all networks. Among other things, we'd confirmed the wisdom of National Football League policy in this area: No wearing of live mikes by players or coaches; no sideline audio from the mikes on hand-held cameras.

The only legal way to catch an NFL profanity is through parabola microphones that audio assistants carry on the field. These dish-shaped mikes are meant to catch a variety of diffuse sounds, rather than a single voice. But sometimes . . .

One Thanksgiving Day in the early '70s, Detroit Lions coach Joe Schmidt saw his running back knocked out of bounds very near a first down. Racing to the scene, he wound up with his face inside a parabola mike. Schmidt demanded of the line judge:

"GIVE US A GOOD SPOT, YA COCK-SUCKER!"

Pro football bloopers rarely climaxed in that kind of profane exclamation. But that's not to say they weren't amusing.

In a 1984 Thursday night prime-time game, Washington at Minnesota, ABC's commentators heard Redskin quarterback Joe Theismann calling "Yellow-30," the dummy audible that he'd explained to Summerall, Madden, Grossman, and me.

O. J. SIMPSON: Just this high—I guess we're about forty rows up—if I was a defensive safety for the Vikings, every time I hear "Yellow-30"—

DON MEREDITH: "Yellow-30"—

SIMPSON: —I'd run to my right side because that's what the Redskins are doing. Now I picked that up all the way up here, Don.

MEREDITH: Yeah, but you're much more clever than a lot of those fellows down there. They've been hittin' each other all night long.

SIMPSON: Let's see if we can hear it.

FRANK GIFFORD: Third down and 6.

JOE THEISMANN: Set! Yellow-30! Yellow-30!

SIMPSON: Uh-oh. A run to the left.

THEISMANN: Hut! Hut! (Hands off to Keith Griffin, who runs up the middle.)

ALL: (Laughter.)

GIFFORD: Griffin up the middle.

MEREDITH: See that. Yeah, I'm glad you picked that up.

I met Madden the next morning at New York Jets head-quarters as we prepared for our weekend game. The moment we saw each other, we stammered incredulously.

"Did you . . . ?"

"I know. Did you . . . ?"

"Can you believe . . . ?"

"No, I can't."

Still, O. J.'s gaffe did not nearly rank with the ABC/NFL bloopers of all time. Most *Monday Night Football* historians would vote for a 1971 night in Houston. The Astrodome was emptying during the final minutes of a lopsided Oiler defeat. One fan, awakening from a brief nap, noticed a camera pointed into his sleepy eyes. "Network assholes," he must have thought, throwing the rude finger. Meredith took one look at him and said, "They're number one in the nation."

Other *Monday Night* observers might vote for the fan in Buffalo, who held up a sign reading, "Cosell for President." Once on camera, the man flipped his cardboard to reveal "FUCK COSELL."

My favorite, however, was the night in Detroit when Howard marveled about a pass reception. "What a catch!" he exclaimed. Then with typical overstatement: ". . . the receiver variously bound and circumscribed by two defenders."

Meredith, pausing only a half-beat, asked, "Aren't we all?"

At NBC, the football blooper of the '80s belonged to a commentator named Reggie Rucker. A former wide receiver with Cleveland and New England, Rucker understood the credibility that attaches to firsthand information. He must have believed our CBS philosophy: "Deliver your research verbatim, chapter and verse. The viewer is reassured to hear you say, 'I spoke to Coach So-and-So last night, and he said . . .'"

Rucker did exactly that one Sunday afternoon during a Cincinnati telecast. Said he'd had dinner the previous night with Bengal coach Sam Wyche and that Wyche had told him x, y, and z. This came as a revelation to the coach. The next day, he told reporters he'd seen Rucker onfield for 30 seconds prior to the game. Period.

At CBS, our commentators had their moments. In 1983, Dick Vermeil observed San Diego's Sam Claphan in a fight with two Dallas Cowboys.

"You don't have to teach him anything about fighting," Vermeil said of Claphan. "He's half Cherokee Indian."

Ouch.

Summerall once heard Madden explain that San Francisco's John Frank, an off-season medical student, kept a daily log of surgeries and other hospital procedures he observed. Translating that ritual to football, he'd begun keeping a diary of practices and team meetings.

"Sort of like the diary of *Anne* Frank," Pat offered.

Ugh. Letter writers correctly pointed out that Anne Frank's life, tragically cut short at 15, was not a frivolous subject. She died in a Nazi concentration camp near the end of World War II. Her diary, found after the war and published as *Anne Frank: The Diary of a Young Girl*, is a story of fear and flight for Jewish exiles in her native Amsterdam, Holland.

One lengthy letter from San Francisco mentioned that John Frank is also Jewish. Another viewer sent me *The Diary* and insisted that I pass it on to Summerall.

For insensitivity, that moment ranked with Tom Brookshier's statement about the University of Louisville basketball team in 1983. After reading a scripted promo for an upcoming Louisville game, Brookshier ad-libbed, "Denny Crum always has a great team at Louisville. They have a collective IQ of about forty, but they can play basketball."

His analyst partner, former Cowboy safety Charlie Waters, may have been a rookie that year, but he recognized a television *Titanic* when he heard it.

"Oh, don't say things like that," he said, throwing Tommy a life jacket.

"It's the truth," said Brookie, leaping into the icy waves.

Only Brookshier, so naive, so sincere the next day in his remorse, could have survived that. And guess whom the University of Louisville invited to tour its campus and speak at that season's athletic banquet? That's right. Our Thomas.

On the production side, our worst moment was a Giants-Rams game produced by Chuck Milton. Late in the first half, Milton came out of commercial to find that a crossbar had broken loose and fallen to the turf. It lay there on its side like a kindergartner's misjudged capital *U*.

Workmen appeared with ladders and wrenches while Milton did eight minutes and 20 seconds of fill. Bemused players sat on their helmets. John Robinson, in keeping with his personality, enjoyed the moment more than anybody.

Finally, the goalpost was fixed. It was time to play ball again. The Giants broke their huddle and came toward the line of scrimmage. But the referee stopped them, waved them back. Milton had suddenly decided to take another commercial. Without a play intervening since the last commercial and *after filling for more than eight minutes!*

Writing about it the next day, Phil Mushnick of the *New York Post* began his column, "Try this on for ridiculous."

When I asked Milton for an explanation that afternoon, he shrugged, "As soon as I did it, I knew it was wrong."

The guy used to drive me wild—a walking, breathing blooper, able to undo an entire staff's good work on any given weekend. Every time I watched his tapes, it gave me a crisis of confidence. Had I lost my ability to teach?

Early in 1983, when the Redskins were defending Super Bowl champions, I called Milton into my office one weekday before his departure for Washington. For reasons previously explained, I asked him to capture the scene in RFK Stadium.

I told him about my days as statistician in the *Monday Night Football* booth—how ABC was in commercial during the best moments of the evening. After Redskin touchdowns, the band would strike up the only truly stirring fight song in pro football. An entire stadium would sing. It was as close as the NFL could come to a collegiate atmosphere.

Even Cosell was moved. He danced in circles, spraying spittle and cigar ashes on everybody as he adapted his own lyrics to serenade Gifford:

> Hail to the Giffer,
> Hail, Gifferoo,
> On, Brave Red Giffer,
> Fight for Gifferoo.

My story brought a smile to Milton's face. But did he understand? America had never *seen* this. And *now* was the time. After a decade of indifferent football in D.C., Gibbs, Theismann, Riggins, and The Hogs had rejuvenated a wonderful tradition. The old George Allen passion was back at RFK.

The NFL, despite its wonderful athletes, has nothing like Texas's "Hook 'Em, Horns" or the "Notre Dame Victory March," or tiger paws on Clemson cheerleaders' pretty cheeks. When we had something remotely similar, I told Milton, we should exploit hell out of it.

He nodded.

All I wanted was for him to place a few effects mikes near the Redskin Band. Then get it on the air once. Just once. Washington was scoring an all-time NFL record number of points that year. The band played after every touchdown and field goal. There would be plenty of opportunities. Just give me one.

He nodded again.

The day after his game, Milton appeared in my office.

"I couldn't get it," he said.

"What do you mean?"

"I couldn't get it."

"You mean they didn't play 'Hail to the Redskins' yesterday? Are you saying that, for the first time since George Preston Marshall recruited a bunch of postal workers in 1937 and formed the Redskin Band, they didn't play at a Washington home game? Is that it? Do we have a big story here?"

Milton grinned and hung his head. "No. I mean I'm sorry. We just couldn't get it."

What do you say to that? I figured I'd try *showing* him.

For the playoffs that year, I had the song's lyrics typed into our Chyron character generator. I asked our audio man to mike the band as if he were doing a PBS telecast of the New York Philharmonic. Then I asked Sandy Grossman to plot a live montage of stadium scenes with his camera crew. This was going to feel like Michigan–Ohio State.

Minutes before the San Francisco–Washington NFC Championship, I stepped into the Chyron trailer. There, I underscored the day's most unusual assignment: Lyrics must change on the beat, keeping pace with the song, just like the old Mitch Miller show. All we lacked was Mitch's bouncing ball.

"Do you guys want Sandy to call the changes?" I asked.

"No," said my production assistant, a young man I'd nicknamed 'The Ohio Rifle' for his wicked tennis serve. "We've got it cold."

" 'Rifle,' one more time, you listened to the song and you're sure you've got the lyrics correct?"

"Absolutely, Terry. You want to see them?"

"No, I take your word for it. And you're sure you can make the Chyron changes?"

"We've been rehearsing all morning. I sing and Bruno [the technician] follows along."

"Okay. You understand this is going to *make* our telecast today?"

"We believe it."

The Redskins cooperated. When they scored their third touchdown to go ahead 21–0, I felt a kind of *now,* a kind of absolute *correctness,* that rarely emerges in the complex, subjective world of live production. Into my headset, I gave the command that everybody had been waiting three periods to hear: "After the [extra] point, 'Hail to the Redskins.'"

A producer works hard to be detached. He must be clinical, unemotional—especially in the game's hottest sequences. Once I came to that understanding, no action on an athletic field ever excited me during air. Even the biggest plays were simply grist for our mill. But, goddamn it, "Hail to the Redskins" sent tingles up my spine.

Sandy was spectacular with his pictures. Our audience was finally enjoying the best scene in pro football. Even our Chyron lyrics were precisely on the beat. At least, they started that way:

> Hail to the Redskins,
> Hail Victory!
> Braves on the warpath
> Fight for old D.C.
> Run or pass and score—
> We want a lot more—
> Beat 'em, swamp 'em, touchdown,
> Let the points soar!
> Fight on, fight on
> Till you have won,
> Sons of Wash-ing-ton.

At that point, the crowd sang, "Rah, rah, rah," and returned to the chorus—the first four lines. But will you believe that "The Ohio Rifle" didn't have a second chorus loaded in his Chyron?

While the crowd reprised, "Hail to the Redskins, Hail Victory," we were still showing "Sons of Wash-ing-ton."

"CHANGE CHYRON!" I roared.

"That's all there is," "The Rifle" protested meekly.

"THE HELL IT IS! LISTEN TO THESE FUCKING PEOPLE! DOES IT SOUND LIKE THEY'RE FIN-ISHED?"

"But . . ."

"FUCK! Sandy, lose the matte."

"But, Terry . . ."

"GODDAMN IT, RIFLE! I DON'T FUCKING BE-LIEVE THIS. I CAN'T BELIEVE WE TALK ABOUT THIS FOR HALF A SEASON AND THEN BLOW IT!"

"Terry, that's all that's in the media guide."

"THE MEDIA GUIDE? THE FUCKING MEDIA GUIDE? YOU TOLD ME YOU *LISTENED* TO THIS FUCKING SONG! JESUS CHRIST, I DON'T BE-LIEVE IT!"

After the game, I thought, "What the hell. Maybe Milton's right. Maybe you *can't* get this song on the air correctly."

Somewhere in the early '80s, I became aware that television wasn't the only medium for our bloopers. As virtually every daily newspaper added a sports television reviewer, the press became a window on some extremely dumb moments. It didn't seem to matter how capable the executive. Look through the clips—you'll find that the biggest names in our business have tasted their own shoe leather occasionally.

Sometimes, the error could be excused as youthful exuberance. For instance, Michael Weisman, executive producer of NBC Sports, is a thoughtful, well-balanced man who now handles the press very well. But in January 1979, he was newly wed, newly promoted, and heavily under the influence of Don Ohlmeyer, the impresario who'd left ABC to make over NBC Sports.

On the morning of Super Bowl XIII, Pete Alfano quoted Weisman extensively in a New York *Daily News* article headlined, "NBC's Ego on Parade."

> Weisman is convinced it's a young man's business. The pay, the glamour and the travel are appealing to a kid just out of school. "I remember when I was single and I would exploit the situation," he says. "If you meet a girl in Kansas City and tell her you work for the Miles Shoe Store, it's not the same as when you say you're a producer for NBC. Then she asks you to dance."
>
> The temptation is to milk it while you can. "I've been called a genius," Weisman said . . .

Yow. But understand, Mike was 29 years old that morning.

Other times, blooper quotes may be put down to competitive fervor and pride of authorship. Ohlmeyer, one of the most respected men in sports or entertainment television, offered an opinion when he first saw our CBS Chalkboard: "It's much ado about nothing—a gimmick that is good for publicity more than anything else."

A week later, Ohlmeyer returned to character, sending us gracious congratulations on our Super Bowl XVI coverage. But his initial reaction shows how vulnerable we all were to the press. Being in your early thirties, reading your name every day, knowing that your little world memorized these quotes every morning—it damaged your thinking sometimes.

The cleverest newspaper columnist to recognize these forces and play on them is Rudy Martzke of *USA Today*. Martzke's column became an industry phenomenon when it first appeared in 1982, in part because his voice is national. By 1988, *USA Today*'s readership was 5.5 million—

the broadest forum ever for daily review of sports television.

Acknowledging his influence, the CBS Sports talent coordinator once stormed into my office and bleated, "Do you realize that Dick Stockton calls him every day? Every single day?"

Like a Boy Scout camping out, Martzke has great facility for spontaneous combustion—rub two network executives together and start a fire. In the spring of '86 for instance, he ran this item:

> As the world turns at NBC: No less than Washington Redskins quarterback Joe Theismann . . . [is] being considered for NFL duty.
>
> Theismann, coming off a severe leg fracture, might not be healthy enough to play this season—or ever. But as an NFL analyst, he appeals to NBC Sports executive producer Michael Weisman: "He will be a very credible broadcaster. He's had a lot of experience and exposure."

When Martzke phoned for my reaction, I asked, "How do you *do* it? How do you get these guys to give you a 'wish list'? When we sign Theismann, NBC is going to look ridiculous."

"What makes you so sure?" he asked.

"Rudy, I don't want to say anything on the record, but Theismann was my classmate at Notre Dame. If I can't get him to come to CBS, I should probably give up this job."

"He what?" asked Martzke. "He was your *classmate*?"

"Yeah, class of '71."

"Oh, wait till I tell Weisman. He'll shit."

CBS signed Theismann a few months later.

Having encountered this routine so many times, knowing it so thoroughly, you'd figure I was not susceptible, right? From an August 1985 Martzke column:

"I've read where people think CBS' [John] Madden and [Pat] Summerall have become No 1," NBC Sports executive producer Mike Weisman said Thursday. "Well, I've told Dick Enberg and Merlin Olsen this year we're reclaiming No. 1 . . . I've never seen Merlin so hungry. . . . I told him, 'It's a Super Bowl year for us, and I want to be No. 1 again.' He agreed. We're going to see a livelier Merlin Olsen."

You'd think I might have been strong enough to withstand such nonsense. Or smart enough to go take a cold shower. But I was upset that Rudy hadn't challenged Weisman, that he'd allowed his platform to be exploited for something so blatantly untrue.

How foolish of me. Rudy's bread and butter was controversy. He wasn't going to edit Weisman, nor muzzle him.

Rather than rebut in *USA Today,* I decided to take my case directly to the viewers in a halftime piece. Goddamnit, I was going to call in the experts—head coaches of the NFL—and assemble their opinions into a monument to CBS football.

Bill Parcells had given me the idea. One Saturday the previous season, he'd ranted to me, "You know those guys from NBC aren't even in the same league with you. They were in here for our Kansas City game last week. I never saw them all weekend. Nobody calls, nobody comes to practice.

"Then we fall two touchdowns behind, and they're on my ass right away. They don't like my offense. I'm 'too conservative.' Hell, they don't even know what we're doing. These guys never speak to me, and yet they go on the air and criticize? You should have heard them bailing out in the fourth quarter when we came back and won the fuckin' game."

After the Weisman quotes appeared, I phoned Parcells

and asked him if he'd paraphrase that conversation on camera. His interview with Joan Vitrano was a classic:

> PARCELLS: Relative to the other coverage in the NFL, I think [CBS's style is] far superior—the diligence with which your people prepare . . . is far and above what I've witnessed. . . . It's like—it's kinda like filet mignon compared to Taylor ham on a hard roll. Just a big difference.

We collected similar sound bites—although none that quite matched Parcells's for distinctive Jersey metaphor—mostly from NFC coaches. The only AFC coach we approached, John Mackovic of Kansas City, came through with a ringing endorsement. He swore that our Dick Vermeil, after three days of film study, was better prepared than some of his own staff. I knew several other AFC coaches who would have joined the chorus. But I didn't want to impose on them, knowing they lived with NBC almost weekly.

Our edited piece was hard-sell, filling the entire halftime of a prime-time, preseason telecast. Not surprisingly, it brought a storm of protest both from within and without. CBS Sports staffers who weren't involved with NFL football thought I was beating my own chest too loudly. NBC, of course, had a predictable response. And Martzke felt attacked on the air, a reaction no television executive should ever engender. Reviewing the weekend programs, as he does every Monday, Rudy wrote:

> **Worst Move:** CBS NFL executive producer Terry O'Neil, normally a class act, allowed himself to be pressured by hyped statements from NBC executive producer Mike Weisman. As a result, O'Neil had the highly respected Summerall narrate a halftime segment Saturday on the Dallas–Houston game in which CBS unabashedly claimed to televise football better. Who said so? Tom Landry, Mike Ditka, Joe Gibbs and Bill Parcells, all

coaches of the NFC, which CBS televises. . . . CBS
should bill itself for the ad

If ever an event seemed headed for the Blooper Hall of
Fame, it was the 1983 Pan American Games in Caracas,
Venezuela.

In essence, the Pan Am Games are an Olympics for the
Western Hemisphere. They include all the Summer
Olympic sports, plus several others that are popular in the
Americas. For the powerful USA team, this competition is
significant in a pre-Olympic year. But for the lesser sporting nations, these *are* their Olympics. In 1983, more than
4,000 athletes from 37 countries were expected to partici-
pate.

Confirming its rank among the three sports divisions in
the '60s and '70s, CBS had become the network of the Pan
American Games. ABC and NBC did the Olympics. CBS
did the Pan Ams. And not well.

Nonetheless, when I was asked, in June 1981, about the
'83 Caracas Games, I replied by memo to our executive
staff: "It would offer a terrific opportunity for us to demonstrate how far CBS Sports has progressed by the summer of 1983." I recommended that we broadcast twice as
many hours as CBS had done from San Juan in 1979.

So I asked for it.

In April 1982, Carl Lindemann and I led a contingent
to Caracas to secure American television rights and work
out a shared broadcast plan with the Venezuelans. Drawing on my four Olympic Games at ABC, I expected to
meet an organizing committee of two dozen or so, each
person responsible for housing, transportation, creden-
tials, security, and so forth.

Instead, we were greeted by two men. Representing the
organizing committee was Dr. Osvaldo Colmenarez,
slightly built, fully gray in his early forties, and dark-
skinned. His eyes were deep brown, heavily lidded, with

large circles underneath, like a basset hound's. His own colleagues called him "Dog Eyes."

Speaking for Venezuelan television was German Landaetta, a 5-foot 4-inch bundle of nerves. Neither man had the first clue about staging or broadcasting these Games.

For one solid day, from 8 A.M. to 8 P.M., I sat in a conference room with them. Nothing of the competition schedule or television coverage had been fixed. It was a rare opportunity to program the Games, the way we did *Sports Saturday/Sunday,* placing glamour events on our weekend air dates for live coverage. These may not have been the Olympics, but at least they could be tailored for maximum effect. No American network had ever enjoyed such a blank canvas in plotting international Games.

As we worked, the two Venezuelans passed from ignorance to skepticism to genuine enthusiasm. They began to see my vision of the first "live" Pan American Games for U.S. television viewers.

"Dog Eyes," in particular, grew intense. He refused any suggestion of breaking for lunch or dinner, instead buzzing his secretary for tiny cups of native cappuccino, heavy as mud, teeming with caffeine.

"They will bring anything you like," he said. "Let's keep working."

Was this a rare, compulsive American personality in the land of *mañana*? Could we be so lucky? I didn't immediately know, but his attitude made me hopeful.

By the time we finished, the morning's hard, equatorial sunlight had been replaced by fluorescent bulbs. The three of us were exhausted, but warmth and partnership were tangible in the room.

Then our CBS business affairs colleague entered and cut what seemed an unfair deal: The Venezuelans would give us exclusive U.S. rights, provide all hardware (cameras, mobile units, microwave transmission, etc.) for the venues and our CBS Broadcast Center, supply technical crews, allow CBS production personnel to produce their "world feed," guarantee my competition schedule to provide mostly live coverage throughout our 16 1/2 hours on the air —all for $900,000. (This was *half* the price of a three-hour afternoon college football game—rights only!) The final nail: Failure to deliver on any aspect of the contract would mean a commensurate deduction in CBS's payment.

Privately, I thought, "Talk about Yankee imperialism and rape of the Third World." But our hosts didn't seem bothered. Colmenarez's "dog eyes" actually seemed expressive for the first time as he proposed a toast. He sent us back to New York with great optimism.

On the return flight, Lindemann said to me, "You know, we'll make some headway with these Games. Once Wyman and Jankowski [our corporate bosses] see the visibility and the profit, maybe we can get this network interested in Seoul [1988 Summer Olympics]."

There followed six months when we heard nothing from Caracas. Then in November 1982, we received a new competition schedule. As Lindemann summarized, "It would appear that everything has changed, including the dates!"

My master plan was in tatters. I wrote "Dog Eyes": "I'm sure you recall the sunny spring afternoon when we labored twelve hours or more. . . . While certain of my colleagues might make this argument on legal, contractual grounds, I appeal to you as a producer: Let the Games unfold *live*. . . ."

But "Dog Eyes" had bigger problems than the start of the high jump and medley relay. In early 1983, a fire gutted his organizing committee offices. Arson was suspected. Two weeks later, the Venezuelan government devalued the bolivar. The free-fall of world oil prices had left his country's one-dimensional economy in ruin. Currency reserves declined sharply, and creditors demanded payment on Venezuela's massive foreign debt.

Amid suggestions that the Games would be canceled, we made another trip to Caracas in February 1983. Our proud hosts rejected the rumors outright. As a show of good faith, "Dog Eyes" asked his architect to take us on a survey of Pan Am venues.

The architect was a very precise, very proper gentleman who wore a Western-style string tie. He puffed constantly through an elegant cigarette holder, pinched lightly by the tips of his thumb and index finger, the way international producer moguls do at the Cannes Film Festival.

He waved an arm sweepingly at the site of his International Broadcast Center. He dramatically unrolled sectional views and detailed floor plans for a ten-story building that would house all the Western Hemisphere's broadcasters.

There was only one problem. The architect was gesticulating at a hole in the ground. The only suggestion of a building was a concrete floor in the subbasement with a few structural rods poking up. No workers were in sight. Yet this man kept insisting that all would be in readiness five months later when we returned.

At my side, a hefty, comforting figure was unconvinced. Joe Aceti whispered to me, "Kid, if you have a choice, take the basement. If they finish anything, they'll finish that."

Thank God, once again, for Aceti. Seven months earlier, ABC Sports had hand-delivered him to us. Not only did they deny him the director's chair on "A" baseball, which he truly merited, but they replaced him on "B" games. When he phoned me with this development, I thought he was joking. But in the coldest tone I've ever heard from him, Aceti said, "Kid, I'm leaving ABC whether you hire me or not." We had him working at CBS within three weeks.

Aceti still called me "Kid" occasionally. But once I passed 30, he added the whimsical alternative "Whitey." It was more than the difference in our flesh tones, said Joe. (He had some Indian ancestry, which explained his copper-colored skin.) It was more a matter of attitude. A street-smart New Yorker, Aceti would observe me in tennis gear or preppy turned-up shirt collars and say, "You know, when God made you, he made the perfect white man."

The young guys at CBS loved hearing Joe call me "Whitey," a nickname they only dared use in private. For my part, I loved hearing Aceti call me anything. With his long experience in blooper baseball, he was perfect for these Pan American Games.

"Would you mind if we survey an alternate site for our broadcast center?" he delicately asked the architect.

Joe then whispered to me, "Whitey, not a fucking chance this'll be ready on time."

Later, we made a tour of competition sites. The 28,000-seat Olympic Stadium was dingy, its infield a mix of bare spots and crabgrass, its track a lumpy mess of cinders and clay. The University gym, site of gymnastics, was actually abandoned. Its floor of two-inch oak strips was badly warped from a leaky roof. There was barely enough house lighting to see each other, let alone illuminate a television picture. Worst of all, at neither site was there a whiff of renovation underway.

Over a drink that night, "Dog Eyes" chillingly answered my April 1982 question about his personality: "You Americans. You worry too much. Everything will be finished when you return for the Games. You will see."

Over the next six months, the Venezuelans made only one concession. In June, they admitted that the architect's new broadcast center wouldn't be ready. But they promised full facilities in the adjacent, government-run Venezolana de Televisión (VTV), Channel 8 in Caracas.

CBS Sports management also made an important concession, allowing me to add facilities and 40 American technicians from F & F Productions of St. Petersburg, Florida. I now understood why we had offered "Dog Eyes" only $900,000. There were added costs. My colleagues had been through this Pan Am scam in Mexico and Puerto Rico. I began to realize these weren't the Olympic Games.

Aceti and I arrived in Caracas on Sunday, July 31, exactly two weeks before opening ceremonies. Without stopping at our hotel, we went directly from the airport to VTV, Channel 8. A guard seemed confused when we asked to see the "CBS complex." Nor did a second guard understand. Finally, their supervisor led us through a maze of hallways to a large double door.

We stepped inside. It was stark *empty.* Nothing. Just concrete pillars and a little soundproofing along the walls. If someone had told us it was a furniture warehouse or a storage area, we'd have believed it. There was absolutely nothing to indicate television—no studio, no control room, no videotape room, no offices, none of the things we'd detailed in April 1982.

Stricken, we went back through the double door into the hallway. Aceti looked out a window at the familiar ten-story hole in the ground. It hadn't changed an inch since our survey in February.

"Cheer up, Whitey," he said. "Look! Our new broadcast center! How'dya like it? Nice, huh? And it'll be ready in two weeks, just like the architect said."

For the next four days, I went to one meeting after another. "Dog Eyes" and his associates were too embarrassed to be straight with me. But from various sources, I learned the awful truth. A U.S.-based representative of Ampex told me the Venezuelans hadn't made a $1.8 million payment on videotape machines. His company had halted delivery somewhere between Redwood City, California, and Miami. A customs official told me that Spanish-built mobile units, assigned to cover the major venues, were impounded in the port of Maracaibo, also pending payment.

Meanwhile, virtually nothing changed in our empty warehouse. Near the end of that first week, I found Aceti as frustrated as I've ever seen him. Slamming an antiquated telephone receiver to the floor, he anguished, "Kid, you want us to make nice pictures fly through the air in eight days, and we can't even get a phone call out of here. We got no fucking chance."

"Jo-jo," I replied, "I think it may be time for my 'ugly American' routine."

That evening, in a meeting with the Venezuelan government minister of finance, the minister of youth, the president of VTV, and "Dog Eyes," I cataloged all their deceptions, all their variances from the April 1982 agreement. While sympathizing with their economic plight, I said, "It would be irresponsible of me not to advise my company to abandon this project, unless I begin to see progress tomorrow morning." I left the meeting and repeated my threat to the press, including *The New York Times.*

From that moment, I became public enemy number one in Venezuela. But we began to see action. Equipment arrived, and our American free-lance technicians, working day and night, built a broadcast center with their bare hands.

At the venues, meanwhile, quite independent of my tantrum, construction workers magically appeared. In the last week before the Games, the Venezuelans poured and painted a synthetic track, sodded the Olympic Stadium infield, replaced the gymnasium floor, hung lighting grids in its ceiling, tiled the swimming pool, and landscaped as best they could, planting flowers until an hour before opening ceremonies.

It was a pretty good comeback, though not perfect. Most neglected had been the Pan American Village, set on baking, barren flatland 18 miles east of Caracas. Arriving athletes were handed room keys, only to find that their units had no doors. Windows had no drapes or blinds. At times, there was no running water, no showers, no flushing toilets, and no breeze in the 90-degree heat. Of course, there was no air conditioning.

Cement dust infiltrated hair, clothing, and bedsheets. The racket of drills and electric saws went on past midnight as workers raced the clock. Athletes were booked eight or ten to a small suite. U.S. boxer Steve McCrory said, "This is worse than living in the ghetto in Detroit or New York."

Some athletes simply moved into Caracas hotels. When several American swimmers arrived at our CBS hotel—the Tamanaco International, said to be the best in town—they were aghast to find hardhats tearing up the lobby with jackhammers. (Commentator John Tesh, stepping out of the elevator one morning, caught a concrete sliver under his contact lens, sending him to the hospital with a damaged cornea.)

When we asked the jackhammer jockeys why they were wreaking havoc in the hotel's busiest month ever, one replied, "Nobody ever thought the Games would happen."

Fear not, the *Juegos Deportivos Panamericanos* were on. Now, about televising them . . .

Since that first meeting in April 1982, the Venezuelans had agreed that the opening ceremonies would be produced and directed for the world by CBS personnel from the largest of their brand-new Spanish mobile units. Now, 48 hours before air, they suddenly reneged in a meeting with Aceti.

The ceremonies were more important to them than any competition. Opening pageantry carried the top ticket price, $2, in a 16-day program where most events were free.

A VTV programming official broke into tears as he explained to Aceti, "You must understand. We may not be as good as you Americans, but we are a proud people. This ceremony *is* Venezuela. We cannot have our compatriots know it was televised by Americans. We would be disgraced."

When Joe told me, I understood. But goddamn, this was a helluva time to be hearing his Simón Bolívar Day speech. Even though Aceti and I had been conducting daily seminars for the Venezuelan, Puerto Rican, Mexican, and Cuban technicians—very important to "Dog Eyes" in the April 1982 agreement—they had no capability of covering the ceremonies to an American standard. We had only one alternative.

"Jo-jo," I said, "how many cameras can we put into our unilateral unit at Olympic Stadium?"

F & F had shipped a miniature "flash unit" that, in truth, was not a television truck at all but a motor home. It had been F & F's first mobile unit years ago, and Caracas was to be its last remote before retirement. Only seven feet wide, it was very cramped, especially compared to state-of-the-art trucks which expand to twice that width.

The motor home was outfitted with two cameras and one videotape machine. From this unit, we'd planned to add American accents to the world feed—introducing our commentators, inserting videotape clips tailored to the U.S. audience. Now we'd have to do everything from this camper.

"You saw it, kid. It's got two cameras."

"Yeah, but how many could it take?"

"I don't know. That's a tiny little switcher. Plus there's only monitors for a few cameras and tape machines."

"Yeah, but what if we added some monitors?"

"Whitey, I know your devious little mind. C'mon, what are you thinking?"

"Jo-jo, we gotta do our own opening ceremonies. We can't take a Venezuelan feed."

"Yeah, but how? We got one day to rebuild a mobile unit that's too small for this. And even if we get enough cameras cabled in there, we don't have enough cameramen."

Three CBS cameramen were on site to shoot and edit taped reports. They had no live experience whatever, but so what? Some spare videotape editors were also available.

They had never operated cameras, but their debuts were about to come on a national telecast.

Aceti protested, "First you want me to teach every technician in South and Central America. Now you want me to make cameramen out of guys who've never held a camera in their lives? Kid, they don't *do* this kind of thing."

One of the marvels of sports television is that free-lance technicians—with no apparent attachment to CBS, Aceti, or me—would catch the spirit of this challenge and work nonstop for 36 hours. George Oregera, president of F & F, had one of his men fly immediately from Florida with cameras and other equipment as personal baggage in order to avoid the normal 48-hour customs hassle. Then, to build an intercom system, he bought out Caracas's only Radio Shack.

His crew worked through the night, jamming nine cameras, three videotape machines, and one Chyron into the mobile home. Its suspension sagged visibly. A family of 15 headed for Yellowstone National Park couldn't have overloaded it more heavily.

How unorthodox was this? Aceti's monitor for the helicopter was a three-inch black-and-white, as opposed to the 13-inch diagonal which is normal. At our towering crane position in one endzone, guide wires for the cameraman's "bucket" were snapped by a careless Venezuelan truck driver. The cameraman grew dizzy, swaying in the wind. But, hell, everybody was dizzy for one reason or another.

I, meanwhile, had another problem. The organizing committee and its choreographer had given me complete freedom in structuring the ceremonies for our two-and-a-half-hour CBS broadcast. My format, precise to the second, hinged on a timely arrival by Venezuelan president Luis Herrera Campins. (The Olympic charter, under which these Games were conducted, said the ceremonies could not begin without the head of state.) But the American ambassador to Venezuela had laughed and shaken his head about the president's perfect record in these matters.

"He's never been on time for anything in his life," said the ambassador. "I'd advise you to make some contingency plans."

I met with Herrera Campins's staff. The reason he was always late, they explained, was that nobody else in the country was on time. The president couldn't be seen cooling his heels. It wasn't dignified. But, they said, if I gave them an exact clocking and guaranteed a punctual start, they'd have him on the dot.

Could I believe them? Could I believe anybody in this insane asylum? Might an intentional snafu in the opening ceremonies be their reprisal for my threats in *The New York Times*?

The U.S. ambassador's words rang in my ears. I gave all the president's men a "false count" of two minutes. Needing their leader in place at 4:07, I said, "Precisely 4:05. In his seat." They agreed.

Despite our last-minute production switch, Herrera Campins was my biggest worry as I climbed into our miniature mobile unit that brilliant Sunday. Actually, it felt more like a *Mercury* space capsule. Aceti's enormous shoulder pressed me hard against the door. Outside, I hung a "DO NOT OPEN!" sign. One twist of the door handle would have sent me tipping into the parking lot.

We took the air hopefully, with a look and feel that said, "Olympic Games." After introducing our commentators and previewing several sports, we rolled a seven-minute tape piece on Venezuela's struggle to reach this moment. It was more construction rubble and last-minute soldering than you ever cared to see.

Following the tape, my format called for a shot of Herrera Campins, freshly arrived, then the Parade of Nations. If he was more than two minutes behind schedule, we would simply start without him. After all, he'd been nearly three hours late to dedicate the Pan Am Village.

With a repeat of that performance, we'd go off the air still waiting for him. "Dog Eyes" had given us cueing control of Argentina, first nation in the parade, and I determined to use it in defiance of the Olympic charter, if necessary.

Admiring the first minute of our comprehensive video-tape story, I was distracted by a rustling on one of the monitors. Crowds were parting decisively, as they do when police take control. Into view burst a small, rotund, officious-looking man in full military regalia.

"HE'S EARLY!" I cried. "THE MAN WHO'S NEVER BEEN ON TIME IN HIS LIFE IS FUCKING EARLY!"

"Don't complain, kid," said Aceti. "It's the first thing that's been early in this whole train wreck."

On headset, I spoke to Pierce O'Neil (no relation), our superb production assistant stationed on the stadium entrance ramp with the first of 4,000 athletes.

"Pierce," I said. "This isn't gonna be easy, but I need you to hold Argentina for five more minutes."

"I don't think it'll be a problem," he said. "We'll keep entertaining them through our translator."

I'd once pulled this trick at a Michigan–Ohio State game. Wanting to show all seven minutes of "Script Ohio" (the dotting of the *i*), I'd false-counted the band director to give myself a margin. Goddamn if he wasn't right on time. I had my production assistant hold the Buckeye Marching Band eerily still and silent for nearly two minutes, before 80,000 bewildered home fans, while we waited to finish a tape clip. The band director stared a hole through my P.A., anticipating his cue. But he waited. Now I needed that same kind of cooperation in a foreign land where I was the "ugly American."

"Hold Argentina," I said to Pierce O'Neil every minute, just wanting to hear myself talk. The tape, which had played so well 30 seconds earlier, now seemed endless.

"Hold Argentina."

Two and a half minutes from the tape's conclusion, our

monitor showed one of the truly incongruous pictures of all time. President Tardy was looking at his watch! He made a gruff gesture, circling his hand to indicate, "Let's go." His assistants reached for their walkie-talkies.

"Hold Argentina," I repeated to Pierce O'Neil.

Flanking Pierce were two uniformed soldiers, the kind we grew accustomed to seeing everywhere in this paramilitary state. These looked to be teenagers, one carrying an Uzi 9-mm submachine gun, the other an M-16 rifle. Each had a saber, a heavy cavalry sword with slightly curved blade, dangling at his waist.

"Hold Argentina."

Now our monitors filled with a commotion on the entrance ramp. As Pierce stood in front of the Argentine flag bearer, restraining him, the rifle soldier stripped his saber from its scabbard. Just as he raised the menacing blade, the other soldier knocked Pierce sideways with the butt of his submachine gun.

"Terry, I can't . . . "

The Venezuelan soldiers flung Pierce against a wall, ordered his hands up, and jabbed the Uzi gun barrel into his chest.

"CUE ARGENTINA! CUE ARGENTINA!" I cried.

No sense getting a production assistant killed for a lousy tape-to-live transition. Aceti covered me, simply picking up the parade with Argentina on the track. If anybody noticed, it wasn't *The New York Times*. Their Lawrie Mifflin wrote, "The production went off without a hitch."

Sure. Just ask Pierce O'Neil.

Our second of three weekends was more routine. The 7½ hours were packed with good action, capped by American Rick Carey's backstroke world record just before we left the air Sunday.

That night, I threw a mid-Games party for the staff. My driver-translator, Carlos, insisted that we use his parents' estate. Why not? It had an eight-lane swimming pool, two basketball courts, and a lighted softball stadium. Hell, it was better equipped than some of the competition venues. This was just what our group needed to recharge for the final week of Pan Am madness.

The next evening, I was still nursing a slight hangover. Aceti and I were having dinner on the hotel's open-air veranda when John Faratzis, our track and field producer, approached with Sam Skinner.

Yes, the same Sam Skinner who'd drafted me as Lee Evans's secretary-stenographer at the Munich Olympics of '72. I'd never forgotten him. When I arrived at CBS, I insisted that all our track and field productions include Sam. As the next several hours would prove, he hadn't lost his nose for big stories.

Faratzis, Skinner, and I greeted each other in our familiar code. I called Faratzis "Dad," a nickname he returned to me. Skinner, a black man, had adopted Aceti's creation and called me "Whitey." He delighted in stunned reactions from people who didn't know our long friendship.

"They can't believe I call the boss 'Whitey,' " Sam would laugh.

Faratzis, unusually serious, said, "Dad, we've got some news. You want to finish your dinner first?"

"No, c'mon, sit down. What's up?"

"Whitey, you're going to like this," Sam grinned.

"Tell me. What's happening?"

"Tomorrow morning early, like before dawn," said Faratzis, "ten or twelve of our track and field guys—some of the big names—are leaving."

"Where're they going?" I asked.

"Home. To the old *Estados Unidos*. They can't pass the drug test."

"Some weightlifters got caught today," explained Skinner. "One of 'em was a Canadian who thought he was clean. The word went through the Canadian and U.S. teams like wildfire. This drug test must be tougher than anything they've ever had."

"So these American track and field guys figure it's better to leave than get caught," Aceti summarized.

"You got it," Skinner affirmed. "If they test positive, they're out of the Olympics for life, and a lot of these guys are looking for a big score in Los Angeles [1984 Summer Games] next year."

"Do the athletes know that you know?" I wondered.

"I don't think so," Skinner replied. "I got it from a guy who wouldn't tell."

"So if we show up at the Village and the airport tomorrow morning, these guys won't be hiding from us? They'll be accessible?" I asked.

Skinner laid his palm open to slap five with me.

"That's my boy, 'Whitey.' "

"Sam," I said, "some day we have to tell these young guys how we owned Munich in '72."

Our ambush the next day at 5 A.M. was a complete surprise to the athletes. One crew recorded their departure from the Village. At the airport, 11 of 12 athletes disembarked from their bus to find another CBS crew. Pole vaulter Mike Tully, seeking an escape, stayed aboard until the bus's next stop. There, he encountered our John Tesh with yet another crew.

Skinner, Faratzis, and the others returned to the hotel suite I shared with Brent Musburger just before 9 A.M. I wanted their eyewitness confirmation before running with the story. They had the exodus on videotape, along with some "ambush interviews" that clearly showed the embarrassment of these men in USA warm-up suits.

We broke the story as lead item on CBS Radio's 10 A.M. newscast: Hours before the start of track and field competition, 12 American athletes had departed Caracas. Sources told CBS Sports that they feared the most sophisticated drug-testing apparatus ever used in international sports. In the past two days, 11 athletes had tested positive, including Jeff Michels of Chicago, who would be forced to return his three weightlifting gold medals.

That evening, our report led the *CBS Evening News with Dan Rather*. For dramatic effect, we displayed a vial of anabolic steroid—the one of 91 banned substances most commonly uncovered in these tests—and a syringe that athletes used to inject themselves.

Anabolic steroid is a catalyst for muscle building. Of itself, it does not add strength. But combined with a heavy training program and a huge intake of protein—five meals a day, in many cases—it helps to build muscle quickly. The drug also speeds an athlete's recovery, so he may train harder and more often.

I knew about steroids from my Olympic research days at ABC. In the early '70s, Al Fuerbach of Emporia State (Kansas) went from 200 to 260 pounds in one year. His personal best in the shotput improved from 60 feet and change to a world-class 70 feet plus in that period. Fuerbach's gain was widely believed to be steroid-driven.

Within 24 hours, some of the departed athletes confirmed our story. Back in the States, shotputter Ian Pyka admitted that "each" of the athletes who withdrew "was concerned about the increased testing procedures." Another of the 12, hammer thrower John McArdle, estimated that two-thirds of track and field's top internationals were taking or had taken steroids.

On a story this big, CBS News would normally fly in one of its producer-correspondent teams. But executive producer Howard Stringer allowed us to run with our newsbreak. And so we did. We made the *Evening News* with follow-up reports the next two days and the *CBS Morning News* three days consecutively.

Our third-day *Evening News* story reported that an American sprinter, Lisa Hopkins, had withdrawn from her race, claiming injury. From several sources, we had information that her coach, Chuck Debus, routinely prescribed anabolic steroids as part of his training program.

Debus was a giant in women's track and field. By '83,

his teams had won 10 of the 12 previous women's national championships. I reached him by phone in Southern California. When he wouldn't give me a clear-cut denial, I decided to go ahead and name him. Sam Skinner said that after years of whispers, this was the first such allegation ever broadcast about a track coach—and on the Dan Rather news, no less.

By the final weekend, we were able to summarize the full story: Seventeen athletes, two from the United States, had tested positive, most for anabolic steroids. Ten of these were medal winners. They were stripped of 21 Pan Am medals, including Jeff Michels's three golds. Altogether, it was the most sweeping disqualification pattern in the history of international sport. Of the 12 American track and field athletes who departed so abruptly, only one returned. Mike Tully, who'd gasped at the early-morning sight of John Tesh, came back to Caracas within a few days, won the pole vault, and passed his drug test.

Our CBS team won raves with its hard-news reporting. *USA Today* headlined: "CBS Newsmen Dig, Break Story of USA Athletes Leaving Games." The *Philadelphia Daily News* added: "CBS Sports Secure Covering the News." The *Miami Herald* wrote: "Against long odds, CBS is winning the Battle of Caracas." Even that noted critic, John Madden, had a review. Back in New York, the first thing he said to me was, "Boy, you guys sure put the frosting on the shit down there."

Even more satisfying was the overwhelming approval we won from U.S. athletes. Steroids had been a source of fear to them. While conclusive medical opinion was still a few years away, some researchers theorized that prolonged use could lead to liver damage, shrunken testicles, and sterility. One doctor predicted that a weightman's heavy steroid program could ultimately enlarge his heart to twice its size.

One athlete told me his experiment with the drug had

caused decreased sex drive, unusual growth of body hair, and varied effects on his vocal cords. He said, "I'm so glad we're getting this out into the open. You can't believe how many [American] coaches tell their athletes, 'You have to take these [steroids] if you want to compete with the Europeans.' You can't imagine the doubt and insecurity, thinking, 'No matter how hard I train, it's useless unless I go to the chemicals.' "

By the end of my month in Caracas, I could have used a steroid program myself. I was gaunt and feeble, having gotten no exercise, lost 10 pounds, and developed a sore back. It took months to collect my thoughts about the Pan American Games. Then, in the third week of November, as linebackers and Chalkboard replays dominated my thoughts, a flashback appeared in the hallways of CBS Sports.

It was "Dog Eyes." We embraced like survivors of a world war, reunited after years of dislocation. He'd come to collect whatever portion of his $900,000 remained after CBS finished it deductions. "Dog Eyes" reached for his wallet and joked, "Maybe they will say I owe *them* money." (CBS ultimately paid the Venezuelans $700,000 and pocketed a $600,000 profit on the Games.)

We laughed about our summertime misadventure. In particular, he recalled my passionate two-hour plea to have the USA-Brazil basketball final restored to a Saturday afternoon for live broadcast. This was yet another broken promise of the organizing committee. In Spanish, nine international basketball officials debated my fate. The clock showed 2 A.M. The chairman asked for a show of hands. I lost, 9–0. Even the U.S. representative voted against me. He said he knew it was hopeless—no sense alienating the rest of the hemisphere.

Only now, looking once again into those "dog eyes," did it seem funny. That afternoon, the sight of him drove me to the typewriter.

November 22, 1983

To CBS Sports' Pan American Games Team:

I suppose it occurred to me that I should write all of you in the week after we returned from Caracas. But my weary mind was unable to concoct anything profound, and I now realize I didn't have much perspective at that point. Somehow this feels like the time . . . maybe because it's Thanksgiving Week, maybe because two survivors of COPAN [the organizing committee] are wandering the office today, mumbling something in Spanish about collecting their money.

At this distance from August, the first thing that strikes me is that we've chosen a most "disposable" profession. Disposable because absolutely nothing lasts. No matter how difficult the assignment, no matter how profusely one bleeds, no matter how large the triumph . . . three months later, the Pan American Games are ether. No less an authority than Billy Packer has called your *tour de force* in Caracas "the miracle of the television year." Yet in the blur of footballbasketballSuperBowl, does anyone care? Does anyone remember?

Well, we should. We should never forget the sight of George Veras, standing at the podium in Olympic Stadium before 5000 Venezuelan children, choreographing the Opening Ceremonies. We should not forget the cramped figure of Joe Aceti, after redesigning his coverage on 48 hours' notice, directing a nine-camera spectacular out of the tiny F & F flash unit.

At least once a year, we should have Pierce O'Neil, Hank Siegel and Ken Torres retell the story of "holding Argentina" against drawn swords. Eric Mann should be made to explain how he did 16½ hours with one Chyron. Richard Drake should recount that telephone conversation from Caracas Airport where he told his wife he'd volunteered to stay another week.

Pat O'Brien and John Tesh will swear that they were thrilled to get up at 4:30 on a Tuesday morning to break the drug story. And David Blatt will recount the reaction of American athletes who thought they were sneaking out of town, only find "CBS is in the Village, at the airport, everywhere we go."

Everyone knows that the real drug stories of these Games were Barreto, Arnold and Musburger. How else could Cathy and Mike have stayed in the Broadcast Center for two-and-a-half days without sleep? And Musburger? All he did was seven hours of live broadcasting on our final weekend, then fly Caracas–San Juan–New York, immediately jump into nightly U.S. Open updates, and cap his week with the season premiere of *The NFL Today*. He's the one whose urine should be sampled.

These tales go on and on, involving every one of you. They ought never to be forgotten, because they're the stuff tradition is made of.

For your refusal to be defeated, for your ruthless dedication to quality . . . my thanks. I'll not soon forget.

Regards,
Terry

8

Part I: TeleGame

BY EARLY 1986, the start of my sixth year at CBS Sports, we had trained a worthy production staff, built the best weekend-to-weekend schedule in network television, and shared the rosy morale that follows a corporate turn-around. In addition, there were these facts:

In my five years at CBS, NFL football programming had earned $91.8 million in profits. Far from the narrow regular-season margin over NBC that we'd inherited (0.3 rating point), our advantage from '81 through '85 was 3.2 Nielsen points.

Pro football ratings were trending down during this period, due mostly to the 1982 players' strike, the advent of the United States Football League, and the explosion of video alternatives. Comparing '81–'85 with the previous five years, ABC's ratings were down 6 percent, NBC's down 6.5 percent. CBS's ratings were up 4 percent.

Sports Saturday/Sunday, in its own way, was every bit as successful, the only serious challenger that *Wide World of Sports* ever had. In 1982, its first full year, *Sports Saturday/Sunday* averaged a 6.9 rating—to this day, the highest ever for an NBC or CBS anthology.

By the early months of '86, *Sports Saturday/Sunday* had reduced *Wide World*'s lead to less than one rating point. More important, the series was projected as a $1 million profit item that year. (*CBS Sports Spectacular* had lagged four rating points behind *Wide World* and been a $4 million loser in its final season.)

There was plenty of critical approval for the new CBS Sports, but most telling, ultimately, were the words of *Detroit News* columnist Jay Mariotti. Chronicling the 1981 makeover, he wrote: "It is not easy for a guy 10 years out of college to walk into a place, bring in his own people and demote longtime employees, some of whom were at the network when O'Neil was in diapers in suburban Pittsburgh."

This was a commentary on the maddening, mysterious sport that television people play: "TeleGame." As Mariotti hinted, it is wholly unlike football and baseball. The TeleGame scoreboard hangs not conspicuously behind the centerfield fence. It etches not crisply with light bulbs in every socket. It posts the game score not every quarter or half-inning, but irregularly—without warning.

The TeleGame playing field is tilted. Competitors must have good footing to remain upright. The unlucky ones, when they fall, often slide all the way to a revolving door that spins them out onto Sixth Avenue.

When I arrived in 1981, CBS Sports was in a dreadful competitive position, badly outflanked in the five major packages of network sports—NFL football, college football, major league baseball, NBA basketball, and college basketball. Other sports—golf, tennis, auto racing, anthologies, and the like—have very limited impact on divisions that air more than 500 hours per year (10 to 15 percent of each network's total programming) and commonly report profit/loss of plus or minus $50 million. Only the big five carry enough program hours, exposure, and profit potential to be meaningful.

At the start of 1981, CBS not only had the fewest major holdings (just NFL and NBA), but its packages were drastically underperforming. ABC (both footballs and baseball) and NBC (baseball, pro football, college basketball) each held three of the five and were exploiting their properties adequately. (What gave ABC its huge advantage was the unique prime-time window of *Monday Night Football* and its perception as "network of the Olympics.")

In the six months from February through July 1981, Van Gordon Sauter turned the three-network competition upside down by acquiring both college basketball and college football. This lifted CBS out of the cellar and positioned it strongly for the rest of the decade. Among major event packages, the count suddenly read CBS 4, ABC 3, NBC 2. Not even Roone Arledge ever had such a dizzying, dramatic half-year as Sauter in 1981.

Then, just as suddenly, he was gone. Apparently, the CBS Broadcast Group's master plan had been to test Van in Sports until June 1982, when Bill Leonard was due to retire as president of CBS News. If Sauter proved worthy, he was to have the prized News job.

But viewers accelerated the timetable, as viewers will do. In March 1981, while I was still finding the men's room at Sports, Walter Cronkite retired, vacating the *CBS Evening News* anchor chair for Dan Rather. Jolted from its comfortable habit, America began "sampling" and found appealing presentations in both *NBC Nightly News* and Roone Arledge's ABC *World News Tonight.* By the summer of '81, Rather had fallen a full rating point from Cronkite's standard. Then in the last week of October, the unspeakable happened. *CBS Evening News* finished third for the first time in history.

Struggling with the turnaround at Sports, I might not have noticed. But "Black Rock," the CBS headquarters building, was fairly trembling. *Evening News* advertising rates were cut roughly $10,000 to an average of $30,000 per 30-second commercial. Far worse was the loss of prestige. The network of Edward R. Murrow, Charles Collingwood, Eric Sevareid, and Walter Cronkite, the network that *invented* electronic journalism, was now last with its flagship broadcast. Unthinkable.

Decisions in a bureaucracy like CBS can take seemingly forever. But in a crisis like this, as Madden would say . . . WHAP! Within two weeks, Gene Jankowski, president of the Broadcast Group, made his announcement: The new president of CBS News would be our own Van Gordon Sauter.

The action had been so frenzied at Sports during Sauter's brief term that few of us recognized his utter singularity until he was gone. In the '60s, network television produced many iconoclasts. What would you expect from an emerging show business form? But as a mature business in the '80s, its odds were a million to one that someone like Sauter could weave his way through natural selection.

The fullness of Van's aberration finally registered on CBS Sports as it gathered in the thirtieth-floor conference room to greet his successor: Neal H. Pilson, 41, tall, bespectacled, and, conspicuously among the sporting crowd, dressed regularly in chalk stripes like the lawyer that he was.

The formative incident of Pilson's CBS career had been the scandalous "Heavyweight Championship of Tennis" series, played 1975–77. Once CBS's "winner take all" claim was exposed as fraudulent, the penalties were far steeper than Broadcast Row jibes and wrist slapping in the newspapers. No, justice was being served in Washington, D.C., of all places.

The Federal Communications Commission (FCC) handed down a short-term renewal (one year instead of the normal three years) to KNXT-TV, CBS's owned station in Los Angeles. In a humiliating March 1978 letter, FCC commissioners scolded the network for abusing its public trust.

Separately, the House Subcommittee on Communications, chaired by Lionel van Deerlin of California, summoned CBS Sports' top managers to Capitol Hill. What a venue for the boys of fun-'n-games TV, who had only been looking for an extra rating point or two.

The task of preparing for this congressional investigation fell to Pilson, effectively CBS Sports' staff legal counsel. Then, after the network adopted stringent, new procedures for disclosing all aspects of its sports broadcasts, Pilson was charged with enforcing them.

Newspaper ads, for instance, began displaying "taped" and "scheduled to appear" disclaimers that, to my shock, were regarded in-house as far more important than the events they promoted. The division was even forced to appoint a "vice president of compliance," surely the most unusual title in the history of sports television. She reported to Pilson, the unofficial "president of compliance."

His supervision of this detail won Pilson approval from corporate management. Further, Jankowski recognized that Neal's natural conservatism was a perfect follow-up to Sauter's radicalism. Having revamped its philosophy and on-air look, having just acquired college football and basketball, the right thing for CBS Sports to do was nothing more.

"Run it like a business" was Jankowski's simple mandate.

Just weeks on the job, Pilson was faced with the most important decision of his presidency. NBA basketball was up for renewal. The league was still floundering, still living down its reputation as a "drug league." Larry Bird and "Magic" Johnson, then starting their third seasons, had not yet made full impact.

Meanwhile, the proposed United States Football League was being offered to all three networks. NBC, heavily committed to baseball, had no room for spring football. But ABC was interested. After eight years, its Sunday tandem of *The Superstars* and *The American Sportsman* was finally dying of natural causes. Inside ABC, Jim Spence argued strongly for USFL football as the ideal replacement.

This word reached us through Chet Simmons, Carl Lindemann's close friend and former NBC colleague, then

USFL commissioner. Wanting to entice two networks, Simmons offered to fit his game schedule around our new NCAA basketball agreement. Retaining the NBA, he suggested—echoing a common argument—would leave CBS overloaded with basketball and stricken with programming conflicts.

Here was a decisive moment in the business. ABC Sports had owned the heavily watched winter and early spring Sunday afternoons *with* NBA basketball up through 1973 and *without* it after '73. Was the self-proclaimed "leader in sports television" about to extend its dominance with another brilliant stroke?

Ten months earlier, Pilson had been dead wrong in arguing that regular-season NCAA basketball would be unprofitable. But this time, he made the right call. He never so much as flirted with the USFL. Instead, he immediately made a four-year deal with the NBA at bargain prices. It was like buying New York City real estate during the recession of the early '70s.

America's number three spectator sport couldn't remain in the doldrums forever. Once Bird, "Magic," Michael Jordan, and other solid citizens retooled pro basketball's image, television ratings soared. In this December 1981 deal, and a renewal in December 1985, CBS earned as much as $15 million a year in profits from NBA basketball.

Spence and ABC, meanwhile, got their USFL. The league premiered against one of our Aspen skiing telecasts in March 1983. I can still taste the gastric bubble that welled in my stomach as I saw that first USFL rating—14.2 in a time period where 6s and 7s were considered excellent. Our *Sports Sunday* skiing rated a 7.3, NBC's *Sportsworld* a 5.0.

"They'll put us off the air," I thought.

But as novelty gave way to numbing mediocrity, the USFL found its level. By 1985, the league's third year of operation, it was playing to vast stretches of empty seats.

ABC's ratings were pitiful 3s and 4s. Spence and the league's leadership began sniping at each other in the newspapers. USFL football never reappeared after that '85 season. ABC Sports' first- and second-quarter Sunday programming has been in disarray ever since.

The pat hand that CBS dealt Pilson prevailed over ABC's limitless antes in two other colossal poker games. In January 1984, CBS dropped out of bidding for the '88 Calgary Olympics at the relatively modest level of $261 million. Spurred by its "network of the Olympics" self-image, ABC dueled NBC to the death in a Lausanne, Switzerland, hotel. ABC "won" the jackpot at $309 million, knowing that the Games required another $100 million in production costs. Four years later, when the Olympic flame died in Calgary, the network estimated it had lost $65 million on the telecasts.

This was a bad period for ABC's Spence and Arledge. In 1983, they spent $575 million for six years of Major League Baseball, 1984–89. What they hadn't calculated was the explosion of baseball on local cable systems and "superstations" like WOR (carrier of the New York Mets), WGN (Chicago Cubs), and WTBS (Atlanta Braves). Suddenly, there was no exclusivity to the regular season. From 10 ratings in 1983–84, *ABC's Monday Night Baseball* slipped to nasty 9s in 1985–86, then egregious 8s in 1987–88. This was in prime-time, where 12s and 13s are average. *Monday Night Baseball* automatically made hits of whatever CBS and NBC scheduled opposite.

Worse were the staggering losses. Printed estimates indicated that, at expiration in 1989, ABC would have lost *$100-to-$150 million* on this agreement. Soon after Capital Cities, Inc., acquired the network in March 1985, its senior managers were dumbfounded to find this kind of red ink on their sports balance sheet. They quickly limited Arledge's duties to News and arranged for Spence's departure.

What a reversal. Since Arledge gave the sports TV business its current shape in the early '60s, his graphs had spiked ever upward. ABC's Olympic agreements, for instance, went from $4.5 million in Mexico City to $7.5 million in Munich to $25 million in Montreal to an astounding $225 million in Los Angeles. Every time Roone prevailed, his competitors screamed, "Overbid." Then ABC salesmen canvassed Madison Avenue and found that Arledge's bravado was again justified.

Who knew that the escalator would jam in the mid-1980s? After 20 years of 15 to 20 percent annual growth, who knew that the sports advertising marketplace would seize up? After the 1984 Olympic bonanza, the market actually contracted in '85 for the first time ever—fewer advertising dollars were spent than in the previous year. This was no time for wild buying sprees.

CBS Sports was sitting pretty as the only network with no baseball and no Olympic Games, but it still needed great luck to report each year of the '80s with black ink.

Our NCAA football pick-up of 1981 may have been a programming coup, but it was a lousy financial deal. In fact, at a negotiating session in Providence, Rhode Island, I found myself in the awkward position of opposing a major property acquisition for event-poor CBS Sports. I authored our counterproposal to the NCAA, putting Top Ten teams on the air more often. But even with that adjustment, the deal was too rich at $132 million each for CBS and ABC, covering four years, 1982–85.

After two decades of single-network exclusivity, this marked the advent of two-network college football. The inevitable process unfolded. Since more games were on the air, viewership declined for each exposure. Since twice as many commercial units were available, advertisers played us against each other, driving prices down. In 1982, CBS lost $2.5 million on college football; in 1983, another $5.1 million. ABC dropped $6.5 million each year.

With rights payments due to escalate in 1984–85 and the marketplace headed for its nadir, total losses on the four-year package would have been devastating for both networks. At CBS, this might have meant paralysis. The Sports division was still earning credibility with senior corporate managers. I could imagine a Broadcast Group financial officer asking Pilson, "Let me get this straight. You're losing twenty-five million dollars on college football and you want me to approve twenty-three cameras for the Super Bowl? We can't do it with fewer?"

But the Universities of Oklahoma and Georgia came to our rescue. They alleged that their football television rights had been appropriated by the NCAA and filed suit to reclaim them. The NCAA countered with two arguments: (1) Its TV plan was necessary to distribute broadcast revenues equitably, thereby encouraging competitive balance. (2) Without its limits on exposure, excessive televised football would drastically reduce in-stadium attendance.

The U.S. Supreme Court didn't buy it. By a vote of 7–2, the television plan was struck down as a Sherman Antitrust violation. Thus ended 33 years of control by the NCAA. Writing for the Court, Associate Justice John Paul Stevens said that neither NCAA argument could justify the "naked restraint on price and output."

It was June 1984. Little did anyone in college football realize that the big winners would be ABC and CBS. Free of their oppressive NCAA deal, they now had leverage on the many conferences and universities that craved exposure.

ABC, instead of paying the NCAA $34 million in 1984, bought a package of College Football Association games —featuring the Big Eight, Southeastern, and Southwest Conferences, plus leading independents such as Penn State and Notre Dame—for $13 million. CBS, relieved of its $34 million obligation, paid $10.5 million for the Big Ten, the Pacific-10, and two games involving independents. Network college football went from financial disaster to a modest profit center. And Neal Pilson, lawyer, had American jurisprudence to thank.

Reading and reacting quickly to this kind of situation was Pilson's strength. On the other hand, as a stylist, he suffered in comparison to Sauter. Probably anyone would have. Whereas Van, utterly self-assured, had simply chosen his people and left them free to do their jobs, Pilson was constantly in your pants.

"Jesus," said Carl Lindemann, "he wants to do everything. Don't be surprised some day if you see him putting clean towels in the men's room."

Pilson's insecurity was understandable. He had been doing an obscure development job for the Broadcast Group while Sauter and I were reshaping CBS Sports. On returning, Neal was openly uneasy with the working structure that had evolved. At management-only staff meetings (producers uninvited), he suggested that newcomer O'Neil had accumulated far too much influence in such a brief time.

Pilson parried by reorganizing production under *four* executive producers—Kevin O'Malley to handle college football and basketball, Frank Chirkinian for golf and tennis, Ted Shaker for *The NFL Today* and NBA basketball, and me to continue with NFL football and *Sports Saturday/Sunday*.

"He wants to clip your wings," Beano Cook told me on emerging from one of Pilson's staff meetings.

This new structure was unknown in sports television, and Pilson admitted to my agent, Art Kaminsky, that it was aimed at me. "Weights and counterweights," Pilson called it, a new formation on the competitive playing field of TeleGame.

Adding to my distress in this period, Pilson used a press gathering in Phoenix to distance himself from Sauter and renounce any attempt at "sports journalism." This must have been baffling to television reviewers who, a year earlier at the same forum, had heard Sauter claim serious reporting as the new "franchise" of CBS Sports.

Pilson told the press, "Journalism, as far as the television medium is concerned, is generally equated with *60 Minutes*. . . . It is not what I have in mind. Sports television is a business where we have out standing well over a billion dollars in program contracts. *60 Minutes* has zero dollars in commitments to anyone other than the American public and CBS to practice journalism. In all candor, it is not our role to practice the kind of journalism that *60 Minutes* practices. We are not equipped to do that. . . .

"Are we going to be soft on the NFL or NCAA because we have a contract? The answer is no. We have set up an editorial distinction between our *Sports Saturday* format and our coverage format. Editorial judgments regarding stories that we might do on college football or in any other sports are handled by our *Sports Saturday/Sunday* operation and are done with editorial freedom."

This, of course, was preposterous. A few weeks later, our *Sports Saturday/Sunday* team produced a feature on pressure in sports—is there such a thing as "choking" for the professional? Pretty tame stuff. Pilson fired off the following memo:

> I am disturbed that a feature on "athletes under pressure" is in our listing for the Saturday broadcast but will not be available for screening until tomorrow morning when the only options will be either to run it or to kill it. . . . Under no circumstances should we, in the future, promote any feature reports unless that report has been viewed by management sufficiently prior to broadcast so that if any changes are required, they can be made.

Pilson wasn't naive enough to think that news gathering and reporting allowed time for management screenings in every case. He simply wanted control.

His intimidation worked with some of my colleagues.

Shaker, assigned to produce pregame and halftime elements of the 1985 NCAA basketball championships, ignored the hottest unfolding story of that month. He went three weeks without a single mention of the Tulane University point-shaving scandal that had broken just days earlier.

Three Tulane players, three students, and a bookie were under arrest, charged with breaking Louisiana's sports bribery law. This was front-page, not sports-page, news all over the country. It involved gangsters and mob figures. It resulted in abolition of Tulane's basketball program. Every coach and athletic director at the tournament was buzzing about it—to say nothing of FBI agents.

The hottest T-shirt in town showed a basketball lathered in shaving cream, a razor blade poised, and—playing on the school nickname, Green Wave—the legend, "Shave with the Wave." But CBS Sports, with more than 40 hours of tournament coverage, uttered not one syllable about it.

For my part, I had no choice but to ignore Pilson. And you know what? He allowed it. Rather than battle every weekend, we settled into a wordless coexistence. He had put me on notice with his Phoenix speech and subsequent memos. I had little doubt that if one of our stories blew up in embarrassment, it would be my ass.

But what else could I do? After a full year of preaching journalism to everybody from commentators to cameramen, was I to tell them I'd changed my mind? Was I to advise them that our principles were under suspension just because we had a new president? Of course not. It was my turn to play TeleGame.

At the Pan American Games in '83, Pilson stood silently and watchfully in the control room as we blanketed all aspects of the drug story, feeding one enterprise piece after another.

Back home, Pete Alfano of *The New York Times* praised our work but remembered the Phoenix speech. Recognizing this paradox, he wrote, "It was just a year ago that Neal Pilson, the president of CBS Sports, appeared to back down on the network's commitment to pursue serious issues in sports."

Pilson's rationalization in reply was worthy of Casey Stengel, baseball's master of doubletalk. *The Times* quoted him:

> When you are sponsoring sports events and generating profits, you can create conflicts and problems. In CBS Sports, we have major business relationships that are worth in the billions of dollars and are renewable. You cannot use the people associated with CBS Sports to investigate the morals of the people you do business with. . . .
>
> We can cover breaking stories like the use of drugs at the Pan Am Games. But basically we are event-oriented. Maybe we shouldn't be, and people will say it's a copout, but that's the business. It doesn't mean, though, that we are not journalists.

Like Jim Spence, Pilson was afflicted with that old canard, "Good reporting will endanger our event portfolio." But there was no more basis for this fear at CBS than there had been at ABC.

See it this way: What's every network's most important package? Pro football, right? At the yearly NFL meetings, I told club p.r. directors that we were going to report all the stories, good and bad. This was our function. They shouldn't take it as a hostile act.

When Detroit running back Billy Sims signed contracts with both the Lions and the USFL's San Antonio Gunslingers, our commentator, Frank Glieber, demanded and got an explanation from Detroit general manager Russ Thomas. When Doug Williams, a black quarterback, found himself at bitter impasse with Tampa Bay over salary, there were racial overtones. Bay Bucs management refused to speak. But our John Dockery obtained Williams's first interview on the subject, print or broadcast, and we played it big.

In Minnesota one year, the Vikings hit a losing streak and Coach Bud Grant thought our commentators were being too harsh. He refused to meet with them one Saturday. I phoned the league office. Did Pete Rozelle complain that we were harassing his coaches? Did he threaten not to cash CBS's $150 million check that season?

Grant turned up for his meeting the next Saturday, wearing resignation where his defiance had been. He told our guys, "The commissioner says he's gonna fine my ass if I don't come talk to you. So here I am."

Contemporary sports operators like Rozelle live in the real world, knowing that contention, human failure, even scandal are just as surely a part of their sports as home runs and touchdowns. No league has ever withheld broadcast rights from a network for documenting these foibles honestly. In truth, sports operators respected television people less for running scared.

In the "communication business," you may find it surprising that Pilson and I never really discussed this. But there was no need. I greatly respected his ability to wring big financial commitments out of the Broadcast Group. And with rare exception, he let me put programs on the air, complete with good reporting. Our differences were ultimately healthy for the organization.

If Pilson was a model of the competence that executive natural selection can yield, his successor was another species altogether. When Neal ascended to a Broadcast Group vice presidency, Peter Lund took over as Sports president.

The new man, at first, appeared too good to be true. He left people and systems in place, pledging himself to noninterference. Asked to describe his contribution to the division, John Madden once said, "He has nice hair. You know, combed to the side, always looks real neat."

Indeed, Peter Lund was fully gray but boyish-looking,

in his mid-forties, with a brush cut swept across his forehead. Always tan, he fancied himself an athlete. His golf handicap hovered between 10 and 12, and his tennis was an upper C club level. But what was his impact on CBS Sports?

In the back of a limousine one afternoon, Madden interrupted Summerall's reading to ask, "What do you think of Peter Lund?"

Pat slowly lowered an NFL press release to his knee as the perfect Summerallian response came to him—terse, whimsical, deadly accurate:

"He spends a lot of time in the neutral corner."

Madden had no regard for Lund whatever. In a hotel bathroom one day, Sandy Grossman mentioned that Korean organizers of the 1988 Seoul Olympic Games were due to meet with Lund. Excited at the prospect of doing an Olympics—the one major gap in his career—Grossman asked me what I knew of the negotiations.

Before I could reply, Madden blurted, "Sandy, let me tell you something. Peter Lund wouldn't know what to do. He'll walk into the room and won't have the first idea —what to say, how to bid, nothing. The idea of him bringing home the Olympics—ha!"

At first, I failed to understand the intensity of John's reaction to this diffident man. Lund came aboard in the spring of 1984 as executive vice president, undisguised on-the-job training. His introduction to CBS Sports was my '84 NFL seminar. He spent those two days sitting silently at the back of the room, next to my secretary, Lori Diver-Ehret. Afterward, she told me, "Peter Lund thinks you hung the moon."

A year later, meeting with the agency representative of Beatrice Foods, a major client, he called me "the best producer in sports television." In a staff meeting, he openly spoke of a plan to make me sole executive producer, thereby eliminating Pilson's four-headed hydra.

He seemed the ideal boss—hands-off, supportive, a man

whose pressure points were clearly discernible. When the NFL began considering television replay as an official's tool, I was the first and loudest to object. Lund called me into his office and gently asked that I cease and desist. He'd heard, indirectly, from the Dallas Cowboys' Tex Schramm, inventor and campaign manager of replay officiating.

"The league thinks you've become the number one opponent of their plan—the guy every newspaperman goes to when he wants a quote," Lund said.

I backed off. This was a small price to pay, and it was so rare that he asked anything of me.

"You know, he's afraid of you," said one of the secretaries.

"What do you mean?" I protested.

"He's afraid of you. He never wants to go into your office. And when he does, he spends a couple minutes outside, pacing, thinking of what he's going to say. All the secretaries notice it and talk about it."

This was at first the blessing but later the curse of Peter Lund. He seemed terrified of running CBS Sports. He'd grown up in Minnesota, been a radio advertising salesman. Riding the broadcast boom, he'd managed radio stations in San Diego and Washington, D.C., then television stations in Chicago and New York.

Some of those situations were like CBS Sports. He'd inherited well-run operations. All his favorite aphorisms were about staying out of the way, not screwing it up. After an NCAA Final Four one year, he came back to the office beaming. He told me how he'd taken over a production meeting and instructed the troops in his philosophy of "K.I.S.S.: Keep it simple, stupid."

Everybody you asked knew him for only one decision. At WCBS, New York, he was the man who decided to kill a local magazine program called *Two on the Town* and replace it with *Wheel of Fortune*. He once told me the decision had taken about 10 seconds once he'd read a market research study. The *Wheel* made nothing but profit whenever it spun, the most successful syndicated game show in history. Somehow, in the puzzling world of network television, this insight qualified Peter Lund to run a sports division.

When Lund's first year passed without noticeable change in CBS Sports, whispers were heard that he was merely a caretaker for success built by others. Lund responded the way a station general manager would—by seeking new on-air talent to put his stamp on the product.

He first went after Bob Lobel, a local sports anchor at WBZ-TV in Boston. Despite an offer of $300,000-plus in salary and Lund's promise of stardom, Lobel turned him down.

Black Rock tittered. With network blandishments, Peter Lund couldn't get a local guy to leave Boston. Next, he pursued Anne Butler, a courtship that defined the vast difference between himself and Van Gordon Sauter.

In 1981, when Sauter announced our need for three new reporters, Anne Butler's agent called. She was then a cohost for syndicated *P.M. Magazine*, an on-air personality of no particular distinction. Van asked me to have dinner with her.

Armed with no sports knowledge but a great desire to please, Butler dominated our dinner with her version of Super Bowl III. She'd rehearsed it pretty well—had the Jets winning over Baltimore, had the game in Miami, had some inkling about the NFL-AFL merger. The only problem was that she kept calling the game's hero "Willie Joe Namath." Not Joe Willie. "Willie Joe."

"Willie Joe was cocky," "Willie Joe guaranteed victory," "Willie Joe backed it up," and so on. Rather than correct her, I kept trying to change the subject. But each time, she insistently returned to the fable of "Willie Joe." This was the one of the longest dinners of my life. Before

I'd even seen the menu, I knew there was no place for Anne Butler at CBS Sports.

Hearing my report the next morning, Sauter typically averred, "Whatever you say, big guy," and called her agent with polite no-thanks.

Segue to the winter of 1986. By then, Butler was working at WABC-TV, New York. Her agent phoned CBS Sports again. This time, the call was answered by Peter Lund. To him, Anne had the rare double virtue of being both black and female. He knew nothing about her ignorance of sports. Without vetting her, he made the hire, then called to tell me.

"Have you ever seen Anne Butler on the air?" he asked.

"Sure, she's the weekend anchor on Channel 7," I replied.

"What do you think of her?"

"I don't know. I've never seen her do more than read a TelePrompTer."

"What would you think about her working here?"

"You know, we actually talked about that once, back in 1981."

"What happened?"

"Peter, she didn't know anything about sports."

"Oh, yeah? Well, you can teach her, because we've just hired her."

Anne Butler strolled into my office a few weeks later. Barefoot, carrying her shoes. I was watching a videotape.

"Track and field," she said brightly. "My favorite sport."

"Oh, yeah?"

"Sure is. Who's that?"

"Mac Wilkins."

"Who?"

"Mac Wilkins, the discus thrower."

"Huh? When was he around?"

"Well, he was at [the University of] Oregon in the early seventies. Threw the shot, discus, and javelin. They called him 'Multiple Mac.' Then he won the discus at the Montreal Olympics in '76. You remember that."

"A gold medal?"

"Yep."

"I *don't* remember. I never heard of him."

Anne Butler was a critical test in TeleGame—a fourth-down-and-inches decision that revealed everything about your essential nature and your play-calling tendencies. She verified not only the difference between Sauter and Lund but also the gap between Shaker and me.

I quietly arranged never to work with her. I admit it. Maybe I'd lost my patience. I just couldn't countenance her. Shaker, however, took her on eagerly. When his staff complained of Butler's incompetence, he railed, "I don't want to hear that. You *make* it work. That's what you're here to do—protect her and make her look good. Peter Lund wants her to succeed, and that means *I* want her to succeed."

No amount of producing, however, could cover an incident in Butler's first football season, six months after her arrival at CBS Sports. It made a November 1986 issue of *Sports Illustrated*.

> Anne Butler of CBS-TV was at Giants Stadium last week to do some feature work on the team. She asked general manager George Young to come to the press room for an interview. Young and Butler had never met, so neither knew what the other looked like. When the G.M. showed up, Butler was on the telephone. Asked Young, "Do you need me?"
>
> "No," replied Butler. Twenty minutes later, the CBS crew phoned Young's office, wanting to know why he hadn't shown up yet for the interview. "I was downstairs and couldn't find her," Young said.
>
> Later, Butler was told that the man she had turned away was Young. "Oh," she said, "I thought he was a janitor."

Embarrassments like Anne Butler led the majority of CBS Sports to Summerall's conclusion—and beyond. Peter Lund wasn't just stationed in the neutral corner. He was asleep there, curled up in the fetal position. Given the ambitious, compulsive people whom broadcasting attracts, that could mean only one thing: While Lund slept, a tag-team, battle royal, Texas death match erupted in the middle of the ring.

Our awkward, four-cornered organizational structure demanded a decisive arbiter, an "executive producer of the executive producers," as we called Pilson. Lund hardly qualified. His weak to nonexistent leadership was not simply ineffectual, it was downright dangerous, leaving a vacuum that everybody wanted to fill with his own self-interest.

Petty squabbles increased over budget, staff size, run-overs, on-air promotion—anything that came from a shared pool. One executive producer tried trashing *Sports Saturday/Sunday* to Rudy Martzke of *USA Today*, saying the series was "dead in the water" and soon to be "deem-phasized" even though it was enjoying one of its finest years. In most corporations, this would have been considered high treason. In TeleGame, it was business as usual.

We had descended to a low form of the sport—mud wrestling—and I suddenly found myself unwilling, *unable* to get dirty. I'd always been competitive enough—some might even say overly competitive—in the four-cornered system. But under Pilson, there was security in knowing that everybody played by the same rules. His decisions stuck. Lund's opinion was ever-changing. The prevailing joke was, "Last man in his office on Friday evening gets his way for the weekend."

I imagined a great injustice in this process. Hadn't I revamped this place? Hadn't I established the methods and philosophy that made us successful? Should I now be forced to play this childish 'Game?

I found myself withdrawing to the sanctuary of line production and colleagues who shared my purpose. More and more, I avoided the office, often working from home by telephone. This was a sizable mistake, supporting a claim by my critics that I was aloof and arrogant.

Part II: Endgame

IN *Bad News at Black Rock,* an inside account of the *CBS Morning News,* Peter McCabe writes:

> For all executive producers, dealing with anchors is a delicate game of negotiation. As Van Gordon Sauter once said, anchors are like Siberian tigers, who would eat their keepers in a second if they ever thought they could. Anchors are paid huge salaries, and they exercise a degree of control and power. When network news organizations are faced with disagreements between an anchor and an executive producer, the easiest solution is usually to replace the executive producer.

Ed Joyce, former president of CBS News, described the same predicament in his book, *Prime Times, Bad Times: A Personal Drama of Network Television.* Caught in a dispute with *CBS Evening News* anchorman Dan Rather, Joyce went to see his boss, Gene Jankowski.

As Joyce reports it, Jankowski's reaction was: "If there's a problem, I'd have no choice. I'd have to make a change. There are lots of presidents. There's only one Dan Rather."

TeleGame in all its forms—news, sports, entertainment, daytime—is rife with such tales. In one week of March 1988, for instance, three such stories were making headlines. Senior producer Richard Cohen departed CBS News after a dispute with Rather. Executive producer Bill Lord was still an item two months after his exit from ABC *World News Tonight* in a long-running battle with anchor Peter Jennings. Meanwhile, in Hollywood, Anne Beatts resigned as executive producer of *A Different World* after a confrontation with series star Lisa Bonet. Reportedly, Bonet's last words to Beatts were, "Get out of my face or else I'm going to slap you."

In all three cases, the departing producer was highly regarded. In Cohen's case, for example, *The New York Times* reported that his "quality of work was apparently never an issue." Translation: He was undone by the relentless politics of network television.

This kind of maneuvering was well known at CBS. In the spring of '81, when *Evening News* ratings dipped immediately upon Dan Rather's succession of Walter Cronkite, Rather's first instinct was to push for a new executive producer. That fall, when Sauter took control of CBS News, Rather got his wish, Howard Stringer replacing Sandy Socolow. Van announced, "I'm married to Dan Rather."

To extend that metaphor, he and Rather were together virtually every day during their honeymoon. They had weekend houses in upper Fairfield County, Connecticut, and socialized warmly. They fished together. Their wives became close friends.

Then in late '84, Sauter made a bad decision in pressing for former Miss America Phyllis George to anchor the *CBS Morning News.* The next year, in Rather's view, Van and his deputy, Ed Joyce, didn't fight hard enough against staff reductions mandated by the Broadcast Group.

The anchor filed for separation from this pair. In December 1985, he forced Joyce out of CBS News. Sauter accepted a second term as News president but lasted only nine months. In September 1986, Rather and allies won a final decree of divorce. They had Sauter removed as well.

None of these history lessons meant much to me, however, until I heard the story of George Merlis. That one chilled me for its parallels to my own situation.

George Merlis was a tightly wound, fastidious man who, in the late '70s, did the improbable. He steered ABC's *Good Morning, America* to outright leadership of morning television, a daypart that NBC's *Today* had owned since it took the air in 1952.

Leaving ABC after a struggle with—you guessed it—an anchor, David Hartman, Merlis was available in early '82 when Sauter went seeking a visionary for his poor stepchild, the *Morning News*. With Van, Merlis worked out a format—the *twenty-first* different approach since CBS first attempted a morning program, with Cronkite, in 1954.

Merlis's *Morning News* was a hit. Its ratings jumped from mid 2s to high 3s and low 4s. For the first time ever, CBS had a competitive entry from 7 to 9 A.M. Instead of an annual $10 million loss, the *Morning News* was headed for profitability. Network affiliates were thrilled, finally, to have a decent lead-in for their 9 A.M. local and syndicated programs. Corporate CBS was relieved that, for the first time in memory, its question-and-answer session at the annual affiliates' meeting would not be dominated by *Morning News* complaints.

But this good feeling did not extend to the production's core. Merlis was besieged by accountants, meddling management, and an ambitious subordinate. Then, fatally, he lost his rapport with anchor Diane Sawyer, who, in this labyrinth of relationships, was a social companion of CBS chairman and founder William Paley. Sawyer observed Merlis's embattled condition and "sniffed blood," according to McCabe. He writes:

Even if the ratings were up—and the *Morning News* was regularly tying *Today* for the first time in thirty years— . . . opinion around CBS News was that anyone could have done it—an opinion that many *CBS Morning News* producers now acknowledge was a big mistake. . . .

And according to one CBS executive, "Sauter wasn't about to go against Diane Sawyer when he knew she was sitting down to dinner with Paley."

Sawyer told Sauter that her executive producer wasn't communicating with her. A few days later, Merlis was summoned to Sauter's office and told he was no longer the executive producer of the *Morning News.* . . .

And so the CBS News management fired an executive producer who had taken the *Morning News* from a 2.8 to a 4.0 in little more than a year.

"Given the opposition he had faced at the company," said one senior producer, "you have to admit that what he did was an achievement. Why they got rid of him in the face of the evidence of his competence, I will never understand."

That Merlis, with his performance record, could have been removed so whimsically was a statement of CBS's particular brand of TeleGame. Just as the San Francisco 49ers play a different style than the Chicago Bears, the sport of TeleGame is played in variations along Sixth Avenue.

At ABC Sports, for instance, the founding father was Roone Arledge, a dominating producer. He allowed producers to run their programs without interference (except for the occasional clash with Cosell) in return for total accountability on every aspect of the production. It seemed to work. So the natural selection of ABC Sports brought forth producers of strong personality.

By the same Darwinian logic, CBS Sports adapted a breed of producers to its circumstance. There, the dominant personality was Brent Musburger—not just as commentator, but in every way. For many years after his arrival in 1975, Brent had very few colleagues who knew anything about sports or broadcasting. For his own protection, he was forced to produce and sometimes direct, as well as anchor and make executive decisions.

Given that burgeoning role, he developed a view of the producer's function far different from Arledge's. In the late '70s, a CBS veteran told me of Musburger's relationship with *NFL Today* producer Mike Pearl:

"We were in the hotel coffee shop on the morning of a [pro football] playoff game. Brent saw Pearl at another table and called him over. Then, right in front of me, he just shredded Pearl's format. Told him to rearrange everything. This is three hours before air. When Brent sent him away, he winked at me and said, 'That'll keep him busy this morning.'"

In January 1984, as CBS prepared to broadcast Super Bowl XVIII, Mark Lorando of the *New Orleans Times-Picayune* spent several days observing our group before writing, "Here's an introduction to . . . the television teams: Terry O'Neil, who coaches the production team; Brent Musburger, who quarterbacks the pregame team . . ." As if *The Super Bowl Today* didn't have a producer other than Musburger.

When I arrived in 1981, neither Brent nor I understood how differently we viewed the anchor-producer relationship. But at the time, it didn't matter. We needed each other. I wanted out of ABC and was drawn to the huge turnaround opportunity at CBS, perhaps the last drastic situation in network sports. Musburger was looking for help, having just committed to four more years with this uninspired outfit.

His public image could hardly have been worse in those days. A few months before I arrived, he'd hosted a *Sports Spectacular* episode called "The Human Fly"—an idiot standing *atop* the fuselage of a flying airplane, unfortunately secured by wires. Brent hyped the hell out of it.

On more conventional events, Phil Mushnick of the *New York Post* called him "a screaming goofball after every layup during NBA telecasts." Musburger's on-air reaction to a 1976 triple-overtime Phoenix-Boston playoff game was nothing short of berserk.

Of his *NFL Today* work, John Czarnecki of the *Riverside* (California) *Enterprise,* wrote, "His outfits, color co-ordinated with the winning teams during the NFL playoffs, were a constant eyesore. . . . Let's face it, professionally Musburger doesn't generate the respect NBC's Bryant Gumbel has received. While Musburger is goofing around with his cowboy hats and Eagles caps, Gumbel simply goes about leaving everyone behind when it comes to objectivity."

When Brent, unaccountably, *sang* a chorus of Willie Nelson's "On the Road Again" to a huge playoff audience, *The* (Baltimore) *Sun*'s Bill Carter was not entertained. He assailed "pre-game, halftime and post-game hijinks of Brent Musburger and the assorted stooges who make up the happy family of *The NFL Today.* . . . Musburger is the man who was once a news anchor in the second biggest TV market in America. Now he flashes cowboy boots on camera and hoots about [Terry Bradshaw's] hairpieces. All this makes CBS's football package hard to take."

The turning point for Musburger's career was *CBS Sports Saturday/Sunday.* When, in the spring of 1981, he suddenly appeared amid the trappings of our newsroom set, reporting basketball scandals at Wichita State and Boston College, exposing cocaine investigations among the Vikings and Broncos, interviewing sports newsmakers, getting mention from the wire services for minor beats . . . when we accredited him as a journalist, people began to remember: "Hey, wasn't that guy once a Chicago newspaperman?"

These were good days for Brent and me. Characterizing our relationship, he told Bill Taaffe of the *Washington Star,* "We think alike—and that helps."

Through our third year, we remained on good terms. In the summer of '83, our news training interlocked wonderfully at the World University Games in Edmonton, Alberta, and the Pan American Games.

In Edmonton, a Soviet diver killed himself by cracking his skull on the concrete 10-meter platform. Musburger fronted our breaking coverage. At Caracas, I assigned him to every CBS News, Radio, and Sports report of the raging drug scandal. To the American audience, it appeared that Brent had broken the story by himself.

'Eighty-four was the year he became more temperamental and our relationship began to deteriorate. His contract was expiring, and, lucky circumstance, Howard Cosell was finally wearing out his welcome at ABC, while Jim McKay was into his sixties. Arledge decided that Brent was the likeliest replacement for both.

In the negotiation that followed, Musburger whipsawed CBS and ABC against each other in the pages of *USA Today*. It was an epic performance, one that later compelled Dan Jenkins to write in *Playboy*, "The editors of *USA Today* will eventually be forced to confirm two rumors: one, that their sports section is a daily memo from CBS Sports, and two, that TV-sports columnist Rudy Martzke is Brent Musburger's agent."

By November, it was clear that the maudlin courtship of two networks, so breathlessly reported, had caused Musburger's personality of the '70s to resurface. For instance, he began second-guessing my distribution of NFL football games. One morning, on entering the Broadcast Center, a technician told me he'd excoriated a Dallas-Buffalo game, my choice as lead regional.

The Bills, still winless on this Sunday before Thanksgiving, were 11-point underdogs, a huge spread for the home team. I'd silenced the office skeptics at midweek by *guaranteeing* that Buffalo would win the game outright. Brent, however, remained unconvinced.

"We got the wrong game going to most of the country," the technician quoted him. "Dallas is gonna blow the Bills out. We should have that Cardinals-Giants game going everywhere."

This was the old Musburger, his omnipotent self-image formed in the barren days when CBS frequently *did* have the wrong game going to most of the country. The situation had changed now. There was competence all around him. But sometimes Brent just couldn't help doing everybody's job.

The scene in frigid, snowy Buffalo was tremendous. A near-capacity house of 74,391 turned out to watch the pathetic, 0–11 Bills challenge the 7–4 Cowboys. On the very first play from scrimmage, Bills halfback Greg Bell raced 85 yards for a touchdown.

In my viewing room, adjacent to Brent's studio set, I jumped up and chortled rhetorically, "Where's Musburger?"

On the "ready list" of TeleGame plays, this was one of the very worst—a guaranteed interception, likely to be run back for a touchdown. But, like Brent, I couldn't help myself. His attitude sometimes infuriated me.

Dallas threatened all afternoon, adding to the excitement, but Buffalo survived for a 14–3 victory. Our rating was through the roof.

Musburger's contract negotiation climaxed in the next two weeks as I was traveling with Summerall and Madden. They devoured newspaper reports—regular and urgent as State Department briefings—that alternately had Brent making his decision (1) in the kitchen of his home, (2) on a deserted Caribbean beach, or (3) on the high school football field in Weston, Connecticut, his hometown.

Madden was then making about *one-eighth* the $2 million per year that Brent was being offered. To Summerall, Grossman, and me, he mocked, "You know, when my contract's up, I think I'll probably go for a little walk on the beach or maybe a football field somewhere. What about you, Pat?"

Summerall's antipathy with Musburger was much deeper, based partly on a suspicion that Brent had eavesdropped on his rehearsals with Tom Brookshier and stolen their information for pregame use. Indeed, as this suspicion deepened in Pat's mind, I had to block our remote feed to New York in order to get a decent rehearsal out of him.

"You know, Brookshier would like to kill the son of a bitch," said Summerall. "Literally wants to kill him."

When Musburger finally signed with CBS for five years (1985–89) at approximately $10 million, he became the highest-paid figure in the history of sportscasting. Interviewed that week, he mentioned not having to worry about college tuition payments for his two boys. This triggered another Madden outburst.

"Can you imagine some farmer out in Nebraska reading this?" John flared. "Some guy who really *does* have to worry about sending his kids to college? And fucking Brent, with his millions, is making a joke about it!"

Summerall replied, "Brookshier always said he's an evil cock-sucker."

Still, this sort of chafing was manageable. Then came '85.

Despite innocent protests, I knew that Brent had begged off *Sports Saturday/Sunday* during his negotiation. This meant that we no longer had any programming in common, indeed, that our only contact was the grinding, inescapable battleground of NFL studio (handled by Shaker) versus stadium remotes.

A constant tug-of-war were the studio updates (Musburger-voiced highlights) inserted between plays of a live game. Brent wanted frequent showcasing in each Sunday's lead telecast. (Bill Taaffe once explained in *Sports Illustrated*, "Two reasons there are so many updates are ego and money. Musburger wants to be on.") Madden wanted no in-game interruptions. I argued for meaningful updates only. But try reaching consensus on that.

In another turf battle, Brent temporarily forced his pregame colleague, Irv Cross, into the critical Saturday meetings with coaches that had been so productive for Summerall and Madden. Besides violating my pledge to the NFL that no information would be revealed before kickoff, Cross simply chilled the meeting, as any newcomer would have.

Pat and John bitterly opposed it. However, their early season producer, Bob Stenner, was a CBS old-timer unwilling to take on Musburger. Privately, he complained to me, "You know, sometimes I think everything we do at the games is just [designed] to make the studio look good." But he wouldn't speak up.

Hitting the road in November, I got an earful of the commentators' resentment. After observing Cross's effect, I discontinued his invitation. Musburger raged. He attacked me savagely to Peter Lund, saying I was disruptive and bent on sabotaging his show.

Lund phoned me in a Washington, D.C., hotel, but, typically, his question was not "What's the issue?" or "What's most effective here?" or "Where's the compromise point?"

Instead, he moaned, *"What're you doing to me?"*

As if it were personal. Lund made clear his disinterest in deciding who was right and wrong. Our product was good enough for him either way. He simply wanted to stop taking indignant telephone calls at home.

I had my neck wrung out a long way. Unlike Musburger, Summerall and Madden had little appetite for office politics. They were 50–50 to back off when Lund called to corroborate my position. As it happened, Madden wasn't in his room, but Summerall supported me, and we carried the day.

Musburger was no graceful loser. He renewed his attack with such ferocity that even Lund, the master of nonconfrontation, mentioned it to me.

"There are some guys here who just don't like you," he

said. "And it's a shame, because you should be president of this place some day."

"How do you mean, they don't like me?" I asked.

"They say, 'Terry's always right.' Or 'Terry doesn't get mad, he gets even.' Or 'Terry always gets the last word.' "

"Peter, may I say that sounds a bit general. Are there any specifics? What's the exact charge?"

He was silent for several seconds, then stammered, "Uh . . . this, uh, this is embarrassing. I call you in here to talk about this, and I can't think of anything specific. All I can tell you is that when you've got one of the 800-pound gorillas mad at you, you've got a problem."

There it was—in Peter Lund's definition, *my* problem. Not *our* problem, not the division's problem. O'Neil's problem. This was the way in TeleGame. You could ask Sandy Socolow, Bill Lord, Anne Beatts, George Merlis, Richard Cohen, Ed Joyce, or Van Sauter.

Lund was effectively announcing his withdrawal, his refusal to be injured in a collision between two other players. This was one of TeleGame's ignoble but widespread features. Jim Spence had shown the same instinct during that Cosell/*Monday Night Football* crisis in 1980, when he wouldn't confront the truth, wouldn't phone Chuck Sullivan or Howard Slusher to get the facts. Then, as now, the issue was so fundamental, it was too hot to handle: *control.*

The next week, everyone still smoldering, Madden reviewed a controversial pass in replay, calling it an interception. At halftime, Musburger led studio guest Matt Snell into a contradiction, ruling the pass incomplete.

Normally, a studio producer would warn the remote producer of such dialogue in advance, leaving the game commentators free to respond. But the studio producers rarely knew what Musburger was going to do. Typically, he dropped his bomb and dumped it back to the stadium, where Madden sat stunned and open-mouthed on the air. When we hit commercial a minute later, John was furious.

"Terry," he demanded, "did you hear that?!"

It was pretty clear that Brent and I needed a meeting. I asked him to lunch.

Before we'd finished our soup, he had (1) threatened to use his influence with Gene Jankowski to have me fired, (2) declared that our exclusion of Irv Cross from the Saturday meetings was potentially a racial issue which might bring an NAACP protest, and (3) admitted ignoring the division's on-air promotion schedule and hyping his *NFL Today* to the exclusion of NFL games. The games, of course, attracted far more audience and advertising revenue. But Brent somehow imagined a challenge from NBC's pregame show and decided to protect himself.

"I just decided I was gonna whale on it," he said.

Despite all this, we left the lunch in truce and, I thought, reasonably good feeling. The next week, I rescued the first 60 seconds of Musburger's pregame. At two minutes to air, he arbitrarily made a format change that paralyzed his producers with indecision. At 30 seconds to air, I offered a solution from the remote that he and his studio people accepted, just so they wouldn't open their show in chaos.

But a few weeks later, at the Los Angeles–Chicago NFC Championship, our cease-fire was broken permanently. About 90 minutes before air, I met Musburger, Shaker, and *NFL Today* guest analyst Bud Grant in the runway leading from Soldier Field to our trucks.

Brent began insisting on his own theme for Summerall and Madden's 60-second insert into the pregame show. By long-standing agreement, this slot had always been mine to format in consultation with Pat and John. But without notice, "The Big Dog," as he called himself, was preempting.

I listened. Brent said his pregame staff had a piece of videotape from the Rams' prior-day practice. John Robinson had positioned his hulking linemen 20 yards from a goalpost and challenged them to hit it with a thrown football.

Was this simply diversion, mere amusement, at the finish of a light Saturday practice? Perhaps for some. But for Musburger, it had deep, hidden meaning.

"The Rams are loose," he said. "We think they're going to win."

Shaker, a dramatic arts major in college, was superb at reading cues from Brent. He nodded, "We don't have room for the tape anywhere else in our show. We want you to use it."

Without saying anything, I thought, "Let me get this straight. After spending all season in the studio, Brent is coming out here to tell Pat, John, and me that we should endorse the Rams, two-touchdown underdogs, just because Robinson had his linemen throwing footballs at the goalpost yesterday? Do I understand this clearly?"

What Musburger didn't know was that Robinson *always* had some gimmick for Saturday practice on the road. He ran a season-long competition between offense and defense. Sometimes, they played volleyball over the crossbar. Before the '83 wild-card game in Dallas, they tried tossing footballs into a garbage bin. One day at the Meadowlands, they tried throwing into the second deck.

Robinson refereed these contests, keeping score creatively so that the competition remained always tight. At season's end, the winning unit, offense or defense, put names in a hat, one lucky player to receive a handsome prize. Peppering the goalpost that Saturday in Chicago, the Rams' defense clinched victory for 1985. Robinson plucked the name of linebacker Mark Jerue, sending him on an all-expense-paid vacation for two to Tahiti.

This gambit, so much in character for Robinson, was good for a few laughs but portended nothing of the coming battle. Did Musburger really think that Jerue had any better chance of stopping Walter Payton this afternoon just because he'd won the Rams' version of *Games People Play?*

I told Brent I'd discuss the piece with Summerall and Madden, then phone his truck. I walked off, knowing this was a precarious TeleGame moment. Was he serious? Or was he trying to position me, hoping I'd defy him and create another entry on his grievance list?

I knew the potential consequences. But there was no decision here. Hell, Madden and I had eaten dinner the previous night with John Robinson and his defensive coordinator, Fritz Shurmur. We knew the Rams' prospects in this game a dozen times better than Musburger—and those prospects sure weren't tied to any Saturday practice frolic. How could I keep credibility with Pat and John if I tried to sell them Brent's approach?

In a brief discussion, Summerall and Madden suggested that the best angle for our 60-second pregamer was the question, "Can Ram quarterback Dieter Brock pass effectively in Chicago's stiff 23-mph wind?"

I phoned Musburger's truck with this decision and sent a hand-held camera onto the field to record Brock's warm-up throws. Shaker responded by sending *his* hand-held camera onto the field for the same purpose. Brock, hopping around our cables, suddenly enveloped by technicians and their hardware, must have thought we'd lost our minds.

As it turned out, Dieter couldn't throw in the wind. Nor could his team run against the Bears. Robinson's Saturday practice might have been a turning point if he'd had Dent, Hampton, Singletary, Wilson, Marshall, and Fencik throwing those footballs at the goalpost—and wearing Ram uniforms. But he didn't. Los Angeles was wiped out, 24–0.

Moments after the game, Summerall, Madden, and I were standing outside our truck, enjoying the glow of a good telecast. Musburger stomped past. His production people had just rolled the wrong videotape several times in

328

an awkward postgame show. I said a cheery hello. Brent responded with a glare.

"What's the matter with him?" asked Summerall.

"I don't know," I lied.

We watched as Brent's agitated form receded, quickly rushing away. From that moment to this, I've not seen him in person.

That night, at a dinner with his *NFL Today* colleagues, Musburger vowed that Terry O'Neil would never sign another CBS contract and further pledged that "1986 will be the year I extract blood from the 'game' people," presumably meaning Pat and John, as well.

Brent and I had one more conversation. Hearing reports of his blow-up, I phoned to allow him ventilation. He refused to take my call. For four days, I kept ringing and ringing at his home until he picked up. I forced him to run through his complaints.

Incredibly, he still defended his pregame idea. Elsewhere in the broadcast, he didn't like our choice of replays at halftime, another area that was none of his business. And he didn't like Madden's Chalkboard of a touchdown scramble by Chicago quarterback McMahon, a play that Fritz Shurmur had feared as potentially game-turning during our Saturday night dinner.

Musburger hung up in a snit. It was January 16, 1986. We never spoke again.

Widening his attack now, Brent ripped me to anyone who would listen. This tactic was prominent in the disenchanted anchor's playbook. It seeded rumors and produced horrific hearsay that would eventually find its way back to management.

In February, a producer who'd worked a basketball game with Musburger told me, "We were on an airplane the other day and he just went wild about you. Loud enough for the whole first-class section to hear. Saying you were poison. You wouldn't believe some of the stuff."

That same month, Lund continued his retreat from me.

I had invited him to speak at the annual *Sports Saturday/Sunday* seminar, pointedly scheduling the meeting around his play in the first AT&T National Pro-Am (formerly the Bing Crosby tournament) at Pebble Beach, California. It was important for our 40 staffers to hear a word of encouragement from Lund. Their series remained a continual underdog in the battle for budget and exposure, despite its fine performance.

On the afternoon before the seminar, when my secretary called to confirm Lund's spot on the agenda, his secretary was surprised.

"Oh, Peter's not going to be in tomorrow," she said. "He's taking a personal day."

The morning after the seminar, Lund appeared at my door, wanting to talk about the 5-iron that he'd flown into the 18th hole grandstand as a national television audience watched.

"I had that thing gripped so tight," he demonstrated, "I was chokin' it . . . By the way, how'd your seminar go?"

I could not conceal my disregard for this man. I felt out of control, more alienated than ever. I knew I was losing at TeleGame.

In March, at the NCAA Basketball Championships, Musburger refused to narrate an announcement that CBS had acquired rights to the 1987 Pan American Games. Assuming (or perhaps fearing) that I would again be executive producer of the Games, he told Lund, "Never again will I do anything that Terry O'Neil is involved in." Lund nodded and assigned Dick Stockton to voice the piece.

Later that month, I was in Geneva, Switzerland, for the World Figure Skating Championships, a *Sports Saturday/Sunday* showcase. A continent away from Musburger and Lund, you might have guessed I was out of harm's way for a week. But this was the venue of my *dénouement* at CBS Sports.

A major story in Geneva was Tiffany Chin, a Chinese-

American skater from Toluca Lake, California. Since a promising fourth-place finish in the 1984 Olympic Games, her career had been in decline. Part of the problem was physical, but another large part, the figure skating community agreed, was Marjorie Chin, "an overbearing mother," as *USA Today* once called her.

Our event producer, David Michaels, and commentator John Tesh had obtained a stunning glimpse of this family contention. During an interview in the Chins' living room, Marjorie stopped Tiffany in midsentence and began haranguing her for lack of effort.

It was a performance Tesh and Michaels had witnessed previously. At practice, for instance, they reported seeing Marjorie vault the rink sideboard, then shuffle onto the ice in street shoes to shake a finger in Tiffany's face. Once, they said, the mother had slapped her teenage daughter.

Mrs. Chin's tirade was fairly obtained—there were no hidden cameras or microphones. In such cases, electronic journalism's general rule is this: When interview subjects invite you into their home, they are free at any point to get up and end the interview. But until then, anything they say or do within sight and sound of your equipment is fair game.

While we prepared in Geneva to air Mrs. Chin's interruption and scolding, Peter Lund was screening the raw recording in New York. He'd been drawn into the matter by Peter Tortorici, the management executive assigned to *Sports Saturday/Sunday*.

Tortorici was the first person I'd hired upon arriving at CBS in 1981. I'd fought for his every raise and promotion until he'd reached his goal of a vice presidency. But in March 1986, he knew of my problems with Musburger. In fact, he'd nodded along with Lund when Brent refused to narrate the Pan American Games announcement. It was now career-smart to separate himself from me—conspicuously, if possible.

Pulling Lund into his office, Tortorici screened the Chin

interview and trumped up the old argument about how Marjorie's upbraiding would be bad for CBS's relations in figure skating. Actually, nothing could have been further from the truth. Mrs. Chin had no standing, no influence, in the sport whatever.

But that wasn't the point. What about the truth? What about the viewer's right to know? What about the question that naturally occurred: Why hadn't Tiffany fulfilled the promise she'd shown in the '84 Olympics?

It took some heavy coercion, but Tortorici finally forced Lund to express an opinion—thumbs down on Marjorie Chin's chastisement.

"Well, if you don't want it to air, you'd better call O'Neil," Tortorici urged in a meeting with two others. "He's over there getting ready to put it into Sunday's show."

Partial scores of this TeleGame sequence reached me throughout the week in Geneva. But by Friday at 5:30 P.M., New York time, I still hadn't heard from Lund. To this day, I don't believe Mr. Neutral Corner would have had the nerve to phone me.

At 5:45, NYT, I got a call from O. J. Simpson. This same day, he'd been removed from the *Monday Night Football* commentary team. ABC Sports wanted him to become its college football analyst. O. J., however, asked ABC to hold its announcement and give him a few days to find work in pro football broadcasting, his first love. Reaching me in Geneva, he was desperate for an immediate indication of CBS's interest.

O. J. and I were longtime acquaintances. I first met him on a golden October Saturday in 1967 when he trampled the Fighting Irish in Notre Dame Stadium. At ABC, we worked track and field assignments together, including the 1976 Montreal Olympics. There, we did so many features on U.S. sprinter Harvey Glance that we inflated him, unreasonably, to a medal favorite in some minds. When Glance finished fourth in the 100 meters—no surprise to track experts—the *Chicago Tribune* messaged its Montreal staff, "Please file 800 words on upset of Harvey Glance in 100 meters."

I wanted to help O. J. but hesitated before phoning Lund. I knew this was an invitation for him to raise the Chin issue, a certain confrontation that I didn't presently need. But after all, it was now 6 P.M. in the office, midnight in Geneva. If he was going to overrule me, surely he'd have done it by now.

I called Lund and told him that O. J. was a perfect in-studio fixture for *The NFL Today*, where his charm and recognizable face would light up the screen. If Musburger needed convincing, I said, I'd be happy to use O. J. as a game analyst for the first year. Lund said he understood the urgency and asked if Monday would be soon enough. I told him I'd pass the word.

Then, *as we were hanging up*, he said, "By the way, I don't want you to air that thing with Tiffany Chin's mother."

What?

We argued. Without ever hearing from Michaels, Tesh, expert commentator Scott Hamilton, or me, without knowing more than Peter Tortorici's shaded view, Lund was issuing a dictum. The unhappiness was evident in my voice:

"We spend all week here, trying to get close to the stories and the personalities, and you preempt us without a hearing? Certainly, we respect your judgment and your right to be involved. You're the division president. But this has never happened before. It must signal some change of procedure. Are there other areas where I should expect to hear from you? Do you want to decide what kind of teases we do on NFL football?"

This was way over the foul line, I knew. But I was prepared for the ultimate confrontation. The status quo was no fun. Peter Lund was now substituting his opinion, from 3,860 miles away, without consulting his well-qualified, well-paid employees. TeleGame be damned; I didn't want to play under these conditions.

That was the last meaningful conversation I ever had with Lund. One month later, April 29, I heard from an unimpeachable source of CBS innerworks that he was planning to fire me. Insultingly, the information had come from an agent, an outsider, with whom Lund and Pilson were close.

There followed an agonizing two months of twisting in the wind. The whole world seemed to know. Newspaper reporters were calling. Producers from other networks heard about it.

In the first week of June, Phil Mushnick wrote in the *New York Post:*

> The hills are alive with the sound of a shakeup coming at CBS Sports that could slay some high-profile executive producer types. Cost-cutting could be a big reason, but not the only one. CBS' exec. producers and their charges carry a lot of emotional baggage. This guy doesn't talk to that guy, that guy can't stand this guy, and it's a highly political, highly divided scene that needs fixing.

This was a replica of language Lund had been using around the office. By leaking the story, he was, in one of his pet phrases, "laying a rail."

The next week, Madden invited me to play golf with him at his new home in northern California before I flew to Pasadena to survey the Rose Bowl for CBS's Super Bowl XXI telecast. I knew John had heard the rumors. To put us both at ease, I raised the topic bluntly.

"What's the reason for this?" he asked. "What possible excuse do they have?"

"I guess I haven't done the political things right."

"Ah, bullshit!" spat Madden.

I gave John the latest scuttlebutt: Lund was going to

offer me a senior producer's role. My unimpeachable source said that CBS expected me to accept, one executive reasoning, "Where else is Terry going to make this kind of money?"

How little they knew me after five-and-a-half years. I was earning a lot of money, but that was not the issue.

"John, you know I can't do that," I said, offering an explanation more with my eyes than my words.

"Of course, you can't," he said, in the perfect reply. "This is a screwing."

Madden offered to intervene, but I dissuaded him. I wanted to see this process run its course and—hard to explain after I'd poured quarts of blood into CBS Sports— I wasn't sure I wanted to work there any longer. Or that I could.

As the certainty of our separation began to sink in, Madden had one final comment: "If they [Lund and associates] do this, they're going to see it on the air."

To this point, I'd refused any reaction to rumors. But now, there was nothing to lose. I had my agent, Art Kaminsky, tell CBS I wasn't interested in being a senior producer.

In the third week of June, two more sources confirmed the inevitable. Van Sauter told Kaminsky, "Peter Lund is being allowed to make this decision and he's scared to death of Terry."

I'd violated one of the axioms of TeleGame: If you're bright enough to be a potential threat, you should be bright enough not to leave your boss feeling threatened. Or your superstar commentator.

There was one last weekend to live with this anxiety. On Saturday night, June 21, I joined several friends at a Jackson Browne concert. Jackson, with a lyric to fit life's every situation, reached me with the opening lines of "For Everyman," his populist anthem that I knew so well:

Everybody I talk to is ready to leave
With the light of the mornin'.
They've seen the end comin' down long
    enough to believe
That they've heard their last warnin'.

"The light of the mornin'" came two days later, on Monday, June 23. When I finished a *Sports Sunday* meeting about 10:45 A.M., Lund entered my office, nervous as a kitten, hammering on his chewing gum. It was startling to see him. Apart from one chance meeting at the elevators, he'd avoided me for weeks.

"T.O., the rumors are true," he blurted.

When he started to expand, I stopped him.

"Peter," I said, "you don't owe me any explanations."

A free man suddenly, I didn't want to hear any more. It felt good to have the crisis ended—for both of us. He scurried out of my office in less than five minutes.

At that moment, another quote was applicable. "All farewells should be sudden," Lord Byron once counseled.

I told only my secretary, Ashley, who immediately broke into tears. I hugged her and, fully composed, went for the door. Walking the thirtieth-floor hallway one final time, I heard *Sports Saturday/Sunday*'s theme music drifting from a screening room.

The elevator door opened. I hustled inside.

Epilogue

BROADCASTING'S obsession with on-air performers was established in the late 1940s by the "Paley raids." In nine legendary months from late 1948 through mid-1949, CBS founder William Paley recruited from NBC an entire lineup of vocalists and comedians for his radio network.

Freeman Gosden and Charles Correll, the voices of Amos 'n' Andy, were first to defect, followed immediately by Jack Benny, forming the axis of CBS's Sunday night programming. Bing Crosby came next in mid-January 1949, then Red Skelton, Edgar Bergen, George Burns and Gracie Allen, Ed Wynn, Fred Waring, Al Jolson, Groucho Marx, and Frank Sinatra.

In later years, as profit potential was discovered in other divisions, this entertainment practice was extended to news and sports. The networks competed hotly for "talent," lavishing it with enormous wages—$36 million over ten years in Dan Rather's case, $10 million over five years in Brent Musburger's case.

The goal of this investment, of course, was a long-term attraction who would generate ratings and thus revenue. It was a thesis and fervent hope that might have been justifiable for singers and jesters, even for the handful of anchors who personified each network's news division. But $2 million a year for a commentator in sports broadcasting where exclusive events, clearly, are the stars?

A CBS-commissioned study in the mid-1980s ranked Musburger no better than ninth on the recognizability/likability index of network sports personalities, despite his extensive airtime. A January 1984 *Sports Illustrated* profile reported that he was basically anonymous, Bill Taaffe writing, "For someone who's on national TV some 275 hours a year, more than twice as much as Dan Rather and five times as much as Mr. T, Musburger's recognition factor in relative terms is zip."

Eleven months later, Brent was presented a $10 million contract. This was the single incident that showed how far out of orbit the television world had strayed in its pursuit of top performers.

Even ungodly money wasn't enough, however, once stars and their agents saw what leverage they'd been granted. Broadcast executives, in their overeager solicitation, had delivered their programs—indeed, their careers—as hostage to "big talent." In effect, they'd announced that the whole television process—programming appeal, audience delivery, advertising support—was driven solely by its on-air frontispieces.

Encouraged by this blunder, talent began insisting on the one prerogative that executive row had reserved for itself: editorial and production control. Ultimately, in their weakness and instinct for self-preservation, the executives surrendered this point as well. Thus was born the all-knowing, ever-fearsome 800-pound gorilla or "anchor monster," as industry insiders have designated Cosell, Musburger, Rather, and their ilk.

Musburger once defined this type when he told me, "You know, I've worked under five division presidents here, and I always thought I could have done a better job than any of them."

The "anchor monster" is fueled by this kind of self-righteousness. He can do vain, outrageous things because the flawed system that created him also grants him total immunity.

338

On September 11, 1987, a papal visit took the *CBS Evening News* to Miami. Sitting on his remote set in the late afternoon, Dan Rather was informed that a long-running match from CBS Sports' coverage of the U.S. Open tennis championships might force him to shorten his broadcast.

Rather, in reply, threatened to leave his chair at precisely 6:30 P.M. if he was unable to take the air as scheduled. His producer informed New York.

At 6:30, with tennis still ongoing, Rather unfastened his alligator-clip microphone and stormed off the set. He left instructions that Sports should fill the half hour until 7 o'clock.

This order directly contravened the written "ground rules" that had been distributed to both News and Sports staffers. In practical terms, there was no chance to reverse the assumptions of dozens of people in New York, Miami, and Flushing Meadow, New York, site of the tennis. Rather had been in television long enough to know this.

Tennis ended a few minutes past 6:30, and Sports left the air. Rather sat boiling in his dressing room, trying to raise a hearing via telephone with CBS officials in New York. Meanwhile, the network sat for *more than six minutes in black.*

Nothing. No programming. The cardinal sin in television.

In the 1988 book *Who Killed CBS?* Peter J. Boyer writes:

> The most telling aspect of the Miami incident was that at the key instant, when Rather said he would leave his anchor chair if the tennis match ran long, no one in authority—not the executive producer, not the president of CBS News, not Gene Jankowski, the president of the CBS Broadcast Group—felt he had the weight to order the $2.2 million anchorman to get back in his chair and read the news.

This was a dilemma that corporate CBS had created for itself. In 1980, faced with the specter of losing Rather to Roone Arledge's aggressive ABC News, CBS granted its star major concessions. One of these was the title "managing editor" of the *Evening News*. This was Rather's pretext for decreeing that *his* broadcast would not air unless tennis finished on time. As one *Evening News* producer later said, "He was the petulant anchorman and the boss at the same time."

Bill Leonard was the CBS News president who'd capitulated in that 1980 negotiation. He later told *Newsweek* magazine, "It's not healthy for him [Rather] to be the final decision maker. I simply gave in to him, and I've regretted it ever since."

But Leonard's was not the only mistake. When Van Gordon Sauter replaced Leonard the next year, Rather was stressed out and failing in his succession of Walter Cronkite. Sauter's solution? To include and invest his shaky anchorman in the revamping of CBS News—to grant him sweeping management authority over personnel decisions, allocation of airtime, and so on.

Rather relaxed. His on-air performance improved. But the institutional effect of this new structure would surface several years later—the lynching of Ed Joyce, the Miami fiasco, yes, even the Hamlet-like destruction of Sauter's own CBS career.

In Peter J. Boyer's analysis, "When, through the conscious decision of management, Rather was given the strongest voice inside CBS News, the potential for disaster was created."

Were these simple misjudgments by Leonard and Sauter? Pilot error in flying their network airplane? Or was it more basic? Was this human weakness, career fear? Whatever, once they left a crack in the cockpit door, their passengers came storming up the aisle.

Rather's success in his 1980 negotiation led Musburger to demand a "managing editor" title in Sports just months later. And in the way that CBS's internal business seems to crisscross and double back with such irony, Brent's wish was granted by none other than Van Gordon Sauter in his first days as Sports president.

Other CBS executives employed this tactic just as wantonly. A significant moment in Peter Lund's failed romance of Bob Lobel, the local Boston sportscaster, was a lunch at the "21" Club next door to CBS. Lund offered Lobel an anchor role on college football pregames and halftimes. The show's executive producer, Ted Shaker, added his pitch.

With Musburger becoming play-by-play voice of the games, the CBS pair said their studio effort needed new direction. Shaker leaned across his salad, peered earnestly into Lobel's eyes, and insisted: "Yes! And you're going to *lead* us!"

Lobel, who'd never worked at a network and hardly classified as a college football expert, looked at the two of them as if they were crazy.

But this was the party line at CBS Sports. Whether from obsequiousness or an ambitious bid to ingratiate themselves, a steady stream of executives had repeated this theme so often that Musburger came to believe it. Ultimately, who could blame him?

Even the secure leadership of ABC Sports occasionally fell victim to this syndrome. Roone Arledge and Jim Spence fostered Cosell's evolution to gorilla size, though Spence's memoir, *Up Close and Personal: The Inside Story of Television Sports,* attempts a revisionist case. Strewn throughout the book are claims that Spence enjoyed a close personal relationship with Cosell from the early '60s, that he was an involved administrator of ABC Sports' day-to-day activities, but that somehow he was unaware of Cosell's regular drinking in the *Monday Night Football* booth until 1984. Under such blind eyes do "anchor monsters" grow big and strong.

To academics and media observers, this television star

system might raise several questions: Is it internally ethical? Is the viewer being well served? Is talent necessarily too involved with on-camera time and other self-interests to discharge overall authority? Can the network's stockholders believe in this process as effective management?

From an artistic perspective, the question may be: Does every dancer need a choreographer, every writer an editor, and thus every commentator a producer? On a professional level: Does the process inhibit creative young people, who should be pushing the medium's frontiers rather than politicking and currying favor?

But within the business, only one question is relevant: What's the efficacy of this system?

Part of that answer is hard to quantify. For instance, I can't prove but will forever believe that Cosell squandered scores of potential *Monday Night Football* viewers with his ignorance and disdain for the game.

He was forever mocking, in singsong verses:

> You isolate the setback
> On the linebacker;
> He dodged a bullet,
> And came to play.
> Just ask the jocks,
> It's holy war . . .

It was one thing for him to do this patter in hotel lobbies. But when his contempt began showing up weekly in America's living rooms, the effect was disastrous. Howard never believed that football, of itself, could compete with entertainment programming. He never seemed to understand the game's nuances, its elements of chess and the military battlefield. He never realized that broadcasters who find this subtlety, and present it understandably, win millions of converts for their network, their advertisers, even for the other networks.

If anybody at ABC ever grasped this, he surely never

342

dared advance it to Cosell. With Chet Forte, his acolyte, Howard the High Priest defiled *Monday Night*'s sacred prime-time altar for 14 years. How many nights did he moan, *on the air,* about a late-running game and wonder whether he'd catch his flight home? To this day, the series struggles under Cosell's heritage of scorn.

Is there harder evidence? When George Merlis departed, the *CBS Morning News* slipped back to its previous audience levels. The program went through several more executive producers and format changes, including a comedy approach in 1987 that was the laughingstock of the industry. The latest version, *CBS This Morning,* looks remarkably similar to Merlis's show. But instead of his high 3s and low 4s, it rates in the low 2s.

At CBS Sports, the 1987 Pan American Games were a minor disaster. On the climactic final day, viewers got no interviews or reaction after Brazil's monumental upset over the United States in basketball, and missed the last two sets of the USA-Cuba volleyball final. Its own scheduling blunder forced CBS Sports off the air just as the Games' two biggest stories were exploding. After promoting volleyball heavily all weekend, CBS missed the USA's thrilling five-set victory.

The sports division president of a rival network called this production "a joke." Despite the home-soil hype of having the Games in Indianapolis, audience levels were 16 percent below the 1983 telecasts from Caracas. And reviews were blistering. *USA Today* panned CBS's leadership for "a disorganized effort" and called the final Sunday "the deepest of downers."

With respect to CBS/NFL football, the 16.2 rating average of my five seasons was followed by a 15.2 in 1986, a 13.9 in 1987, and a 13.8 in 1988. *CBS Sports Saturday/ Sunday* dropped from that all-time high rating of 6.9 in 1982 to a 3.9 in 1987.

More striking to the home viewer was coverage of Super Bowl XXI, the Denver Broncos versus the New York Giants, in January 1987. In the second quarter, Denver leading 10–7, CBS missed what is arguably the most important replay in the history of televised football.

The correct angle of a John Elway–to–Clarence Kay pass would have overruled an on-field incompletion call, transforming it into an important Denver first down. But the CBS producer this day was an old-timer who had never fully embraced the production system installed in 1981. Relying on associates, he wouldn't find the critical replay until nine minutes later.

On the very next snap, the Giants sacked Elway for a safety. Instead of leading 10–7 and driving for more, Denver was clinging to a 10–9 margin and kicking to resurgent New York. The Broncos never regained their momentum, losing 39–20.

At the next year's Super Bowl, Brent Musburger was talking to a CBS football analyst about network sports executives, past and present. Musburger told his colleague, "You know who was the best guy we ever had? Far and away, not even close. Terry O'Neil."

I did not blush, as if complimented, on hearing this story. Instead, I recognized it as the peculiar, mystifying logic of "anchor monsterism." The present circumstance is never acceptable. Nothing is ever satisfactory.

I was reminded of George Merlis. Mere months after he left the *CBS Morning News,* Diane Sawyer was already "bitterly at odds" with his replacement, according to Ed Joyce's book. She and coanchor Bill Kurtis sat in Joyce's office, complaining that their new producer "lacked the spark of George Merlis, who was now being canonized in absentia by them both."

Merlis often admitted bewilderment over his departure from CBS. I knew what he meant. For the first two years after leaving, my reflections brought forth no conclusion, either. But finally, in the summer of 1988, there came a series of revealing incidents and the perspective to connect them.

NBC News announced a new president in July 1988. The *Washington Post*'s well-connected Tom Shales reported:

> Tom Brokaw helped engineer the ouster of NBC News President Lawrence K. Grossman, according to NBC sources at various levels of the company. When Grossman's resignation was revealed yesterday, it was a signal to some that Brokaw's power within NBC has become immense.
>
> "An 800-pound gorilla has been allowed to grow into a one-ton gorilla," one unhapy NBC veteran said. "Tom was clearly a prime mover in getting Larry out of there and was active in the selection process for his own new boss."

The new man, Michael Gartner, was an attorney and career newspaperman taking his first job in television at the age of 49. Gartner told reporters that he expected his longevity at NBC would be a function of job performance. This quote was seen by his good friend Richard Wald, a former president of NBC News.

Gartner later smiled, "Dick Wald called me up. He said, 'Even if you do it right, they'll get rid of you.' "

An NBC News staffer concurred in the *Washington Post* report: "That guy [Gartner] hasn't got a chance either. If Brokaw doesn't like him, he'll have him fired, too."

The startling aspect of this episode is that Brokaw is one of the *good guys*, widely regarded in the industry as a class act. If he, too, is engaged in this behavior, it may be time to throw up one's hands and accept the problem as inevitable, incurable. Perhaps the pressures are so great, the stakes so high, that even the noblest among us may be expected to use their influence in pursuit of self-interest.

Two weeks before the change at NBC, an executive shuffle was announced up the street at CBS. Howard Stringer succeeded Gene Jankowski as president of the

CBS Broadcast Group. This was apparently unrelated to the Brokaw-Grossman flap. Or was it?

For longtime observers of Stringer, a charming 45-year-old Welshman and Vietnam veteran, his promotion was no surprise. He, more than any of my contemporaries in the industry, had shown a deft hand with television politics since the day in 1965 that he began as a CBS researcher.

Recall that in 1983 Stringer was the CBS News producer who allowed our Sports staff to run with the Pan American Games drug story. That week, he warmed Musburger's and my Caracas hotel suite with a personally crafted telex of thanks and congratulations. We were ready to run through walls for him.

Just three years later, it was Stringer who followed Ed Joyce and Van Sauter as president of troubled CBS News. The once fabled institution of Edward R. Murrow was then a mine field of factions. Stringer stepped carefully. He solicited the "old guard," principally Walter Cronkite, at well-publicized lunches. He escorted the new CBS chairman, Laurence Tisch, on a tour of European bureaus.

Importantly, he *produced* his way out off this morass, steering *West 57th* and *48 Hours* onto CBS's prime-time schedule and reclaiming the weekday two-hour block for *CBS This Morning*. Following the Joyce-Sauter era of drastic budget cuts, these programs meant new jobs, restored prestige, improved morale.

All of this served to fortify and insulate Stringer from the "anchor monsterism" that had ravaged his two predecessors. He'd earned the support of chairman Tisch above, a reinvigorated staff below, and anchor emeritus Cronkite —a notorious "loose cannon"—to the side. Closing the circle, he even won Dan Rather's gratitude by conjuring up a public defense for those six minutes of black from Miami.

Stringer's slick coalition stood in contrast to reports about Larry Grossman's shop. The *Washington Post* report quoted one of Grossman's NBC associates: "He alienated people above him, and he alienated people below him. In the end, he was friendless above and below."

Larry Grossman was not the only man to have learned this painful lesson past the midpoint of a successful career. About this same time, political analysts were remembering a similar comeuppance for Michael Dukakis. On the eve of Dukakis's coronation at the Democratic national convention, *The New York Times*'s R. W. Apple, Jr., recalled that the nominee had "learned to be a politician late and learned it the hard way, losing a bid for reelection as governor of Massachusetts."

That was 1978. Opponents called him "aloof" and "arrogant." *The Times*'s Apple reported that Dukakis "had an imperfect understanding, to put it kindly, of the way power, patronage and policy interact."

In his own words, Dukakis summarized, "When people walk into the voting booth and say, 'We want this guy, not you,' that's a pretty strong statement. I had blown it."

How devastating, facing the likelihood that his political career was ended at the age of 45. The humbled former governor took a teaching job at Harvard University. He rode to work on a bicycle, carried his lunch in a brown bag, and began to retool his personal style. An entire commonwealth seemed to notice. In 1982, offering himself as a bridge builder and seeker of consensus, Dukakis won back the governorship.

Only six years later, as he confidently accepted nomination, I could not resist the parallel with CBS's nominee, Stringer. Just as the television executive knew that his business was far more than airing good programs, Dukakis had learned, in the words of his biographers, Richard Gaines and Martin Segal, "that good government was not enough, that to be a good governor one had to be a good politician."

It was a seemingly obvious point, but in the election

year of 1988, not every candidate seemed to understand. Even before his fatal tryst with Donna Rice, Gary Hart had felt the sting of "aloof" and "arrogant." His own speechwriter, Peter Tauber, characterized him in those terms.

Tauber departed Hart's campaign after just one week, unable to make the Colorado senator see "the difference between running for smartest kid in the class and for President of these people."

No, in this year of enlightenment, not every politician seemed to learn. Donald Regan published his number one best-seller *For the Record* in the spring of 1988. Regan had been both treasury secretary and White House chief of staff under Ronald Reagan. His book, at one level, is a searing indictment of personal politics in Washington, a score-settling account of Nancy Reagan's campaign to have him ousted.

For the Record evidenced a stellar résumé, but there was a fatal gap in the author's experience. Despite a Harvard education, a Marine command in World War II, and corporate success on Wall Street, Regan arrived in Washington unprepared. He had not learned, in the words of political columnist Morton Kondracke, "the arts of negotiation, alliance-making and warfare-by-publicity that were necessary for exercising power (indeed, surviving) in the White House."

Nor was he inclined to admit these failings once he departed. Asked by interviewers if he could cite any personal failures during his term in the White House, Regan sniffed, "Well, I guess I was naive about politics, though some people would tell you that's not necessarily a failure."

"Aloof" and "arrogant" are accusations that I recalled from my network career. These are frequently hung on the very capable or the charismatic. In the summer of 1988, Jesse Jackson was such a man. I liked Ted Koppel's viewpoint on this issue one night on ABC News' *Nightline:*

348

It is the very level of passion generated by Jesse Jackson that carries such a price. It is the dullness of a [Michael] Dukakis or a [George] Bush that contributes to their acceptability across such a wide spectrum. It is Jackson's passion that causes him to be adored, but sometimes also feared—viewed with such total trust by some, and such absolute cynicism by others.

"Aloof" and "arrogant" are adjectives not restricted to politicians and television producers. Bill Walsh has suffered this attack at various times in his career.

In December 1975, Walsh had every reason to hope that he would succeed the retiring Paul Brown as head coach of the Cincinnati Bengals. Walsh had labored eight long seasons on the Bengal staff, devising the team's futuristic pass offense and developing quarterbacks Ken Anderson, Virgil Carter, and Greg Cook.

But when it came time to name a successor, Brown chose not Walsh but "Tiger" Bill Johnson, an unimaginative line coach who would last less than three seasons in the job. On some level, Brown was intimidated, or unwilling to trust his more acclaimed assistant. As Kenny Moore portrayed Walsh's reputation in *Sports Illustrated*:

> Word got about that there was something different about him, something that unsettled owners and general managers. He had a mind that saw deeply and in detail, they said; he could encompass two or three sides to a question. In the euphemistic world of football, that meant he was indecisive. They said he was a good, humane teacher, and that meant he was soft. They said he was a genius, and that meant he was too abstruse.

Was it fair for Walsh's character to be assassinated in that way? Certainly not. But was this a widespread perception within the NFL? Sadly, yes. He was 44 years old when the Cincinnati opportunity passed. Would he never be a head coach in the NFL?

Walsh spent a year on the San Diego Chargers' staff, then went to Stanford, resurrecting its program and winning bowl games in both seasons despite personnel rated far below his competition. At Stanford, something else happened. Walsh's oldest son, Steve, said he saw his father relax.

After 11 years in the NFL, campus life was meditative, educational—even for a man in his mid-forties. By the time the 49ers called in December 1978, Walsh had evolved an engaging, communicative style to go with his ambition and his x-and-o brilliance. He never looked back.

In the summer of '88, lining up the careers of Walsh, Dukakis, and Stringer in parallel, I began to see. Businesses so human, so collaborative as football, politics, or television demand that a personal balance be struck—a style that is not pandering, not false, but inclusive, effective.

At CBS in 1986, I had not understood this. Through my last tumultuous months, a large part of me desperately hoped that performance would be enough. As I edged closer to the brink, I always believed that somebody in the CBS hierarchy would finally look at ratings and profits, compare them to the years before my arrival, and say, "Fellas, we can't unload this guy. He puts numbers on the board."

This was naive. "The game behind the game" is as fundamental to broadcasting as the cathode ray tube or the on/off switch. One need not relish that, but one may not ignore or pretend to be above it, either. Everybody whose name is on the roster must recognize the sport and play hard, every day. Nobody earns an exemption for good work.

If I'd had this perspective in '86, you ask, would I still be working at CBS? I don't think so. Given our differing backgrounds, I don't believe that Musburger and I were destined to coexist much longer on the same transmission circuit. Were I still at CBS, for example, the anchorman and I would be headed for a collision over the 1992 Winter Olympic Games.

CBS went from "no factor" to "leading contender" in Olympic television negotiations when Chairman Tisch saw what devastation ABC's 1988 Calgary Games wreaked on his prime-time entertainment schedule. His angry reaction became Neal Pilson's mandate to lock up the 1992 Winter Games in Albertville, France. Nothing could have pleased Pilson more. After a decade of feigning CBS's interest at Olympic meetings, he was finally being bankrolled. His aggressive bid to the International Olympic Committee, $243 million, carried the day by *$68 million* over NBC. (ABC had dropped out before the process began.)

Sobered by this embarrassing overbid, CBS will be questioning every expenditure in its $100 million Olympic production budget over the next three years. Meanwhile, given NBC's disappointing ratings at the 1988 Summer Games in Seoul, advertisers will be demanding hard assurances of audience levels before they commit to expensive commercial buys. In this climate, the question of the prime-time anchor is sure to be raised.

Somebody at CBS should be responsible and courageous enough to insist on a "likability" study of the top anchors in sports. This audience survey would probably reveal that CBS should pursue ABC's Al Michaels or NBC's Dick Enberg, not Musburger, as its lead Olympic personality. After 20 years of taking its Games from Jim McKay—kindly, soothing, even grandfatherly in his later years—America is not prepared to invite someone marginally abrasive into its living rooms four hours per night for 16 nights.

But this study is unlikely to be commissioned by CBS Sports. Brent still makes the decisions he wants to make. And take my word, he wants to be your host from Albertville.

Recreating in chapter 8 my little disputes with the anchorman, they now seem so trivial, so manageable. Why did we declare World War III over this minutiae? But that's a view from outside the cauldron. Inside, you'd be surprised how aggrieved you can be at the tiniest transgression.

The good, creative people of television—Musburger included—are every bit as passionate as Jesse Jackson. This is the fuel that sustains them through overnight edits, through countless miles of air travel, through the tense moments of live performance. At the slightest provocation, their passion can sour to self-righteousness. They can turn on each other with the same fury they unleash on a difficult broadcast. Channels of communication close. Positions harden. It gets personal. There is impasse.

The challenge of network management is to recognize this natural process and prevent it. Especially now, in this new era of corporate ownership, there is such need for enlightened leaders who will run meritocracies and demonstrate care for quality. The television executive of the '90s should be personally dynamic, fully self-secure, determined to nurture his creative people and manage their differences, rather than pit them against each other in a debilitating endgame.

Otherwise, this art form, this thoroughly American expression, will ultimately be passed to the television politicians. You'd be surprised how many of them occupy desks in network skyscrapers—people without the slightest hint of artistic or journalistic intention, waiting to inherit the earth. They have no skill other than their ability to navigate among the raging fires of self-interest. Without a creative contribution to make, they believe that politics *is* the game, an end in itself.

Synthesizing these notions near the end of 1988, I didn't know whether to smile or grimace at the comments of Candice Bergen. Ms. Bergen was brand-new to television in '88, star of a CBS prime-time series, *Murphy Brown,* in which she plays—double irony—a television anchor. The daughter of ventriloquist Edgar Bergen and wife of French film director Louis Malle, Candice had spent her whole career in cinema. But even before her first sitcom aired on the small screen, she had seen enough to reach an unsettling conclusion. She was quoted, "Television really rewards mediocrity. I just don't think they want people with rough edges."

One afternoon in Washington, the Redskins were pounding the Rams 51–7 in a playoff game. Both coaches cleared their benches. This meant that the two quarterbacks were Bob Holly of Princeton and Jeff Kemp of Dartmouth. Going to commercial, John Madden told Pat Summerall, "Pat, before the season, if I would've said, 'You're gonna have a playoff game and both quarterbacks are gonna be ex–Ivy League quarterbacks,' you would've said, 'Nah, no way.' "

The moment we hit commercial, he erupted, "Hey, Terry, I bet your guys at the Greenwich Country Club loved that one!"

This was one of those singular moments, so exclusively reserved for the people of network sports. It was also the kind of personal aside that gave our jobs a fraternity-house quality.

Saturday nights after the production meeting, too tired to move, never aspiring to better company than each other, we'd sit for hours. My hotel room would be a bombsite of papers, press releases, team rosters, videocassettes, film cans, soft drinks, and half-eaten room service food for 12. Amid this wreckage, we could talk for hours in the strange language that football coaches had taught us:

"That Johnson is a *load,*" Summerall would volunteer. "Did you see the legs on him?"

"He's a full bucket," Sandy Grossman would concur.

Relaxed in this way, Madden would unsheath his ever-sharp needle. One Saturday night, he asked me if I'd heard about Grossman's new training regimen:

"Terry, did you hear that Sandy's become a jogger?"

"Oh, fuck you, John," bantered Grossman.

"No, I swear," protested Madden. "He told us last week. He said, 'No matter how far I run—a mile, two miles, three miles—I always kick it home the last two hundred yards.'"

Madden's Irish face was wrinkling with amusement. His eyes were nothing more than slits of mirth.

"Can you imagine? Little Sandy? Those little legs? *Kicking it home?!*"

None of us was immune from this treatment. One year at the mid-March NFL owners' meeting, Madden watched my winter-encrusted tennis game crumble in a doubles match against Will McDonough of the *Boston Globe* and Carrie Rozelle, wife of the commissioner. The next football season, in Bill Walsh's hotel suite, Madden had just the audience he wanted for this story—Walsh and his wife, Geri (both avid tennis players), Summerall, Grossman, and me.

"I'm out there," he recounted, "rootin' for my guy. You know, I'm CBS. Terry's CBS. I'm sittin' there with Marianne Noll [wife of Steeler coach Chuck Noll], and I'm tellin' her, 'Watch this. This is my guy.' Terry's got the tennis shorts, he's got the socks. (Rises to gesticulate.) He's got the sweat bands. He looks great! He's got the whole outfit!"

Madden sighed and hung his head with great exaggeration:

"But ultimately and eventually, you have to *play!*"

This was the fun of it. Not the limos and the first-class air travel. Not kudos in the newspaper. Not even seeing your Super Bowl credit reach 40 million homes. This stuff.

The moments immediately after a quality broadcast were so delicious to share. All your senses were still on fire, your pores wide open, your ears ringing, your mind still racing with hundreds of split-second decisions.

Madden would slump into the car and groan, "God, I'm tired." Then, brightening suddenly, he'd say, "Boy, we sure sucked that thing dry, didn't we?"

After a Rams game at Anaheim Stadium, Summerall and I once rode north toward Los Angeles International Airport. Drunk with the nectar of a great collective effort, I drained three or four beers in 60 minutes.

A few miles from the airport, I asked the driver to stop. Then Summerall and I stood on the shoulder of the San Diego Freeway, relieving ourselves so long and so hard, it was blissful. Horns honked at us. It was still daylight. We laughed like a couple of schoolboys.

On the evening of that 1985 "Angus" game in San Francisco, Grossman, Vitrano, and I had a leisurely four hours before catching our "red eye" flight back to New York. I asked those two to join me for dinner, along with Summerall, Madden, and Al and Linda Michaels, who lived in nearby Menlo Park.

Despite their prominence in the business, Summerall and Madden had somehow never met Michaels. It was a glorious coming together of the good guys.

At one point, Pat and John wanted to hear some stories of my days at ABC. Michaels obliged happily. Madden reciprocated, mimicking my telephone instructions to a CBS production assistant:

"Mike, this is Terry calling. I got a little assignment for ya here. Nothin' to it, really. You know, Mike, for this week's tease, I remember a shot from 1959. I was just in grade school at the time, but I remember it perfectly. It was a low, tight shot of Jimmy Brown against the Steelers. The game was in Forbes Field. I think the date was October 11. . . . "

The skillful roasting, the mix of good friends, the tension release at season's end—they all combined to leave me giddy. Later, after Grossman, Vitrano, and I had departed for the airport, somebody said, "I've never seen Terry laugh so hard. I've never seen him so happy."

Index

Sports Immortals

FROM ST. MARTIN'S PAPERBACKS

LANDMARK BESTSELLERS
FROM ST. MARTIN'S PAPERBACKS

HOT FLASHES
Barbara Raskin
_____ 91051-7 $4.95 U.S.   _____ 91052-5 $5.95 Can.

MAN OF THE HOUSE
"Tip" O'Neill with William Novak
_____ 91191-2 $4.95 U.S.   _____ 91192-0 $5.95 Can.

FOR THE RECORD
Donald T. Regan
_____ 91518-7 $4.95 U.S.   _____ 91519-5 $5.95 Can.

THE RED WHITE AND BLUE
John Gregory Dunne
_____ 90965-9 $4.95 U.S.   _____ 90966-7 $5.95 Can.

LINDA GOODMAN'S STAR SIGNS
Linda Goodman
_____ 91263-3 $4.95 U.S.   _____ 91264-1 $5.95 Can.

ROCKETS' RED GLARE
Greg Dinallo
_____ 91288-9 $4.50 U.S.   _____ 91289-7 $5.50 Can.

THE FITZGERALDS AND THE KENNEDYS
Doris Kearns Goodwin
_____ 90933-0 $5.95 U.S.   _____ 90934-9 $6.95 Can.

Publishers Book and Audio Mailing Service
P.O. Box 120159, Staten Island, NY 10312-0004

Please send me the book(s) I have checked above. I am enclosing
$ _____ (please add $1.25 for the first book, and $.25 for each
additional book to cover postage and handling. Send check or
money order only—no CODs.)

Name _____

Address _____

City _____ State/Zip _____

Please allow six weeks for delivery. Prices subject to change
without notice.
                                        BEST 1/89